Communication and Interpersonal Skills in Social Work

Communication and Interpersonal Skills in Social Work

Third Edition

JULIET KOPROWSKA

Series Editors: Jonathan Parker and Greta Bradley

LearningMatters

First published in 2005 by Learning Matters Ltd.
Reprinted in 2006
Reprinted in 2007
Second edition 2008
Reprinted in 2009
Third edition 2010
Reprinted twice in 2011

© 2010 Juliet Koprowska

British Library Cataloguing in Publication Data
A CIP record for this book is available from the British Library.

ISBN: 978 1 84445 610 9

This book is also available in the following formats:
Adobe ebook ISBN: 978 1 84445 741 0
EPUB ebook ISBN: 978 1 84445 740 3
Kindle ISBN: 978 0 85725 011 7

Cover and text design by Code 5 Design Associates Ltd
Project management by Deer Park Productions
Typeset by Pantek Arts Ltd, Maidstone, Kent
Printed and bound in Great Britain by the MPG Books Group

Learning Matters Ltd
20 Cathedral Yard
Exeter EX1 1HB
Tel: 01392 215560
info@learningmatters.co.uk
www.learningmatters.co.uk

Contents

Acknowledgements

First, I would like to thank the service users and students with whom I have worked, for all they have taught me about communication and interpersonal skills. Special thanks are due to Una McCluskey for her intellectual acuity and vision, and her personal support. I also wish to acknowledge the members of the Northern Attachment Seminar, and mentors, peers and friends in the SCT® community, particularly Yvonne Agazarian, Claudia Byram, Fran Carter, Susan Gantt, Dorothy Gibbons, Doug Johnson, Jon McCormick and Anita Simon. I thank my colleagues at the University of York who made it possible for me to take study leave to complete this book, and the Sisters of the convent of Santa Brigida in Rome where I spent three weeks peacefully writing. I also thank the unnamed multitudes from whom I have learnt how not to communicate.

I also want to thank Ray Haddock for his sustaining presence during the work on the second and third editions.

Series Editors' Preface

The Western world including the UK and England face numerous challenges over forthcoming years. These include dealing with the impact of an increasingly ageing population, with its attendant social care needs and working with the financial implications that such a changing demography brings. At the other end of the lifespan the need for high quality child care, welfare and safeguarding services have been highlighted as society develops and responds to a changing complexion.

Migration has developed as a global phenomenon and we now live and work with the implications of international issues in our everyday and local lives. Often these issues influence how we construct our social services and determine what services we need to offer. It is likely that as a social worker you will work with a diverse range of people throughout your career, many of whom have experienced significant, even traumatic, events that require a professional and caring response. As well as working with individuals, however, you may be required to respond to the needs of a particular community disadvantaged by world events or excluded within local communities because of assumptions made about them.

The importance of social work education came to the fore again following the inquiry into the death of baby Peter and the subsequent report from the Social Work Task Force set up in its aftermath. However, it is timely to reconsider elements of social work education – indeed, we should view this as a continual striving for excellence! – as this allows us to focus clearly on what knowledge is useful to engage with in learning to be a social worker.

The books in this series respond to the agendas driven by changes brought about by professional body, Government and disciplinary review. They aim to build on and offer introductory texts based on up-to-date knowledge and to help communicate this in an accessible way preparing the ground for future study as you develop your social work career. The books are written by people passionate about social work and social services and aim to instil that passion in others. The current text introduces you to the important area of communication; developing and using your interpersonal skills to forge relationships, engage in dialogue and develop shared perspectives on issues of concern to those people with whom you will be working. Communicating with others is something we do everyday, but using your interpersonal skills as a professional social worker is complex and demanding. This book offers a comprehensive introduction to these skills from which you can build and expand your proficiency.

Professor Jonathan Parker
Greta Bradley

Introduction

This third edition is primarily addressed to social work students studying at both under-graduate and postgraduate levels, and it will contribute to preparation for practice learning. It may also be of value to newly qualified and experienced social workers and other health and social care colleagues.

Good communication skills are essential to any form of social work practice, from therapeutic interventions through to the most mundane bureaucratic activities. Whether you are dealing with a complex family situation, or phoning the local council on their behalf about non-payment of rent, or writing a letter to the health visitor who referred them, you need to be able to communicate well. This one example gives an idea of the diversity of communication, and shows that social workers need to be able to move flexibly between different modes of communication and use them all effectively.

In everyday life, a 'good' relationship is characterised by honesty, trust, concern for each other, mutual understanding, the shared enjoyment of activities, and the persistence to get through difficult times and resolve conflicts. In personal life, relationships may last a lifetime. A social work relationship is both similar and different. Our ability to build rapport, show friendliness and warmth, have faith in people, tell the truth, and show reliability and persistence are similar to the qualities and skills on which friendship is founded.

Relationships in social work also have a defined purpose, with boundaries that limit the degree of mutuality that is desirable. The relationship may be brief (for example, an assessment for a package of care under the NHS and Community Care Act 1990), defined by specific time limits (such as Core Assessments with children) or long term (as in the case of some work with children, families and people with mental health problems). We may have to be bearers of bad news or hard truths. And we need to be mindful that not all service users are to be trusted. They may wish to pass themselves off as good enough parents or well intentioned carers or as capable of looking after themselves, when the truth is that abuse or exploitation or self neglect is taking place. Occasionally they may even mean us harm. Optimism, hope and idealism are valuable attributes in social work, but naivety is not.

Requirements for social work education

The book aims to meet the Department of Health requirements for the honours degree, which state that students need to learn how to communicate effectively with children, adults and those with special communication needs. The National Occupational Standards expect social workers to be able to:

- prepare for and work with people to assess their needs and circumstances;

- plan, carry out, review and evaluate social work practice;

- support individuals to represent their needs, views and circumstances;

- manage risk;

- manage and be accountable, with supervision and support, for their own social work practice;
- demonstrate professional competence in social work practice.

The 2008 academic subject benchmark statement identifies five core areas in which students need to acquire knowledge, understanding and skills:

- social work services, service users and carers;
- the service delivery context;
- values and ethics;
- social work theory;
- the nature of social work practice.

Within the benchmark, communication skills are a key part of social work practice. The Social Work Task Force report (DCSF, 2009) also names communication skills as essential to good social work practice.

Communication and interpersonal skills

Skills cannot be learnt solely from reading a book, however interactive the book may be. It is in the nature of skills that they have to be practised in everyday life – try learning to ride a bike from looking at a manual! Much of your learning and assessment of communication skills will take place in practice settings during encounters with service users and fellow professionals, but a good deal is usefully undertaken in private study and in the academic environment, where there is less immediate worry about 'getting things wrong' to the detriment of service users. This book will help provide you with the foundations and scaffolding you need so that you will be able to build on your skills when you go out into practice.

We currently lack a knowledge base for the best ways of learning and teaching communication skills, since the learning processes involved are complex and have rarely been evaluated (Trevithick et al., 2004). Richards et al. (2005, p.410) cite research by Collins and Bogo (1986) and Dickson and Bamford (1995) which suggests that evaluating the *transfer of learning to practice settings poses methodological challenges*. This is not to say that learning is not transferred; the issue is that we do not know exactly how. My own research suggests that studying and practising skills within the university environment at least enhances students' self-efficacy – their confidence about their skills (Koprowska, 2010).

Interpersonal skills are very different from the motor skills involved in riding a bike. We use our minds and our feelings far more than in cycling, and we continually have before us many choices about what to say or do next in any given situation. This is because communication is inherently interactive, so the scene is continually changing. The behaviour of other people in an interaction is much less predictable than road surface or wind direction, and our behaviour has an impact on the other person or people with whom we are working. We therefore bring consciousness and deliberation to interpersonal skills, and we constantly reassess what is happening, from moment to moment. This happens between people all the time, not just in social work encounters.

For this reason, this book draws on a wide range of literature, including communication theory, linguistics, systems theory, social psychology, neuroscience, and empirical research in health care, social work and psychotherapy. The aim is to promote your thinking, reflection and curiosity. As far as possible, the approaches suggested have some basis in research evidence about what appears to be useful and acceptable to service users, and it is grounded in social work values of respect for persons – including ourselves.

The Social Work Task Force Report

The Social Work Task Force Report (DCSF, 2009) was produced to consider why professional social work, despite its importance, was not thriving, and to make recommendations about improvements at every level. The recommendations, if fully implemented, would create considerable change in social work education, in conditions of employment, in the career structure for the profession, and in how the public view social work. The implication is that social work would become better able to meet the many challenges it faces and work more effectively with the members of the public who need our services.

Book structure

Chapter 1 introduces some of the core concepts which underlie the other chapters, drawn in particular from systems theory. It provides an understanding of communication as interaction, and explains how feedback continually influences that interaction. It shows how in social work contexts, social worker and service user form a communicative system, and their interactions with each other constitute a continuous stream of feedback to each other.

Chapter 2 introduces the working alliance, the product of a good enough working relationship combined with sufficient skill to enable service users to identify and achieve goals and consolidate changes made. Drawing on research studies, you will also learn about what service users want from social workers, and about where things go wrong.

Chapter 3, which has been substantially updated for the third edition, includes material on the role of mirror neuron systems in our understanding of other people's actions, intentions and feelings. It discusses the expression and regulation of emotion and non-verbal communication.

Chapter 4 takes you through the skills needed to make initial contacts by letter, phone and in person. This is a very practical chapter with plenty of suggestions.

Chapter 5 leads on to the skills involved in maintaining and ending working relationships. It introduces you to a method for analysing verbal interaction to guide your understanding and help you plan your verbal contributions in social work encounters.

Chapter 6 focuses on children's communicative abilities and the skills needed to work with them. It describes a number of methods for engaging children.

Chapter 7 discusses the skills needed in working with more than one person at a time, and includes working with mothers and infants, families and groups.

Chapter 8 addresses the skills needed to work with people with special communication needs, and asks whether it is in fact the social worker who has the needs.

Chapter 9 looks at aggressive behaviour – when we might expect it, how to guard against it, how to recognise warning signs and how to behave in the face of it. It also considers how service users may use deception.

Chapter 10 discusses some of the challenges we face in interactions, in terms of our assumptions, our own negative feelings, and the emotional demands of social work. It also looks at how social workers sustain themselves in the role, and how we and our colleagues can use interpersonal skills to make the workplace a humane place to be.

There is a glossary at the end which provides brief definitions of the concepts that appear in the book.

Learning features

The book contains activities and case studies to enable you to participate in your own learning as you progress through the different chapters. Some expect you to work on material presented in the chapters themselves; some involve observation of other people in life or on television; some ask you to think about yourself and your assumptions about the world. Many you can do alone, but others will be more interesting and more fun if you do them with another person or a group. Engagement with the case studies and activities is designed to increase your self-awareness, consolidate your understanding of the concepts presented, and enable you to practise skills in communicating.

A final comment

In 2005, Richards et al. suggested that we were faced with a dilemma about interpersonal skills in social work education, since much social work practice is characterised by bureaucratic activities, the filling in of forms, managerial preoccupations with efficiency, a shortage of resources, and pressured working environments in which time for individual service users is short. The Task Force Report highlighted some of the same concerns. The report indicates that *there are certain areas of knowledge and skills which are not being covered to the right depth in social work initial training* (DCSF, 2009, p.18). Of those they name, *communication skills* and *managing conflict and hostility* are of special relevance to this book. The report also emphasises the importance of research-informed practice, the value of supervision, and the need for social workers to have adequate time *to carry out the analysis and reflection that lead to good judgement* (p.28).

These are issues of great importance, and your reading of this book will be the test of whether it meets your needs in present-day social work contexts. The book is based on the following contention: that engaging with people sensitively makes a difference, to them and to us, whether we meet them briefly to discuss practical needs or explore profound emotional experiences over months or years. Test the validity of this as you progress through your degree.

Chapter 1

Communication skills: don't they just come naturally?

A C H I E V I N G   A   S O C I A L   W O R K   D E G R E E

This chapter will begin to help you to meet the following National Occupational Standards:

Key Role 1: Prepare for, and work with individuals, families, carers, groups and communities to assess their needs and circumstances.

- Prepare for social work contact and involvement.

Key Role 2: Plan, carry out, review and evaluate social work practice, with individuals, families, carers, groups, communities and other professionals.

- Interact with individuals, families, carers, groups and communities to achieve change and development and to improve life opportunities.

Key Role 5: Manage and be accountable, with supervision and support, for your own social work practice within your organisation.

- Manage and be accountable for your own work.

It will also introduce you to the following academic standards as set out in the 2008 social work subject benchmark statement:

4.7 Defining principles.

5.1.4 Social work theory.

5.1.5 The nature of social work practice.

5.5.4 Intervention and evaluation.

5.6 Communication skills.

Introduction

In this chapter, some of the key concepts to be used in the remainder of the book will be introduced and explained, with practice examples to help you make sense of them. There will also be exercises and case studies to help you engage with the subject. The chapter lays the foundation for two themes which will keep emerging in the course of the chapters to follow.

The first is that *communication is by definition interactive and always takes place within a relationship*. This means that we need theories of interaction to make sense of it and to distinguish between effective and ineffective communication. It also means that the quality of the relationship and the quality of communication are deeply connected with each other.

The second is that *communication is context-related*. It does not happen solely within the confines of a relationship, but in a larger world which affects both the nature of the relationship and the nature of the communication that properly takes place within it.

Communication undoubtedly 'comes naturally' to human beings, since we are a social species: we seek out the company of other human beings and rely upon our connections with each other for both our physical and psychological well-being. If you stand in the street watching how people behave, you will notice that they are frequently in communication – making eye contact, smiling, touching, talking, phoning, texting, signing. In infants, the stark need for successful communication can be witnessed. Before a baby is born, the mother's body meets the baby's requirements without her conscious involvement. Prospective mothers often communicate with their unborn children, by singing to them, talking to them or feeling them through the stomach wall, and these activities may well contribute to the baby's development. After birth, though, communication becomes essential since the baby's survival depends upon someone older being able to understand and meet its physiological and emotional needs. This is also the beginning of the baby's learning how to communicate and how to read other people's signals, in which mutual imitation plays an important part. There is a growing body of evidence that the human brain needs to be in communication with other human brains to develop, and that this depends on appropriately loving contact, which indicates how profoundly 'wired' for communication we are. This will be discussed further in Chapter 3.

Communication is so central to social life that Paul Watzlawick and his colleagues famously declared: *one cannot not communicate*. They reach this conclusion by way of the following argument:

> *behavior has no opposite . . . one cannot not behave. Now, if it is accepted that all behavior in an interactional situation has message value, i.e., is communication, it follows that no matter how one may try, one cannot not communicate.* (Watzlawick et al., 1967, pp.48–9)

In this sense, communication just is, and is happening all the time when people are together. Every social situation entails communication and therefore calls up communication skills. Even when we are trying to avoid communicating with someone, we are communicating something (*I don't want to talk to you right now*, or *I'm angry with you*, or *I'm avoiding you*, etc.). To describe how strangers sharing public space communicate without becoming involved, Goffman (1963) coined the term *civil inattention* (p.84). This denotes acknowledgement of the other's presence without fear or hostility, followed immediately by *withdrawal of one's attention* (p.84). So from the intimacy of the early relationship of mother and newborn baby, through to the much more attenuated 'connections' between strangers in public places, people are using interpersonal skills. Most social work activity takes place somewhere in between these two extremes. So how do we begin to build on all the knowledge and experience we already possess about communication and think about its dimensions from a social work perspective?

Metacommunication, rules and habitus

Through the experience of living in social environments we learn a wide range of social cues and behaviours. Watzlawick et al. (1967) argue that although we communicate all the time, we have little conscious awareness of the communicative rules that we are putting into practice. We know how to do it, but our behaviour is taken for granted and goes unexamined. Much of what we know is not obvious to us, and we have difficulty in identifying, naming and discussing how we are communicating. The problem arises, they say, because we can only communicate about communication by communicating – so it is easier to become confused than, say, when we are communicating about geography. They give this special form of communication about communication the name *metacommunication*, which indicates that they are taking a bird's-eye view of the process. They are particularly interested in understanding the rules of communication, the pattern rather than the content.

Stephen Pinker (1999) offers a somewhat different slant in considering linguistic rules. He explains that we do not learn language solely by imitation; we absorb and apply the rules which govern the use of language early in our learning. So a child will hear both the words 'walked' and 'ran', but will spontaneously say 'walked' and 'runned' instead, applying the rule that adding the sound of '-ed' to a verb turns it into the past tense. I have occasionally heard adults make this same error when flustered. Interestingly, children first learn correct forms and then begin to make errors, suggesting that a process of *reorganisation* is happening (Pinker, 1999, p.193). Evidently, our minds are not just recording machines; we engage with what we learn, and we apply the rules we already know, though not very consciously. Watzlawick et al. and Pinker concur that our grasp of communicative rules is largely outside of our awareness.

Bourdieu, cited by Thompson, uses the term *habitus* to denote all the 'taken for granted' aspects of culture, including our ways of thinking, feeling and communicating (Thompson, 2003, pp.21–2). We tend to become aware of our own habitus when we encounter someone whose habitus differs. This may be another way of indicating that the rules which govern not just language, but broader aspects of our communication and behaviour, exist outside awareness. The process of learning new communication skills necessitates a greater level of self-awareness, and it is arguable that, as social workers, we should retain a level of self-awareness that is not needed in all the everyday transactions of life, as we are always working with new people, and dealing with the unexpected.

The communication skills which come naturally are an expression of habitus, being those we use all the time in navigating round our lives and relationships. We have learnt them in a whole variety of environments, in our homes, with our friends, in school, in work. The ones which come less naturally are the ones which take us beyond habitus into new areas, where we need to learn new rules, and may at first make mistakes in applying them as we reorganise. The concept of metacommunication helps us to understand and analyse the pattern of what happens, and revise our behaviour in response.

I find it helpful to think in terms of first- and second-order skills:

- *First-order skills* are those required in direct communication itself, with service users, colleagues and others;

- *Second-order skills* are those employed in planning our communication strategy, thinking about what we are doing, observing interactions, paying attention to feedback, reviewing what has happened, and modifying our next and future communications accordingly.

(Koprowska, 2000)

First- and second-order skills are both essential to social work and the terms 'first' and 'second' are not evaluative. The two types could equally be called 'skills' and 'metaskills', as second-order skills are skills in thinking about skills. Second-order skills are akin to the essential professional activities which Donald Schön (1984) refers to as reflection-in-action and reflection-on-action.

ACTIVITY *1.1*

Imagine you work in a community mental health team. Amina has been admitted to the acute ward several times in the last year with depression, and the psychiatrist thinks that marital problems could be part of the cause. You arrange a home visit to see the couple together and after introductions, you say, 'I understand you have some difficulties in your marriage. Perhaps we could talk about them?' Amina and her husband exchange a look and then they both say, 'What are you talking about? We don't have any problems in our marriage at all. Not at all'. The interview comes to an abrupt close.

Let's assume that the psychiatrist's hunch is correct. Use your second-order skills to review how the interaction went, and to devise some different approaches to this delicate subject.

COMMENT

Service users may reject the idea that they have problems, as this is shaming. A focus on improving matters or relieving stresses may be more palatable.

General systems theory

All theories are lenses through which we organise our vision of the subject under scrutiny. Theories are thus never the truth; rather they represent our best effort yet at making sense of the world. Thomas Kuhn (cited in von Bertalanffy, 1971) proposed that when a theory can no longer expand to incorporate new ways of seeing, a new paradigm is needed. Systems theory was just such a new paradigm at its inception, and it has continued to develop since.

Systems theory has its origins in the 1920s, when individuals working independently of each other in a range of different fields began to turn away from a classical scientific approach. Classical science examined the parts of things (cells in biology, individual human beings in psychology, sovereigns or other rulers in politics), on the assumption that each element, right down to the smallest, needed to be understood thoroughly in its own right. Classical science also conceived of cause and effect as a one-way process.

Systems theory takes as its focus not the individual parts, but the relationship and interaction between them to understand how they work together as a whole. Its premise is that things cannot be understood in isolation, but only through their relation to each other. The 'exploded' pictures of car components familiar to anyone who has pored over a mechanic's manual reflect this well; the pictures are there because when the individual pieces are separated on the driveway, they could go back anywhere you fancy if you don't know how they relate to the others. This premise is also related to the Zen question, *What is the sound of one hand clapping?*

Systems theory, unlike classical science, regards cause and effect as mutually interactive, not one-way. Take the case of a child who will only go to bed if the parent lies down on the bed until the child falls asleep. When the tired parent does this, they fall asleep too, and end up going to bed at whatever time it is. As a result, the parent, who wants to stay up, keeps the child up late. The child, meanwhile, almost falls asleep independently several times during the evening, only to be stirred into wakefulness by the parent who is not ready to go to bed. Having missed several opportunities to fall asleep, the child is fretful and alert at the parent's bedtime and needs comforting for some time before it finally settles. If we only looked at one set of behaviours, we might hold either parent or child responsible for this unhappy cycle; by looking at the mutual cause and effect, the problem will be better grasped as a predicament rather than a reason for finding fault (though of course the parent has to take steps to act).

General systems theory (GST) is the expression of principles which have general application to many different kinds of systems in different fields of enquiry.

RESEARCH SUMMARY

General systems theory

Open and closed systems

Open systems exchange across their boundaries with the larger environment, and their boundaries are thus said to be permeable. All living systems are open systems. At an individual physiological level, humans take in food and excrete waste, inhale and exhale, and we also exchange information, ideas and affection. A human system can be an individual, a pair, a family, a group, a society. Closed systems, by contrast, operate within prescribed boundaries; the province of physics is said to deal with closed systems.

Isomorphy

Isomorphy describes those aspects of systems which they have in common. Literally it means 'equal in form'. Mammals, birds, reptiles, fish and insects share certain isomorphies: all these creatures are symmetrical from the midline; legs, flippers, wings and fins all correspond. Thinking of human social systems, while there may be differences between, let's say, a family group and a multidisciplinary team, the similarities in the ways in which they function are isomorphic. Examples would be: a need for both privacy and companionship; a need for autonomy and shared responsibility; executive decision-making resting with few members (parents, the managers). Isomorphy can also be seen in small systems and larger ones, so the competitive behaviours which we witness between individuals are isomorphic to those we see between political parties, for example.

Self-regulating systems – primary regulation

Living systems are seen to be self-regulating. Physiologically, our bodies take care of themselves, when all is well. We digest food, we breathe in and out, our hearts beat, our temperature is regulated (in older children and adults), all without conscious will on our part. In addition, we develop psychologically self-regulating systems, if we have

Continued

enough appropriate regulation from others as we mature, so that when we get somewhat anxious, we can comfort ourselves; when we get tired, we can allow ourselves to rest and sleep. These are regulating activities which take place inside me and inside you, as individual systems.

Feedback – secondary regulation

Feedback is said to happen when information crosses the system boundary and creates a response. Body temperature is a self-regulating system which is stable within a narrow range when a person is well. If the weather is suddenly much warmer (stimulus), then the skin (receptor) sends a message to the 'thermostat' (control), which sends a message to the sweat glands (effector) to produce a response. The body then cools and this provides a new stimulus, which is feedback. If feedback is that the body is still too warm, it will continue to sweat, until feedback that it is cool enough arrives, and then sweating will stop. The occupant of the body may of course hasten the process of cooling by removing a layer of clothing, going for a swim, or having an iced drink! We will see that the concept of feedback is essential to understanding the human interactions at the heart of communication.

Homeostasis

Homeostasis refers to the propensity of systems to maintain a steady state. The example above in relation to feedback illustrates this exactly: it is essential for all warm-blooded animals to maintain body temperature within a narrow range, or organs begin to get damaged. Although the concept of homeostasis has been applied to the nature of healthy family functioning, for example, von Bertalanffy was cautious about this application long ago. The idea that the human norm is to seek a steady state is contradicted by our powerful impulses to learn, explore and engage in new activities. Von Bertalanffy suggests that homeostasis has limited applicability to human endeavour as it cannot embrace creativity, spontaneity, or self-directed activity.

Information theory

Information theory was developed by Shannon and Weaver (1964); *it is a mathematical theory which, in everyday language, states that the chances of all the information in a message being received increase according to how complete, yet uncluttered and essential its components are. At one end of communication is a transmitter, which sends information to a receiver, and the more noise there is in the transmission, the less of the message gets through. An easy example is actual noise when a radio or television station is badly tuned.*

The theory is framed in terms of energy and the second law of thermodynamics, and von Bertalanffy not only questions its validity but notes that it had not been much applied to understand human communication systems. Since then, it has been taken up by a systems theorist and psychotherapist, Yvonne Agazarian, and is widely used in her model for systems-centred practice. Noise is defined as ambiguity, contradiction and redundancy.

Continued

RESEARCH SUMMARY *continued*

Ambiguity *refers to vagueness, lack of specificity, mumbling, hinting, things half-said.* Contradiction *refers to making internally contradictory statements* (I'm fine; I only nearly died yesterday), *or to contradictions between words and non-verbal communication.* Redundancy *refers to repetition and other unnecessary statements* (I'm sorry, I expect this is really silly, you know what a dunderhead I am, but could I just ask . . .)

(von Bertalanffy, 1971; Agazarian, 1997)

Before going on to consider some of these concepts in social work practice, there are some other aspects of communication which need to be brought in, concerning the non-verbal elements of spoken language.

Paralanguage, multiple meanings and emotion

Spoken messages are like a braid of which only one strand is the words themselves. The other strands are pitch, volume, speed and tone, sometimes referred to as *paralanguage* (Thompson, 2003). And, as Pinker so eloquently puts it, *People are infinitely creative with the sounds they use in conversation. They salt their speech with gestures, sound effects, foreignisms, names, and quotations, all as if they were actual words* (Pinker, 1999, p.152). Take a few minutes to think of some examples, or take the chance to observe people's paralanguage in a café or bar.

In addition to this use of gesture and sound as word substitutes, the message will also be accompanied by other non-verbal behaviour (e.g. eye contact, shrugging, fidgeting). Words, even when they convey feelings, are not the thing itself: just as the word 'blue' is not necessarily blue, and the word 'perfume' is not scented, the word 'angry' is not anger itself. In linguistics, this reliable relationship between words and the things they represent is known as the *arbitrary sign*, a term created by one of the earliest and most eminent thinkers in this field, Ferdinand de Saussure (Pinker, 1999, p.2). The sign is arbitrary because the word and what it represents have no natural association. (There are less arbitrary signs, such as onomatopoeic words like 'boom' and 'whisper', and symbolic sounds which evoke the thing they represent – Pinker (1999, p.2), suggests that 'sneer', 'cantankerous' and 'mellifluous' fall into this category.)

These ideas throw light on some regular forms of miscommunication, particularly those which arise from misinterpreting the use of words, or being on the receiving end of messages whose elements contradict one another. Take the fact that some words have several meanings, i.e. a sound is an arbitrary sign for a number of different things. When I had not long been working in a Mother and Baby Home, one of the pregnant residents came to me saying, *I've lost my plug!* I thought she seemed unduly agitated over the loss of an easily replaceable household item from her wash hand basin – but that wasn't it. It wasn't her hairdryer either. *Never mind, we'll get you another one,* wasn't the right response at all, as the plug in question seals the womb during pregnancy and its loss is the first sign of labour.

As for contradictory elements in the message, these arise when language and paralanguage or another non-verbal strand of the braid don't weave in together. In the story above, I knew the young woman was anxious because she spoke with urgency, moved from foot to foot on the spot, and held her hands curled up in front of her chest (try this out and see how it feels). I saw the signals and paid more attention to the words, at least at first.

Emotion is felt, expressed and seen in the body. It is possible to say *I'm really angry* in an angry way, or not. Tone and pitch, volume and speed can be congruent with anger, accompanied by gestures (a grimace, a clenched hand, pointing) and other involuntary non-verbal signals (bulging eyes, a red or pallid face) indicative of anger. *I'm really angry* can also be said in a flat voice, or even with an ingratiating smile. When the two don't match, we have an incongruous message to unravel. Do we believe the words or the gestures? The importance of recognising non-verbal information, especially for understanding the expression of emotion, and for warning signs of aggression, is discussed further in Chapter 3 and Chapter 9 respectively, where there will be more practice examples.

Finally, in the research summary I referred to self-regulating psychological systems such as self-soothing when anxious. Nearly all of us experience the need for others to 'regulate' our psychological states at times. Small children taking a slight tumble will often cry and seek a hug for comfort, and we learn to manage these minor to moderate experiences, but if you think of the last time you hurt yourself badly or felt really unwell, you probably wanted someone else to show concern and offer comfort. Service users often face such challenges to their self-regulating capabilities, and some have had very little opportunity to develop their self-regulating systems at all. In these situations, we will be called upon to offer some form of support and regulation, and this too will be addressed in more detail in Chapter 3.

Feedback and homeostasis in social work practice

As can be seen from the research summary, the meaning of 'feedback' here both relates to and differs from its common use, which is to give someone information about an experience. Students are constantly asked for feedback about modules and courses; groups will sometimes give feedback to each other about progress, or about personal characteristics; staff usually provide feedback on students' assignments. Here, though, we are talking about something much less deliberate and often more implicit.

Clearly human beings and our relationships are even more complex and certainly more conscious than the self-regulation of body temperature used as an example in the research summary. We do quite a lot more than heat up and cool down and, in the process of communicating, there is always a great range of choices about how to respond.

These concepts are invaluable in thinking about communication skills in social work, both in examining snapshots and in looking at progress over time. In an exchange between two people, each person's 'turn' is a form of feedback to the other person's previous statement.

$A \Rightarrow B \Rightarrow A \Rightarrow B \Rightarrow A \Rightarrow B \Rightarrow A$ and so on.

ACTIVITY *1.2*

Sometimes feedback is implicit in the way the person responds rather than shown explicitly in the words. Consider the following contrasting interactions between a social worker, SW, and a service user, SU, and think about what the pattern of responses says about the feedback each is giving the other. The service user is in hospital after a knee replacement, and the social worker is going to assess for home care services on discharge. Use second-order skills to write down what you think each person is feeding back to the other in the two interactions.

Interaction 1

SW: Do you live on your own?

SU: I do now; ever since my wife died. The house . . .

SW: When did she die?

SU: It's only six months ago. It feels like yester . . .

SW: Do you have any children?

SU: Yes, one daughter. She's very good to me but it's just not the same without her mother.

SW: So your daughter helps out with things, does she?

SU: She does, she does her best, but . . .

SW: So you probably won't need much help at home when you get back. What do you think?

SU: Well, I don't know really.

Interaction 2

SW: Do you live on your own?

SU: I do now; ever since my wife died. The house feels ever so empty without her.

SW: It sounds very lonely. Were you a close couple?

SU: We were – been together since I was 16 and she was 15. We were always together, when we had our shop, you know, and then when we gave that up and retired out in this direction.

SW: When did that happen, then?

SU: Only two years ago – it was always her dream to have a place with a bit of land, and 18 months later, she was dead. I can't believe it. She was only 63.

SW: That's young these days, isn't it? How did it all happen?

SU: It was a Friday she took ill . . .

And so on

COMMENT

The more personal nature of the second conversation will help the service user feel more relaxed and better understood. You will still be able to make plans with him.

In Interaction 1, SW's responses to SU seem to say: *I'm not really interested in you. On no account tell me anything about your feelings of loss.* The social worker appears to need to keep in a steady state as an individual system, and cannot respond warmly to SU. SU's feedback is something like: *I really need to talk about this so I'll keep trying. OK, I'll give up.*

In Interaction 2, SW responds to both emotional and factual elements of the interchange, and seems to say: *I'm interested in you and concerned for you. I want to understand how things are for you.* SU responds by volunteering both his story and his feelings about it. His feedback is: *I really need to talk about this, I can tell you're interested so I'll carry on.*

It is also valuable to consider how communication changes over the life of a working relationship. A social worker might initially undertake to advocate for a service user if the service user lacks the skills or confidence to do so for themselves. Over time, the social worker's role may be to work with the service user to advocate for themselves, so that the service user's skills and self-confidence are enhanced. The social worker would be preventing the service user from reaching their potential if they continued to take on the advocacy role.

Linked to this is the notion that homeostasis is not in itself always desirable. Service users are often seeking help with change in their lives, because the homeostasis which exists concerns the maintenance of very distressing difficulties. If feedback has the capacity either to maintain or to disrupt a steady state, then we need to intervene carefully to maximise its impact in the direction that we and the service user have agreed to go. The goal will be to establish a preferable steady state.

Context, role and goal

A theme that will run through this book is the importance of context, and the related notions of role and goal. These concepts are systemic in nature, as they consider how different parts of systems interact and influence one another. Context is the environment in which activity takes place. It is usually a physical place, and always a social and psychological space which conveys certain expectations. Context is a major determinant of behaviour – some would argue, a more powerful determiner of behaviour than our individual attributes (Agazarian, 1997). The kind of behaviour appropriate to a given context relates to the goal of that context.

Conversely, similar behaviours can be appropriate to many different contexts. Keeping quiet is not only expected during recitals but also in the reading areas of university libraries (where the goal is for people to concentrate on their studies), in hospital wards (where the goal is for sick people who are often in pain to rest and recuperate), and during prayer in religious observance (to enable people to concentrate on their spiritual experience).

Test these assertions by imagining your behaviour(s) as a member of the audience in the following contexts:

- *watching television at home alone;*

- *attending a Live Aid concert;*

- *going to a football match;*

- *attending a recital of a Schubert song cycle.*

When is it appropriate to stand up or sit down? be quiet or join in? get up and dance?

What do you think would happen if you displayed out-of-context behaviours in any of these situations?

COMMENT

This activity highlights the influence of context. We become self-conscious if our behaviour is markedly out of keeping.

Behaviour is also influenced by the role you occupy. Silence at the Schubert recital is required of the audience – but not the singer. Football crowds are meant to stay in the stands and let the players score goals. When you shop in a supermarket, you expect to take things off the shelves, not stack them on. Supermarket staff, however, sometimes become customers at the end of a shift, and may react unhelpfully if you approach them as a person in uniform when from their point of view they are not working, but in 'shopper' role. Role transitions are not always easy to make, and communicative mistakes take place when people are unclear about role, a theme that recurs in subsequent chapters.

The primary goals of social work have been expressed by the International Federation of Social Workers (2001) as follows:

> *The social work profession promotes social change, problem-solving in human relationships and the empowerment and liberation of people to enhance well-being. Utilising theories of human behaviour and social systems, social work intervenes at the points where people interact with their environments. Principles of human rights and social justice are fundamental to social work.*

These are the goals of the profession and, like the Codes of Practice, operate at a higher level than the goals related to any particular social work context. If an agency we work in violates these goals or the Codes of Practice, we should question its activity.

At one level below that, there are the goals determined by current social policy, legislation and political ideology. We need to act within the law, and we will only be entitled to implement the law if we are employed by an agency which has this right. At the level of ideology, we are in an age which regards placing people in institutions as a last resort: children are to be looked after by their own family or by a substitute family; older people are to maintain their independence in their own homes; people with learning disabilities are to live in ordinary houses and engage in ordinary life. These goals are not purely 'evidence-based'; they are a product of protest and concern about the quality of care in institutions; of service users' human rights agenda to choose how they live their lives; and of political and economic expediency (caring for people never comes cheap, but institutions are extremely costly).

At the next level down, social agencies and organisations have goals which will contain both common and diverse elements, with specific goals relating to service user groups served, funding, and so forth. The goals of voluntary organisations may have more in common with each other than with those of statutory agencies working with the same user group.

These contexts and goals therefore determine the roles that are required meet the goals, and the roles have associated behaviours which, when put into practice, realise the goals of the context.

The relationships described here between context, goal, role and behaviour are abstract in that they provide a conceptual framework for thinking about these elements in any system. In a sense they describe how things ought to work. In fact, the nature of a context, its goals, the roles within it and their relevant behaviours are often not spelt out explicitly, though many organisations are working towards more explicit statements about these issues, through mission statements, job specifications and policy and procedure manuals. Even these may not adequately reflect what is expected of people and much may remain undocumented and invisible. Dress codes, for example, are rarely made explicit. It is also the case that how people actually work in an agency does not necessarily make a good fit with its explicit goals. I used to work in a social services mental health team whose remit was to work with people with 'severe and enduring mental illness' yet many service users did not strictly fit this category. Quite a few had severe and enduring emotional difficulties, rather than symptoms which met the criteria for diagnosis for mental illness, and there was debate within the organisation about whether these service users were entitled to this particular service.

Communication in context

Natural though communication is, it is contended by a range of writers that communicative incompetence is widespread (Spitzberg, 1994) and mistakes are common (Watzlawick et al., 1967; Ekman, 2003). The implications of communicative incompetence are considerable. Spitzberg (1994) reports that it affects well-being and has a detrimental effect on the skills and qualities available to people in their personal and working lives, as well as in the larger world of political decision-making. He argues that people often make context errors – they use perfectly good skills in the wrong context. Take the following illustration: most people during their working lives will encounter a colleague who, rather than dealing with conflicts in a fairly rational, task-oriented way, instead sulks or resorts to personal insults – just as if they were having a row with their partner. This kind of behaviour isn't that pleasant at home, but it is certainly out of context at work.

A limited understanding of goal will also give rise to errors. An error of this kind takes place when a student goes to see a service user with a list of assessment-related questions, and on finding that the service user is not in a position to answer the questions as asked, gives up and arranges to go back another day. The mistake is to think that the goal is to get the questions answered, rather than to make an assessment. The use of other questions, a discussion which ranges more freely, and attention to observation may mean that the original questions do indeed get answered – but not through asking them.

Again, lack of understanding of role will present problems. Sometimes people confuse their personal feelings with their role. For example, you are affected by a service user's story, which has echoes in your own, and you tell them about your similar experiences. While there are certainly occasions when this kind of disclosure can be made well and meaningfully, it is a minefield. Here are a few of the potential risks:

The service user may:

- feel that you are so deeply affected by the issue that you cannot tolerate hearing about their experience;

- think your experience was worse than theirs and they are just not coping;

- idealise you for how well you coped and feel ashamed;

- think you mishandled your situation and lose confidence in you.

Another kind of misunderstanding is not knowing the limits of a role, so its remit is construed too narrowly or too widely. Remembering that role is defined by context and goal, the social work role will have different meanings in different places. In some contexts, it may be part of the social work role to help someone to learn how to do their own washing. In another, this would be done by a less well-qualified member of staff and it would be considered a waste of resources to employ a social worker to do it. On occasion, people refuse to undertake work which is clearly part of their remit – something that in the longer run could become a disciplinary issue. Organisational change often leads to a reconsideration of the remit of various roles in an agency, and may give rise to a flurry of resignations as conditions of employment are altered. In learning to become a social worker, there will be times when you do not know what falls inside the boundary of your role, and what falls outside.

ACTIVITY **1.4**

This could be done when you are undertaking preparation for practice, shadowing a social worker, or visiting an agency prior to or during practice learning. You will need to devise a set of questions for yourself.

What is the context in which the person works? (Statutory or voluntary? Individual or group-care? In people's own homes or residential? Long term or short term? And so on.)

What are the main goals of the agency? Are they written down? How well do they fit with the context?

Continued

ACTIVITY **1.4** *continued*

What is the role of the social worker (or other social care worker) in this organisation? How do they see it? How does this compare with your own observations?

What kinds of behaviour and activities does the role involve? How good a fit do these make with the role, the goals of the agency and the context? Are there contradictions or anomalies that the person is aware of, or which you have observed?

How might your role as a social work student be affecting what you see and how you understand it?

If there are contradictions or inconsistencies, imagine writing a letter to the manager of the agency to explain your thoughts. How would you try to communicate them so that the message could be heard?

COMMENT

The activity helps you take a bird's eye view and hone your observational and reflective skills.

CHAPTER SUMMARY

In this chapter we have begun to differentiate between those aspects of communication which come naturally to most of us, and those which are usually outside of our awareness. We have turned to the major tenets of systems theory to view communication as an interactive phenomenon in which participants continually influence each other. We have also looked at the relevance of the concepts of context, goal and role to begin to establish that social work takes place in a wide range of contexts with differing goals, and where our roles as social workers will be quite diverse – and our communication skills need to recognise and encompass these different demands.

FURTHER
READING

Payne, M (1997) *Modern social work theory*. 2nd edition. Basingstoke: Macmillan.
A good all-round introduction to theory, including systems theory.

Thompson, N (2003) *Communication and language: A handbook of theory and practice*. Basingstoke: Palgrave Macmillan.
The theory section of this book is particularly enlightening.

Chapter 2

What do we know about effective communication?

ACHIEVING A SOCIAL WORK DEGREE

This chapter will begin to help you to meet the following National Occupational Standards:

Key Role 1: Prepare for, and work with individuals, families, carers, groups and communities to assess their needs and circumstances.
- Prepare for social work contact and involvement.
- Work with individuals, families, carers, groups and communities to help them make informed decisions.
- Assess needs and options to recommend a course of action.

Key Role 2: Plan, carry out, review and evaluate social work practice, with individuals, families, carers, groups, communities and other professionals.
- Interact with individuals, families, carers, groups and communities to achieve change and development and to improve life opportunities.

Key Role 6: Demonstrate professional competence in social work practice.
- Research, analyse, evaluate and use current knowledge of best social work practice.

It will also introduce you to the following academic standards as set out in the 2008 social work subject benchmark statement:

4.7 Defining principles.
5.1.4 Social work theory.
5.1.5 The nature of social work practice.
5.5.4 Intervention and evaluation.
5.7 Skills in working with others.

Introduction

Over recent years, the evidence base for social work and other helping professional activity has taken centre stage. This preoccupation is reflected in book titles such as *What works for whom*? (Fonagy and Roth, 2005), *What works in leaving care?* (Stein,1997*)* and so forth. Champions of evidence-based practice argue that professional practice should be grounded in proof that this way of working makes a difference: the rhetoric needs to have some reality. If everyday communication skills were good enough for social work, why would you take the trouble to learn anything else? So, how do we know 'what works' in terms of communication skills in social work?

This is not an easy question to tackle, for three reasons. First, there is a distinction to be drawn between what matters and what makes a difference, and this inevitably raises the question *What matters to whom?*, which is dealt with in the second point below. It might matter to me that the greengrocer is pleasant, but if she isn't, the lettuce doesn't actually wilt under her gaze (though I do). So is there a relationship between what matters to people – in particular, to service users and carers – and what makes a difference? We will find that it usually does, but it doesn't always make a difference that makes a difference.

Second, what matters, and what differences you want made, depend very much upon your perspective (in other words, on how you view the world from your context and role). Parent, child, social worker, manager, local councillor, politician: their views about what matters in social work are likely to diverge. A mother with mental health problems related to her childhood experiences of sexual abuse may want long-term supportive counselling from a social worker to help her recover and to enable her to take better care of her children. If her care for her children is good enough for them not to be considered children in need under the Children Act 1989, and if government policy does not include her in its definitions of mental illness, she will not be considered a priority for such a service (Hooper et al. 1999).

Third, evaluation of social work practice is inherently complex and is still a developing area (Shaw, 1999). This is the case for social work as a whole, of which interpersonal and communication skills are only a part. We simply do not have a body of literature which puts communication in social work under the microscope – so we need to think more broadly about how to get at relevant information.

In this chapter we will consider the nature of research, we will look at the relevance of a new concept – that of the working alliance – and we will consider the findings of a number of studies in social work and one in social care. The concepts introduced in Chapter 1 will be brought in to make sense of the findings from the studies.

Does skilled communication make a difference?

The short answer to this question is a resounding *Yes*. We know this from a number of different sources, and while the picture could be described as something of a patchwork, only a limited number of patterns are represented. The studies I have chosen to discuss relate to social work or social care, but there is valuable research in social care, psychotherapy, counselling, and medical and health care, and you may want to read some of this literature as well. I have not attempted an exhaustive trawl of the field, but instead selected studies which explore the experiences of a number of different service user groups in a variety of ways. As is often the case, many different kinds of research have been undertaken in this field, so one study may have little in common with another, and we need to be cautious in our conclusions. On the other hand, if studies conducted with diverse groups from the perspective of different investigators using a variety of methods arrive at common results, then we can have considerable confidence in the findings.

Just to give you an idea, here are some of the differences you might encounter in reading research studies.

First of all, how many people are involved as subjects, i.e. who was asked questions or studied in some other way?

- This could be anything from one to several thousand.

Who are the subjects?

- Service users – real or role-played.

- Carers.

- Service providers (students, qualified staff, and managers).

- Observers.

Who are the investigators?

- Academic researchers, including students.

- Service users.

- Service providers (students, qualified staff, and managers).

What methods are used?

- In-depth exploratory interviews.

- Focus groups, where people discuss the topic together.

- Questionnaires using closed or open questions, or both; often completed anonymously and may be posted or collected.

- Observation of interaction where one or more observers rate what they see according to criteria which have been developed for the purpose.

- Scrutiny of records (for example, to see if people improve and cease to need a service).

- Single case studies.

- Narrative accounts (sometimes a service user telling the story of their experience).

In each case, there may be combinations of subjects (e.g. service users and staff), investigators (e.g. academic researchers and service providers) or methods (e.g. focus groups and questionnaires). In an ideal world, research would be large scale and all possible perspectives would be taken into account. In reality it is conducted under constraints, so choices have to be made about numbers, methods, who to investigate and who to employ as investigators.

In some respects, considering research in this way is isomorphic to many social work activities. When we read a previous social worker's record of contact, meet a service user, talk with their carer, contact the health visitor, we too are trying to understand a situation from a number of perspectives. We have to consider whether they seem to be similar, or whether they contradict or otherwise obscure each other, and develop ideas about why this might be. Like researchers, we have to draw conclusions of our own, and in some cases base recommendations on our conclusions. The following activity therefore has a broader applicability than just to research.

1. *Take one of the categories above, of subjects, investigators, and methods. Take each item in the category by turn, and draw up a list of advantages and disadvantages of restricting research to this item. If you are conducting this exercise in a pair or group, don't try to reach consensus – list all the advantages and disadvantages you think of.*

2. *Share the advantage/disadvantage lists with other individuals, pairs or groups and see whether they have other ideas to add.*

3. *Again as individuals, pairs or groups, think about how the three categories relate to each other. Explore the match you would make between subjects and investigators. Then pay particular attention to the methods you think would be appropriate. Consider the reasons behind your preferred approach, and prepare to argue your case.*

4. *Exchange ideas.*

COMMENT

Understanding different kinds of research is of increasing importance in social work practice (DCSF, 2009).

The working alliance

Before considering the individual studies, I want to introduce a conceptualisation of working relationships known as the therapeutic alliance or the working alliance, against which we will able to consider the findings from social work research. The working alliance has been researched widely and has been found to be independent of any particular therapeutic model or technique, hence its relevance to how we establish working relationships in social work, even though most social work activity is not 'therapy'. Another strength of alliance research is that it has examined and compared client, therapist and observer perspectives. (In this research, people whom social workers would currently call service users are sometimes described by the more medicalised term 'patients'.)

The concept of the working alliance has been developed most fully by Adam Horvath. He attributes the origins of the concept to Sigmund Freud in particular, to work dating from 1912 and 1913. Freud, who could be called the 'father of psychoanalysis', was the first to propose that the relationship between therapist and client was an essential part of the healing process (Horvath and Greenberg, 1994).

The methodological problems referred to in the research summary are these. First, most alliance research has been conducted in the early stages of its formation, less in the middle stages and almost none at the end of working therapeutic relationships, so we know most about its nature and impact in the early stages. Second, the alliance has been measured using a range of research tools which are not always comparable, and client, therapist and observer perspectives may need different types of enquiry. Finally, results depend on whether alliance is subjected to microanalysis in a single session, or measured over a longer period of time. Even in the face of these problems, the association between good alliance and good outcome is strong and commands our attention.

The working alliance

The working alliance is, first and foremost, collaborative. The relationship between therapist and client is that they are on the same side, forming a partnership against the common foe of the client's debilitating pain. Neither a good relationship nor therapeutic skill on its own is enough to form an alliance or bring about change; they are thought to interact together (Horvath and Greenberg, 1994, p.1).

The primary activity in the early stages is to agree on a change goal that is clearly understood by both parties. Ruptures and strains can be recovered from once the alliance is established, but not before (Bordin, 1994).

Despite methodological problems in the research, there is strong evidence that a good alliance predicts good outcome (Horvath and Greenberg, 1994).

Therapist, observer and client perceptions of the alliance all predict outcome, but the client's perception is the best predictor. The alliance appears to have three main components:

1. The necessity to establish an at least partly positive relationship with the therapist.

2. The expression by the patient of the patient's conflicts and the working out by the patient and therapist of ways of coping with them.

3. The incorporation of the gains of treatment so that they are maintained after its termination (*Luborsky, 1994, p.47*).

Success outcomes are associated with clients seeing the therapist as warm, attentive, understanding, respectful, experienced and active. In difficult cases, where therapists were able to offer warmth and exploration, patient involvement improved and outcomes were better than predicted.

Negative and hostile attitudes to the client lead to poor outcomes even where the therapist is technically skilled. Studies of therapists and university teachers known to be understanding sought to compare their ability to work with different kinds of patients. With well-motivated patients, the therapists did better than the teachers, but with patients with personality problems such as pervasive distrust and hostility, they did not. Surprisingly, therapists did little to adjust their methods in response to difficulties; rather they responded with hostility of their own (Henry and Strupp, 1994, pp.53–7).

The early establishment of goals that are agreed between therapist and client is a vital feature of successful work, and this should not be underestimated. The other central message is that the therapist needs to demonstrate both personal qualities and technical skill in order to be effective. By implication, this body of research recognises that therapists are only human, and have the full range of human feelings and attitudes, but highlights that certain human qualities really do make a difference. Warmth, attention, respect and understanding, when coupled with active and skilled interventions, enable people both to feel better and to manage their lives better. Some of the more depressing findings regarding the effect on client outcomes of therapists' hostility, negativity and inability to adapt their style are salutary. Clearly these attributes also make a difference – but very much the wrong kind. These issues will be taken up again in Chapters 3 and 10.

So, what does social work and social care research have to say about the impact of interpersonal skills?

Research in social work and social care

Some of the studies discussed below are specifically focused on interpersonal elements; others enquire more broadly into how services are experienced and what might improve them, but I will, in the main, concentrate on the interpersonal aspects.

The first major UK study

I have decided to discuss this study in some detail, as it is something of a watershed. It was conducted by John Mayer and Noel Timms (academic researchers), was published in 1970, and is of particular interest for two reasons: it was the first major UK inquiry into service users' experience of social work services, and it shows how important interpersonal skills are, even when the problem is a practical one. There is a research summary below.

RESEARCH SUMMARY

Mayer and Timms (1970) interviewed 61 recent clients, mainly women. Two kinds of help had been sought: with interpersonal problems *and* material and economic problems.

With interpersonal problems, these factors led to satisfaction in the sense of:

- relief from unburdening *(including experiencing the worker's approach as* unhurried*)*;

- emotional support *(referring not just to listening, but also to* expending energy*)*;

- enlightenment *(greater self-awareness, improved understanding of own situation)*;

- guidance *(suggestions, advice and recommendations, especially when these did not conflict with the views of the client's formal and informal network). (pp.81–8)*

With material and economic problems, satisfaction resulted where the social worker:

- *provided material assistance;*

- *was friendly,* interested, trusted them, *took time and was* active *(e.g. contacting the client's landlord);*

- lessened their feelings of shame *by taking an interest in other aspects of life, by discreetly handing money over in an envelope, and by reassuring the client that they were not begging;*

- *let them know early on whether financial assistance was likely, or not;*

- *made it possible to talk about personal problems as well without being intrusive – allowing the client to choose;*

- *made a* meaningful *response to new or personal material. (pp.106–12)*

Continued

With both kinds of problem, dissatisfaction resulted where:

- *clients and workers differed in perspective, attitude to problem-solving, and understanding of the causes of problems;*
- *these differences were not recognised, acknowledged or explained;*
- *clients felt the worker doubted their story, wasn't interested in them, or lacked authority to act.*

In addition, those seeking material help were dissatisfied when the social worker:

- *asked about their personal life (with clients finding this distressing) while failing to recognise their financial problems (sometimes making the matter feel unmentionable to the client);*
- *did not say early on whether help, including financial help, would be forthcoming;*
- *repeatedly asked the same questions and did not seem to grasp the detail of the person's financial problems;*
- *made suggestions about how to solve financial problems which the client resented.*

The study revealed that clients seeking help for material and economic problems often felt ashamed and were fearful that their privacy would be violated. Those who were dissatisfied were mostly the people who had been refused financial help; however, interpersonal skill in terms of sharing information, understanding the client's perspective and sensitivity to their feelings evidently influenced client perceptions.

The lack of a shared understanding about the purpose of contact, and approaches to problems and solutions, is noteworthy. It would seem that mutually agreed goals, as suggested by the alliance research, had not been established. On occasion, the client recognised the worker's intention, but was dissatisfied when it contradicted their own wishes. Now, social workers do sometimes have to say unpalatable things or turn down requests for help, inevitably leading to some dissatisfaction on the part of service users. But even more valuable is the insight that social worker and client did not recognise or acknowledge that they had different points of view. Both parties apparently assumed that the other knew where they were 'coming from', and did not perceive the pitfalls in their communication.

For example, the social workers in this study were trained in case work, which was a social work approach informed by psychoanalytic theory, and social workers regularly took detailed personal histories in order to formulate ideas about how the clients' early experiences could be linked with current problems. Clients, though, could be puzzled when the social worker asked for information about their childhood as this seemed to them to have no bearing on their current difficulties. This looks like habitus at work, where the social worker has forgotten that in the context of making a social work relationship, doing things in a taken-for-granted way isn't enough. Purpose and goals need explaining, checking out and agreeing, and these behaviours have to be engaged in deliberately by the social worker, as the client is unlikely to raise the issue.

It is a limitation that the study was not able to include interviews with the social workers as well, so inevitably I am speculating here about what was happening for the social workers. Interestingly, though, these were experienced practitioners, and it is quite likely that their familiarity with a particular approach made them lose sight of how mysterious it would seem to service users.

Perhaps for different reasons, inexperienced practitioners make similar errors, often because they are feeling their way, rather than due to the habits of habitus. I have seen student social workers ask a series of questions which the service user dutifully answers, without explaining why they are asking these particular questions or why they think the process will be of use and, in addition, without finding out whether the approach makes sense and is acceptable to the service user. If the questions happen to link in to the service user's concerns and way of thinking, this might not present problems, but if they don't, the service user may be left bewildered and irritated. The imbalance of power between social worker and service user means that responsibility rests with the social worker to be explicit and to check out whether the service user has understood and agrees with the way that they are working together. Chapter 4 offers further ideas about how to overcome obstacles of this kind.

People with mental health problems and their social workers

The second study I wish to describe in some detail is a survey of adults with mental health problems and their social workers (Fisher et al., 1984), which confirms some of Mayer and Timms' findings and adds some new insights. It is an important study in part because it paints rather a bleak picture. Social work teams were generic at that time; that is, they undertook work across the spectrum of service user groups, and people with mental health problems carried quite low priority, especially in contrast with child care and protection (though some parents with mental health problems also had child care needs). The team of academic researchers spent time in the offices of the social work teams, so they had the opportunity for informal discussion and observation as well as conducting formal interviews with service users, carers and social workers. For a variety of methodological reasons, the clients interviewed were all long term, having been receiving a service for at least one and half years.

Some clients had initially requested help with practical problems, and were appreciative when the social worker took an interest in other aspects of their lives and showed an understanding of the persistently stressful and distressing circumstances of their lives. Other clients had requested help with stressful relationships, and unsurprisingly, these individuals too welcomed the emotional support and interest provided by the social workers, and also benefited from practical assistance. Once again, there had been no formal discussion or negotiation over the agreed purpose or goals of contact. The terms of the relationship had evolved into a supportive, friendly and open-ended form of contact which clients who appeared to feel *supported* understood.

Striking by its absence was any concerted effort to alter *the behaviour-patterns of clients which contributed to the degree of stress they experienced* (Fisher et al., p.113). At times of particular stress, contact was increased to provide more of the same. The researchers concluded that the social workers were perceived as a form of compensation for the clients' stressful and difficult lives, rather than as facilitators of change which might have reduced the clients' need for this compensatory support. In terms of the working alliance, it appears that the social workers possessed the personal qualities needed but lacked the requisite technical skills.

In systemic terms, the social workers did not seek to alter the unhappy homeostasis with which these clients lived, but instead became a semi-permanent part of the system itself, helping it to run a little more smoothly. Watzlawick et al. (1974) refer to this as *first-order change* (p.10), where efforts are directed at change within the system, while the system itself remains unaltered. The worker thus becomes a member of the system without significantly influencing how it operates. Contrasted with this is *second-order change* (pp.10–11), which changes the system itself. Watzlawick et al. (1974) argue that successful therapeutic interventions frequently rely upon bringing about second-order change, and this holds good for social work as well.

Bateson (1972) describes second-order change elegantly and simply as *a difference that makes a difference* (p.315). First-order change can often feel as though it is going to make a difference, and sometimes it requires us to look at a situation over time before we realise that nothing much is happening. Probably most of us have at times undertaken work where we might have been able to make a difference that made a difference, but have failed to do so – and failed to notice that we were just treading water. If we did notice, we may have been able to reverse the trend, or found ourselves too entrenched in the pattern to alter it. Bringing about second-order change is almost certainly reliant on second-order skills: that is, we need to think about and observe what we are doing and what is happening or failing to happen, and use supervision as well to help see the bigger picture.

Returning to Fisher et al.'s (1984) social workers and clients, clients who felt themselves to be *unsupported* experienced the social worker as failing to recognise critical aspects of their circumstances, and their feelings of distress. The relationship was characterised by early misunderstandings which were never resolved. Clients felt criticised, ignored and made to feel like a child. Where the primary reason for contact was the provision of a practical service such as day care or child care, the discomfort engendered by the lack of interpersonal connection diminished the value of the practical help, leaving them feeling short-changed, unconvinced that the social worker had done their best for them, and with no confidence that they could be relied on. Tellingly, these clients felt at best indifference and in some cases hostility towards the social worker (p.118). The study does not record clients resorting to hostile acts, but this finding gives us powerful reason for considering the quality of our skills, not only for the service user's sense of well-being, or even for the sake of effectiveness, but for our personal safety. Chapter 9 discusses working with (and reducing the likelihood of) hostility.

Unlike Mayer and Timms, Fisher and his colleagues were able to interview the social workers, so what did they have to say about their professional activity with clients?

Common to the different kinds of cases (older people with dementia, socially isolated adults and families under stress) was that the purpose and goals of work were seldom negotiated or clear. Although the social workers sometimes had goals in mind, such as reducing social isolation or promoting independence, they were largely unsuccessful in communicating them to the clients and unskilled in methods of intervention likely to bring them about. The social workers did link clients to practical services and advocated success-fully with, say the Benefits Agency of the time, but more often they seemed to occupy a place usually filled by informal networks, such as offering emotional support and checking up on people with dementia to ensure they were safe. The researchers perceived them as frustrated and weary, with low expectations of clients to whom they felt shackled despite their inability to bring about change. The social workers tended to see the reasons for this inability to effect change as resulting either from the clients' irretrievably damaged backgrounds combined with current stresses, or in the clients' personalities, and some were *moralistic* in their attitudes (p.132). Perhaps unsurprisingly, they did not have a conception of second-order change, nor how to bring it about. Thinking about the working alliance, some of these social workers had the kinds of attributes that helped but lacked skill; others, perhaps demoralised by their lack of skill, seem also to have had the negative attitudes and inability to adapt their approach known to be associated with poor outcomes.

Echoing Mayer and Timms' enquiry, social workers and clients appeared to have different perceptions of the relationship and its purpose. On occasion clients were satisfied with social work support but social workers were disheartened by the intractability of the situation. Many of the clients had many years of contact with social services and had seen social workers come and go. Perhaps their behaviour reflects habitus, in that they were accustomed to having supportive yet rather unclear and directionless relationships with social workers, and took this for granted.

This study offers strong confirmation of the alliance research, as it shows that while forging a friendly and supportive relationship is essential for effective work, there are few situations where this alone is enough to create change. The good relationship is necessary but not sufficient. It also confirms, from the experience of unsupported clients, that the absence of a good quality connection taints whatever else is offered.

ACTIVITY 2.2

Think about the following scenario. You have recently taken over as the family's social worker.

Gina is a Brazilian woman who has lived in England for 14 years and speaks good English. She came to the UK to marry an English pen friend she had never met, and the marriage was not a success. The couple now live separately, and their son Harry, aged 13, lives with Gina. She has been depressed for most of her time in England, and misses her family back in Brazil, but has never earned enough to afford to visit, and they have never come to England. Gina has mainly used the previous social worker as a sounding board for her unhappiness.

Continued

ACTIVITY *2.2 continued*

Harry likes going out with his friends, riding bikes, skate-boarding, getting chips. Gina expects him to be in by 8.00 p.m. and Harry has a watch and knows this. He is persistently late by half an hour to an hour, and always has an excuse. After a while, Gina grounds him for a night, and then he comes back on time for a couple of days before being late again. So she grounds him for two nights; and so on. Now he is out one night and in for the next five, and recently he slipped out without her noticing. Her ex-husband tells her she is just weak and Harry needs a good hiding but Gina does not agree.

Gina is operating first-order change, i.e. doing the same thing even though, far from helping, the situation is getting worse.

In the role of their social worker, think about how you might negotiate agreed goals of work with Gina. Then work out two different suggestions which might bring about second-order change in the pattern she has with Harry.

COMMENT

Possible answers to the activity include:

- *reward for coming in rather than punishment for staying out;*
- *reward for two arrivals on time;*
- *negotiate a 'late' time at least once a week;*
- *negotiate later time during school holidays;*
- *reward with later time in exchange for homework or contribution to household, e.g. dishes, errands.*

Foster parents

I now want to turn to a large study of foster carers conducted by an academic research team which included an exploration of the helpfulness of social workers to foster carers (Fisher et al., 2000). Typically, foster carers had two types of contact: first, with the specialist fostering social worker, whose role was to support them; and second, with social workers allocated to the foster child or children. Overall, they prized social workers who shared information, valued the foster carers' contribution and views about the placement, listened to their concerns and those of the child, were approachable and responded to requests, were reliable (i.e. turned up on time, returned phone calls, did what they said they would), and had time to attend to concerns – all interpersonal skills. The converse of all these qualities led to dissatisfaction. Their experience of the fostering social workers was somewhat better than that of the children's, and this may be to do with the fact that the goals and role were better defined in these instances. The children's social workers naturally enough prioritised their work with the children, but on occasion foster carers felt excluded or sidelined, and it may be that the children's social workers were unsure of their role. Two examples were when the social worker undertook direct work with the child, and foster carers were given no information at all about this, and when children made complaints which the foster carers weathered without support.

Those who were satisfied with social work contact were less likely to be considering leaving fostering; although the authors did not think this had a large effect on the numbers willing to foster, they did see it as important given how scarce a resource foster carers are. Finally the authors noted the value of telephone contact, which sometimes led to a visit but equally could be sufficient in itself to resolve problems and provide support.

Young people leaving care and staff

On the other side of fostering are the children and young people who are fostered or otherwise in care. The study under discussion (West, 1995) is interesting in part because it employed young people who had themselves been in care to interview care leavers. They also decided to interview social services staff. The final report was written up by a researcher, who is eager to stress that the researchers did not have the time to do this but were consulted at every stage. Factors such as low income, huge variation in leaving care grants, unsuitable housing, lack of education and support, inadequate preparation for leaving care, poor relationships with the police and discriminatory public attitudes had a major impact on the young people, with those from black and minority ethnic groups more disadvantaged than their white peers. The young people saw social workers and social services as able to help in nearly all these areas. The area particularly related to inter-personal skills was the young people's wish to have support, by which they meant having someone who would listen, be there for them when they needed someone to turn to, and offer advice and advocacy but not take over decision-making. Lack of choice was a common theme. For example, those who received help to furnish and equip a new home were rarely given the money itself, and thus had no opportunity to choose their own things. This is clearly an issue of respect, empowerment and trust as well as choice.

Although the Children Act 1989 allowed social services to provide support, including financial support, for young people in care up the age of 21, and longer for those in full-time education, it did not impose a duty on them to do so. As a consequence, there was considerable latitude in the way that social services departments, managers and social workers took up their roles in relation to care leavers. Shockingly, young people in the same area could be given wildly differing care-leaving grants. Perhaps goals at different levels of the social services system conflicted with each other, so that one social worker was more conscious of the goal to support care leavers and get them established independently, and another was more conscious of financial constraints. The implementation of the Leaving Care Act (2000) and the work of leaving care teams has gone some way towards ameliorating these problems.

Older people, carers and staff

Finally, I want to look at a study which investigated home care rather than social work itself. It was designed to establish the outcomes of home care for a range of older people (Qureshi et al.,1998). Outcome is related to the idea of goal. If a service is functioning well, what will it be achieving with its service users? What do people want to be able to do that a service can help them to accomplish? These are outcomes, and once they are identified, services can be designed to maximise the chances that they will be achieved.

The study was undertaken by a group of researchers, and their subjects were service users, carers and staff. The service users were people over 65 years old with physical disabilities, mental health problems or dementia, and included those who used day care, and those who came from a minority ethnic group, all in an area covered by one social services department. The study draws together their views with those of carers, frontline staff and managers. They distinguished three types of outcome: those associated with creating change, so that the service was no longer needed; those associated with maintaining quality of life even when improvement would be minimal or non-existent; and those associated with the process of delivering the service. It is this last category which has most relevance to interpersonal skills.

Competence of staff was important, as well as the interpersonal qualities of kindness, sensitivity and an unhurried pace in the provision of practical and personal care (Qureshi et al., p.6). Once again, people wanted choice and control over how services were provided, and care managers (who would typically be social-work qualified) played a critical role in sharing information about options and consulting individual service users about their preferences.

Overall, service users in the study wanted to:

- be *valued and treated with respect*;
- be *treated as a person*;
- have *a say in services*;
- get *value for money*;
- receive services which made a *'good fit' with existing care giving and receiving within the family*;
- receive services which made a *'good fit' with cultural and religious preferences and requirements*. (pp.11–12).

In summary, these studies suggest that interpersonal skills which create good working relationships are as follows:

Sharing of information
This could include providing information about confidentiality policies, complaints procedures, services available and any costs attached, the time available for discussion.

People might include advice here, and it is worth noting that 'advice' has two meanings in everyday language. One is to provide information, in just the way described here. The other is to tell someone what they should do, which is clearly unwelcome to many people, and social workers tend to see this kind of advice as conflicting with the aim to empower and liberate others. We need to take care not to moralise about people who seek this kind of advice, though, as they may never have had the opportunity to make their own decisions, and there may also be cultural differences. Sue and Sue (2002), for example, suggest that Chinese-Americans seek advice from professionals, and that it is a sign of respect for the expert, but US ideologies are geared to promoting independence and can see this as dependent and 'weak'.

Developing a shared understanding of what the working relationship is about
This implies that purpose and goals are defined and negotiated. They can of course be reviewed and adjusted if they stop being a good fit. It also involves understanding people's perspectives and feelings.

Maximising choice and control
Most people want to feel in control of their lives and their decisions, and many service users have histories of being deprived of choice, by family, by professionals and by institutions. Enabling other people to make choices can be time-consuming and takes patience. You may need to take someone to several groups or day centres or classes or residential homes before they feel they can decide what to do. With someone who understands little speech, offering pictures to represent activities or foods creates the possibility of choice. It takes longer than deciding for them – but is far more commensurate with their human rights.

Responsiveness
This can be fairly practical, like returning a phone call, or more emotional, in terms of sensitivity to the person's feelings in the moment, or remembering personal information in contexts when it may be aroused. Responsiveness could lie in non-verbal recognition that the person has chosen the picture of the activity they want to do, without making them go through the whole gamut just for the sake of it.

Reliability
This means doing what you said you'd do, when you said you'd do it – or having good reasons why you haven't been able to do so. Reliability significantly affects people's trust and confidence in you and in the service you represent, thus it is linked with the Codes of Practice which expect us to instil confidence in our services (which can only be done by proving ourselves worthy of that confidence).

Honesty
Honesty in terms of not stealing from or otherwise harming service users goes without saying. Here the meaning is more to do with people knowing where they stand. Can you secure them a place in a nursing home or not? What are the chances of their child being returned to them if they solve particular problems? Will you support them in opposing their detention under the Mental Health Act at this time? Can they see their father?

Unhurried pace
Several of the studies referred to the importance of feeling unhurried. Although real time makes a difference, pace changes the quality of whatever time you have available. Pace is a non-verbal communication and it can be hard to control if you are genuinely in a rush and late for your next commitment. Even then, an explanation and an agreed time limit will help, and help you to calm down too. Not only do people feel offended or that they don't matter if you are rushing them, they will usually communicate more clearly if they feel they have your attention and you are present. So not rushing someone may actually mean you get to the point more quickly. This will be discussed further in Chapter 3.

Respect

In a sense, everything else listed here refers by implication to a respectful approach. It is an overarching concept which relates to values, and the respect we accord to every person just by virtue of their presence in the world. Respect may have context-specific forms as well. For example, have you ever been to a meeting where people don't introduce themselves, use jargon or acronyms which are unexplained, refer to mysterious others by first names only, so you don't know who they are talking about, and make decisions without consulting everyone? All these behaviours show a lack of respect. Respectful behaviour will be discussed in Chapter 4.

ACTIVITY **2.3**

Work in threes. Take turns so everyone has a chance to be the service user, the social worker and the observer. When you are the service user, choose one of these thumbnail sketches as your starting point, or take the situation of a service user you have worked with.

- *Joe (or Jenny) is worried about money. He/she wants help with debts, paying the rent, fuel bills and so forth.*

- *Linda's (Len's) daughter is 14 and has stopped attending school, instead spending all her time with her 21-year-old boyfriend.*

- *Sindy (or Simon) provides shared care for Tom, aged 34, who has physical and learning disabilities. When they were out recently, a group of young people taunted him about his disability and made racist comments.*

First time round (3 minutes or less for each turn. Keep it short – it won't be pleasant)

A is the service user and B is the social worker. Without actually being impolite, B behaves disrespectfully, i.e. doesn't share information, tells A what to do, doesn't agree goals, tries to make decisions on their behalf, misses emotional cues, doesn't answer questions, and rushes the pace.

After each turn, make a few notes about how it felt for you as the service user, the social worker or the observer. Be honest.

Second time around (5 minutes for each turn)

A is the service user and B does their best to behave respectfully.

After each turn, make a few notes about how it felt for you as the service user, the social worker or the observer.

Discuss the differences between the two experiences.

COMMENT

Being on the receiving end of disrespectful and respectful behaviour is salutary. It helps us see where we might unwittingly be disrespectful.

CHAPTER SUMMARY

The studies here were selected precisely because they arise in different contexts with different goals, where the social work role carries different expectations, yet common themes emerge about the value of communication skills. Whether people are seeking help with interpersonal or practical problems, their satisfaction with services hinges significantly on the interpersonal behaviour of the staff they encounter.

We have seen that a satisfactory sense of interpersonal connection between social worker and client is the foundation for their work, and that this needs to be established early on. But a good connection is not, on its own, enough to produce change. One of the main impediments to forming a good working partnership is lack of clarity about the goals and purpose of contact, and these too need to be established early on, as it becomes increasingly difficult for social workers to challenge the orthodoxy of the relationship once it has evolved. Social workers also need skills in a range of interventions, and whatever models for practice are employed, the interpersonal skills discussed in this chapter are needed to implement them effectively. Collaboration, mutually agreed goals, respect, attention, adaptability – all these are relevant in any form of intervention.

There are important penalties for both parties where negotiated goals are neglected. Service users may become frustrated and even hostile to social workers. While some will be vociferous about their dissatisfactions, others will quietly wait, maintaining contact in the mistaken hope that what they want to happen will somehow take place. If they want assistance or a service which is in fact not available or falls outside the social worker's remit, then they will feel let down that this was not clear from the outset. Likewise, for social workers, the misery of working ineffectively yet not being able to disentangle themselves from contacts that feel fruitless should not be underestimated. It is less well documented than service user experience but common sense suggests it has a bearing on social workers' general well-being and the retention of staff, making it a matter for both individual and organisational concern. The kind of weary frustration described by Fisher et al. (1984) is a recipe for burnout and important to guard against. Still less has been said in the literature about the rewards for social workers of knowing their work is effective. This will be discussed in Chapter 3.

FURTHER
READING

Cheetham, J, Fuller, R, McIvor, G and Petch, A (1992) *Evaluating social work effectiveness.* Buckingham: Open University Press.

Lishman, J (2009) *Communication in social work.* 2nd edition. Basingstoke: Macmillan. Chapter 2 considers clients' views on social work.

Shaw, I and Lishman, J (1999) *Evaluation and social work practice.* London: Sage. These two books both offer valuable accounts of the concepts, problems and methods related to evaluating social work.

Chapter 3

The human face of social work: understanding emotions, intentions and non-verbal communication

Introduction

Relationship is the momentary and cumulative result of the reciprocal messages, primarily non-verbal, exchanged between the two interactants.

(Kiesler, 1979, p.301, quoted in Henry and Strupp, 1994, pp.64–5)

In Chapter 1 we considered the question of whether communication skills come naturally. In this chapter we will examine in more detail the exceptional abilities we are endowed with to recognise and understand other people's actions, intentions and feelings (Hurley and Chater, 2005). How we accomplish this has been the subject of much philosophical, psychological and scientific enquiry. During the last 20 years, neuroscientists have begun to provide us with explanations. Two linked areas of particular interest to social workers are our innate use of *imitation* and the presence of *mirror systems* in the brain, which appear to explain our extraordinary ability to understand other people and to learn from them. First of all, this chapter will discuss the centrality of emotion in non-verbal communication. Then it will explore imitation, mirror neurons, cultural and gender differences in everyday body language, and affect regulation. The review of research data will be accompanied by ideas about practical application, exploring how this knowledge may equip us better to manage interpersonal relations in social work.

The contribution of Charles Darwin

First, I will introduce the work of Charles Darwin, best known for the publication in 1859 of *The Origin of Species*, in which he set out the evidence for his theory of evolution. Darwin's writing was based on detailed observations made by himself and other people, and this method was followed again in the work first published in 1872: *The Expression of the Emotions in Man and Animals* (Darwin, 1998). This was the first major book in English about the expression of emotion. It synthesises wide-ranging accounts from around the world with domestic observations of the behaviour of his much-loved children.

Darwin demonstrated that certain emotions are universal; in other words, all humans feel and express them in the same way, and recognise them in others. This was quite a radical thesis at the time, and it was rejected until the 1960s on the grounds that emotional expression was thought to be learnt and culturally determined rather than innate and universal. As Ekman (1998) points out, this was part of a larger debate about whether human beings are the product of nature or nurture. The number of emotions considered universal varies. Six are always included: happiness, sadness, fear, anger, surprise, and disgust. Sometimes contempt is included (Ekman, 2003), and pleasure and pain (Damasio, 1999).

Some of the innate spontaneous emotional expressions which Darwin described are as follows. When we are frightened, we all widen our eyes and open our mouths, and yes, our hair really does stand on end; blushing never spreads lower down the body than the top of the chest; just as dogs do, we communicate a threat when we draw back our upper lip to reveal a canine tooth. He also noted that smiling and laughter are innate rather than learnt, citing the story of a deaf–blind woman who had neither seen nor heard these expressions of emotion, yet who showed signs of joy *when a letter from a beloved friend was communicated to her by gesture language* (Darwin, 1998, p.195). Genuine joy can be distinguished from a social smile by the involvement of particular muscles around the eyes which are only deployed when genuine emotion is experienced. Think of smiling at a stranger, and then think of something that makes you really happy. Can you feel the difference in your face? Ekman's extensive cross-cultural research in the 1960s, and that of another scientist working independently, Sylvan Tomkins (Ekman, 2003), finally confirmed the validity of Darwin's work.

Darwin's observations make the link between motion and emotion. Emotion could be said to be 'written on the body', to borrow the title of a novel by Jeanette Winterson, as it is visible through posture, movement and changes in complexion. Everyday phrases reflect this common knowledge: people slump in despair, get frantic with anxiety, wring their hands in agony, jump for joy, go grey with fatigue or white with fear (a Eurocentric description; people with black or brown skin show pallor that is more grey than white). Can you think of any more phrases like these?

In summary, Darwin established that there are universal emotions in humans which are expressed in the same way and are readily understood by other people, which has survival value – see the Research Summary.

Darwin's ideas have been extended, for example by Damasio (1999, p.50), who uses the term *primary* rather than *universal*. He also names *secondary or social emotions* including *embarrassment, jealousy, guilt and pride*, and *background emotions* such as weariness, relaxation, tension, excitement, well-being, which shape posture, level of animation and body movement. Fortunately, as Damasio observes, we do not live in the drama of primary emotions, which tend to be fleeting, but in our background emotions.

RESEARCH SUMMARY

Emotion and survival

Emotion aids survival, for the individual and for two-person relationships and groups. The good feelings we experience in relation to food, companionship and sexual relationships motivate us to keep healthy, stay safely with others and reproduce the species. Anger helps us to protect ourselves through fighting; fear protects us through freezing as a means of concealment, or running away. Disgust helps us avoid contaminated, toxic or rotten substances. Secondary, social emotions also serve to shape and maintain relationships with other humans.

In emotional states, brain and body work in concert to ensure survival. Colour drains from the face in fear as part of the redirection of blood to the arteries in the legs to make running away possible. Emotion involves specific patterns of physiological change which enable action to be taken (Damasio, 1999, pp.50–2).

Universal emotions also have communicative survival value in a different way: an angry face may frighten off an attacker without a fight; a fearful face warns others of potential danger.

So patterns of physiological change also communicate our state to others (Darwin, 1998). We can also use our cognitive reasoning to decide whether or not to take action when the impulse seizes us (Damasio, 1999). Spontaneous emotion cannot be faked, but we have partial control over its expression.

Imitation

It is ... extremely difficult to prove that our children instinctively recognise any expression. I attended to this point in my first-born infant, who could not have learnt anything by associating with other children, and I was convinced that he understood a smile and received pleasure from seeing one, answering it by another, at far too early an age to have learnt anything by experience … When five months old, he seemed to understand a compassionate expression and tone of voice. When a few days over six months old, his nurse pretended to cry and I saw that his face instantly assumed a melancholy expression.

(Darwin, 1998, pp.353–4)

Darwin's genius as an observer meant he noticed a phenomenon we are now in a much better position to explain. He was addressing a conundrum known as the *correspondence problem* (Hurley and Chater, 2005), that is, how we are able to perform actions, including facial expressions, purely on the basis of observing someone else. How do we transform a visual image into an action? The groundbreaking studies of Meltzoff and Moore from 1977 onwards are widely accepted as having proved that even newborn infants who have never seen their own faces in an actual mirror will imitate the facial expressions of adults (Meltzoff, 2005).

The word imitation is used in a specialised sense here. It means the inherent capacity to reproduce in oneself what one perceives in others. We know that *Imitation is rare in the animal kingdom* (Meltzoff, 2005, p.55), while humans are supremely good at it. Meltzoff believes that infants are born with a capacity to recognise other humans as 'like me'. When an adult sticks out their tongue, an infant 'knows' that its own tongue corresponds to the adult's, and begins to move it. Meltzoff views our capacity to imitate from birth as the basis of our understanding of other people, other minds (sometimes referred to as mentalisation or theory of mind). Critically, as we develop, we also come to understand that other minds differ from ours – other people have different experiences and perspectives (p.57). This understanding is essential in social work.

Imitation is central to learning – Meltzoff calls it *no-trial learning* (p.55). In a sense this seems obvious – how often do we want someone to *show* us how to do something rather than *tell* us? This is why we cannot learn skills solely from a book.

Imitation leads to liking. Meltzoff (2005) describes how infants, by about nine months, will imitate an adult, and then deliberately change tack, watching the adult carefully for imitative behaviour. They enjoy being imitated, gazing and smiling more at someone who has imitated them. Dijksterhuis (2005) confirms that this is not confined to infants: imitation builds rapport between adults. When people wish to be liked, they unconsciously imitate more, and imitation can be used purposefully. He cites a study by van Baaren et al. from 2003 in which waitresses were instructed to imitate customers by repeating their orders back to them verbatim on some days, and not to on other days. They received larger tips on imitating days.

Mirror neurons and actions

First, a word about neurons. Our brains consist of billions of neurons which form networks. Their activity is not separate from what is happening in our bodies; it is connected to what we see, hear, do and feel. Ramachandran and Blakeslee (1998) describe how our conception of brain functioning has oscillated between two viewpoints. One proposes the idea of *modularity*: that different areas of the brain have specialised functions for, say, *memory* or *facial recognition*, and they do not relate much to each other. Another view proposes *holism* or *connectionism*: that everything is connected and *many areas ... can be recruited for multiple tasks*. They suggest that both views have some truth and merit in them (Ramachandran and Blakeslee, 1998, p.10). There is certainly differentiation between the two hemispheres, with the right brain being involved in the production, expression and recognition of emotion (Schore, 2003). As social workers, we do not need detailed knowledge of the structures and functions of the human brain (but see Farmer 2009 if you want to know more). We do need to know enough to avoid wild assumptions based on modest understanding. The researchers cited here are scrupulous about the conclusions they draw from their experiments. I will make the distinctions clear too, between what is known, and what remains a hypothesis.

So, how do we know what face to 'make' when we see another's expression? The answer seems to rest in large part with the presence of *mirror neurons* in our brains. The name is slightly confusing, as it suggests a special class of neuron whose function is mirroring, but this is not the case. At its simplest, when I perform an action, certain neurons fire; when I observe you performing the same action, my same neurons fire. See the Research Summary.

RESEARCH SUMMARY

Mirror neurons for action

Mirror neurons were first discovered in macaque monkeys by a group of Italian researchers at the University of Parma in the early–mid 1990s. When a monkey grasped or ate a piece of food, certain neurons discharged. These same neurons fired when the monkey observed another monkey, or a human, grasping or eating a piece of food. The researchers named these mirror neurons. *In what turns out to be an interesting contrast with humans, the monkeys' neurons only fired in object-related actions. If the monkey was shown food (the object) which was then hidden by a screen, it responded on seeing the experimenter reaching for the concealed food. But if the monkey was shown that there was nothing behind the screen, there was no neuronal response to the experimenter reaching behind it, even if the gesture was identical. So the macaque did not mirror all actions – only goal-directed actions.*

(Rizzolatti and Sinigaglia, 2006)

These researchers went on to study humans, in whom single neurons are not studied. Evidence from different kinds of brain imaging strongly suggests the presence of a mirror system in the human brain, sited similarly to that in the monkey brain: the action mirror system responds when executing or observing actions. The researchers found that humans, unlike macaques, also respond to mimed movements and to gestures with no object-related purpose – meaningless movements.

(Rizzolatti and Sinigaglia, 2006)

They also describe canonical neurons *(Rizzolatti and Sinigaglia, 2006, p.79) which respond not to actions, but to the sight of three-dimensional objects, such as a cup, or a tool. Canonical neurons 'prime' the muscles for the right kind of grasp for that object, so that*

Continued

the hand is readied to hold it. Mirror neurons also prime muscles ready for action. These automatic responses are simultaneously inhibited, so we do not copy everything we see, although some people with rare types of brain damage do.

(Ramachandran and Blakeslee, 1998)

Mirror neuron systems seem to exist for hand, mouth and foot actions. Mirror neurons related to mouth movements respond to the sight of food, and also to the sight of movements resembling speech.

(Watkins et al., cited in Gallese, 2004)

ACTIVITY **3.1**

The food test

Get a friend to eat something that you both like, but don't have any yourself. Sit and watch your friend eating. Can you almost taste and chew the food? Do you notice an impulse to reach for it?

COMMENT

This exercise its designed to raise your awareness of your physiological responses and begin to sense your own mirror neuron system.

Mirror neurons and intention

After finding a mirror system which codes *actions*, investigators began to explore whether there was coding for *intentions*. Iacoboni and colleagues set up an experiment known as the Tea Party (Iacoboni, 2009), using video clips, and measuring the neuronal response in viewers. Among other things, the video clips showed a real human hand removing a cup from a scene which either looked set out for tea (*Before tea*), or as if tea was over (*After tea*). The most powerful finding was that there was a stronger neuronal response to the sight of someone picking up a cup in the *Before tea* scene than in the *After tea* scene. The researchers concluded that the neurons responded to the implied intention – either to drink the contents of the cup, or to clear it away. Iacoboni (2009, p.130) observes: *This result ... made sense, since drinking is a much more primary intention than cleaning up.*

Apart from providing a neuroscientific justification for the piles of washing up to be found in sinks up and down the country, this experiment shows that people have an immediate understanding of the intentions of others.

This is the key finding – that our understanding of each other happens instantaneously. It happens because our brains recognise and respond to what we see (or hear), and the response is felt almost imperceptibly in our own body. We do not have to work it out: oh, Jane is picking up a cup, is she going to drink the contents, smash it on the floor, wash it up? We usually just know. What is more, we are specialised to understand other humans (though we respond to a lesser extent to other primates). But when we see a dog bark, this does not spark a mirror response for speech (Watkins et al., cited in Gallese, 2004). We can learn, by cognition, that this is a form of communication, but we do not just know it.

The drink test

Next time you are in a café or a bar, watch the behaviour of people who are standing or sitting together (this could be your own group), drinking or eating. Look out for the following behaviours, as they may show the mirror system at work.

When one person picks up a cup or glass, do you know what they are going to do with it? If they drink from it, does another person reach for their own glass or cup almost immediately? Do you notice an impulse in yourself to reach for your drink?

When one person reaches for food, does another do the same? Do you notice any sensations in your own mouth or hand indicating that you too might reach for food?

How often do two people start talking simultaneously?

COMMENT

You might think that people are behaving very similarly because of context – in a café, of course people will be drinking. Pay attention to pauses in the activity, and see whether there are defined sequences of 'not drinking' and 'drinking'. Attending to your own responses will help you see if your own impulses are triggered.

Practice application

When we work with people with addictions, we may advise them to avoid spending time with people who are still using the substance in question. *If you are giving up smoking, stay away from smokers. To kick your heroin habit, stay away from friends who use.* Might this be wise advice because of the mirror system? I assume that if I see someone pull out a cigarette, my canonical and mirror neurons fire, priming me to reach for one myself – especially if I have performed this action thousands of times myself, so my response is well-established.

The fact that we 'just know' so much about other people's actions and intentions is very economical. We do not have to work everything out every day as we go about our business, and it makes it easy for us to learn from each other. The slightly unnerving adage used by medics – *See one, do one, teach one* – has at least a grain of truth in it.

It is also the case that we can make errors of judgement, and people are sometimes successful in masking their real intentions. At times this might put us at risk. If you think someone is reaching into a bag for a pen but instead produces a knife, you are unprepared. We will return to this subject in Chapter 9.

Mirror neurons and emotion

Schore (2003), reports that there are specific patterns in the brain for different emotions, and these 'light up' whether we are experiencing something in the here-and-now, imagining or remembering events, or responding to the same emotion in another person. Anecdotally, most of us have felt tears rise in our own eyes when someone we care about is crying.

Gallese (2004, 2005), and Oberman and Ramachandran (2009) offer the hypothesis that mirror responses enable the automatic understanding of others' emotional states. They cite experiments showing that observing physical touch stimulates the same neuronal responses as experiencing the touch; observing and experiencing disgust activate the same responses. Perhaps most compelling is a study of pain:

> *Both the experience of a physically painful stimulus and the knowledge that a loved one is experiencing the same painful stimulus activates the anterior insula and rostral anterior cingulated cortex bilaterally (Singer et al., 2004). These areas were also correlated with individual empathy scores, indicating that the more an individual was able to use this shared network of cortices, the better his or her ability to empathise with others.*
>
> (Oberman and Ramachandran, 2009, p.49)

In addition, Oberman and Ramachandran (2009) suggest that autism may stem from differences in the mirror neuron system, since people with autism have difficulty in understanding other people's minds and emotional states.

The term *mirror neuron* has been exclusively used to describe neurons in brain areas related to motor activity, so to encompass the way that we understand *others' mental and emotional states,* Oberman and Ramachandran suggest *that the term 'mirror neuron' should be used for any neuron which is capable of remapping an observed state in another onto the observer's own representation of that state* (2005, p.51). Under this definition, we become free to talk about a mirror neuron system for emotion. We come full circle to Darwin: we instantly respond to emotion in others, and the hard science is now only a step away from claiming how that occurs.

Some cultural and gender differences in non-verbal communication

Non-verbal communication contains innate behaviours, learnt behaviours which become automatic and unconscious, and deliberate behaviours which may have particular social or cultural significance. Expression of intense emotion happens spontaneously, but more often, emotional expression is unconsciously tempered by the social environment and is context-related, a phenomenon which Ekman (1998, p.383) describes as *display rules.* For example, in some studies people show greater facial emotional expressiveness in the presence of friends than while alone or in the presence of strangers (Knapp and Hall, 2006), suggesting that we show emotions more in situations of trust. In a contrasting study comparing control over expressed emotion in Russians, Koreans, Japanese and US

Americans, Matsumoto and colleagues found that Russians exerted most control, Americans least. Women exerted control over all expression *with family members,* and otherwise over *anger, contempt* and *disgust,* with men *exerting more control on fear and surprise* (cited in Matsumoto, 2006, p.226). The fact that women concealed their emotions in front of relatives is interesting – why do you think this might be?

Many aspects of non-verbal behaviour, such as proxemics – which refers to how close we get to other people – are culturally determined and habitual. They vary according to gender too – although boys and girls in Western societies behave similarly, men and women diverge (Hall, 2006, Matsumoto, 2006). Studies suggest that women are better encoders and decoders of nonverbal communication than men, and tend to show more of the behaviours which build rapport. Women smile more and receive more smiles; exchange more gazes at close quarters; orient towards the other person; use more *listener responses* such as 'Mm'; notice and decode non-verbal cues; have more expressive faces, hand gestures and voices; and recognise faces more. Men tend to be both more restless and more relaxed, are more expansive in occupying physical space, and show more *speech disturbances* (Hall, 2006, pp.203–8). Ambady et al. (2002), cited in Knapp and Hall (2006), studied the facial expressions of physiotherapists working with older people. They found that *facial expressiveness (smiling, nodding, and frowning) was associated with increases in functioning* (p.326). In other words, expressiveness in the therapist was not just a social nicety, it enhanced recovery.

Learnt cultural behaviours become automatic (part of habitus), and meeting people from other cultures can catch us out. In the UK, we nod to indicate *Yes,* in Greece, people bow the head to indicate *No.* The degree of eye contact considered socially acceptable between different groups of people varies greatly from culture to culture. (See Matsumoto, 2006, and Knapp and Hall, 2006, for more detailed discussion.)

Face-to-face contact is especially important for people with hearing impairments, both to take in non-verbal information and to lip read, if they do so; they may also need to sit nearer than a hearing person and use touch. For other people, reading faces is difficult. People with varying degrees of visual impairment will take in only partial information, or none at all, and are more attuned to tone of voice, pace of speech, and larger body movements which can be seen, heard or felt. People with autism find face-to-face contact disturbing or even painful, and have difficulty in recognising the expression of emotion. If you are fully sighted and well accustomed to face-to-face communication, you will find this strange until you find ways of making contact.

ACTIVITY 3.3

Responding to non-verbal communication
Do this in a pair, with each of you taking turns to be the service user.

Choose a subject to discuss.

The service user's job is to make only fleeting eye contact at first, otherwise looking down at the floor. Only start to make eye contact when you genuinely feel the social worker has made a connection with you.

Continued

ACTIVITY 3.3 *continued*

As the social worker:

- *How does the lack of eye contact make you feel?*
- *What does it make you want to do? (Be honest.)*
- *What are you telling yourself about why the person is behaving like this?*
- *What happens to your body language as you try to communicate?*
- *Try sitting next to the person. What happens?*
- *What difference would it make if:*
    - *You were a middle-aged woman and the service user a 14-year-old boy?*
    - *You were a white man and the service user a Muslim woman from Pakistan?*
    - *You knew the service user was depressed?*

COMMENT

Lack of eye contact may be accounted for in many different ways.

A 14-year old boy might be scared, shy, defiant, or doubtful that a middle-aged woman could understand him. Trevithick (2005) suggests making deliberate errors about age, for example, to coax a silent person into speech, and this might work here. You're very tall for a 13-year old …

A Muslim woman from Pakistan might feel uncomfortable about being with a man who is not a relative, if her family observes traditional gender divisions. She may be showing respect; or she may be afraid of men, if she is being subjected to domestic abuse. You might ask if she is comfortable with you or would rather see a woman.

If someone is depressed, then showing interest and empathy in your voice will be needed first of all, and then it will become possible to ask for eye contact.

Attachment theory and communication

I now want to turn to another rich source of knowledge about human behaviour and development – attachment theory. Thanks to Freud and other psychoanalysts, we know that early relationships profoundly shape who we are and how we relate throughout life. Attachment theory, originally conceived by John Bowlby, and developed by numerous others, began to explain how and why this was the case. Attachment theory flows from Darwin's work on evolution in recognising that survival is the bedrock of infant behaviour. Although Bowlby has been criticised for his original view that a one-to-one mother–child relationship was essential to satisfactory development (as discussed by Crawford and Walker, 2010), there is no dispute that without someone older to take care of them, human infants perish.

Infants therefore possess instinctual care-seeking behaviours which prompt reciprocal care-giving behaviour on the part of adults (Bowlby, 1988). The baby cries and the adult goes to the baby to try to put it right. If this is successful, the baby's care-seeking system has met its goal, and so has the adult's care-giving system. These instinctual biological systems for preserving the life of infants are thus said to be goal-corrected. When an infant's care-seeking needs are met, its natural state is exploration, which is essential to learning.

Care-giver distress has an important function, because it helps them to persist. Supposing I am taking care of a baby who becomes upset, and I try to feed it, but it remains upset. If I were to feel satisfied with this outcome, I would give up immediately. Instead, I try something else, such as changing the baby's nappy. If everything fails, yet the baby doesn't seem ill, I may give up. I put the baby to bed and after 20 minutes it stops crying and goes to sleep. At least I experience relief that it is no longer crying, but not the pleasure of successful care-giving. These are the kinds of situations which often arise for parents having trouble with parenting, and their efforts to be sensitive to the baby and reach a satisfying point for both are short-lived. (The reasons may be many, including fatigue and other stresses, substance use, lack of experience and confidence, or more profound problems relating to their own unmet care-seeking needs.)

Dorothy Heard and Brian Lake (1997) extended attachment theory in a number of ways. Heard and Lake suggest that when care-seeking and care-giving meet their goals success-fully, both parties feel pleasure and relief, in adult–adult interactions as much as adult–infant interactions. When it goes wrong, the goal-corrected systems do not meet their goals and this is distressing for both. Heard and Lake (1997) propose an instinctual system for self-defence which, when care-seeking or care-giving fails, may be activated. This is not a conscious choice, but the activation of a goal-corrected, self-protective system. In a parent, the cognitive manifestation may be to blame the baby in age-inappro-priate ways (*She's always winding me up*, or *He's just like his father, nothing's good enough for him*), or feeling that the baby dislikes them, and that they are no good (perhaps echoing what they were brought up to feel). For the protection of children, and for the promoting of more beneficial relationships between parents and infants, we need to recognise these communicative failures.

The other aspect of attachment theory central to the argument here is the idea of internal working models. Bowlby believed that we internalise our early relationships as working models in our minds. Our expectations of and behaviour in relationships are coloured by those early ones. If my early relationships led me to feel inferior to others, this would become my habitus and I would continue to expect to feel inferior in future relationships. Heard and Lake extend Bowlby's internal working models to *internal models of experience in relationships* (Heard and Lake, 1997, p.84). This term captures the idea that we internalise a number of relationships, and several aspects of our relationship with one person. So your mother may have been loving and sensitive, angry and hot-tempered, and angry and cold. These are all internalised and may be triggered by subtle communicative signals in the present.

It is vital not to take an overly deterministic view: Heard and Lake (1997) believe that the internalisation of relationships continues throughout life, so that where there have been early difficulties, subsequent good relationships may displace, if not eradicate, earlier problematic ones. Herein lies the power of therapy (or a good partner relationship).

Affect regulation in early life

Just as Ekman's research finally vindicated Darwin, modern neuroscience provides significant support for Bowlby's formulations (Schore, 2003). Consider the following statement:

> *It is characteristic of mammalian brains that they develop in co-ordinated systems with other brains.*
>
> (Pally, 2000, p.13)

This means that our brains are profoundly social and communicative from the start, as we have seen from Meltzoff's (2005) work.

The emotional aspects of development take place in the right brain, and this happens sooner than the development of the left brain which, among other things, is dominant for language. The right brain is activated when emotion is felt in the body, and is the site for visual recognition of faces, facial expressions, emotional expression and gesture. It 'hears' the emotional content of language, known as prosody (the emotional music of language, similar to the term 'paralanguage'), though words themselves emanate from and are interpreted by the left brain. The right brain develops sooner in baby girls than boys (Schore, 2003).

Schore argues that it is through the emotional interchange between mothers (and other adults) and babies, that infants' emotional capacities form. Just as babies cannot regulate their own physiological systems, they cannot regulate their emotional systems. An upset baby needs the comfort of communication with someone older, and for this to happen successfully, that someone needs to be sensitive to the baby's signals. This mostly happens spontaneously when the relationship is good enough, and the baby acquires the capacity to regulate its own emotional states. It is through this developmental process that we learn to recognise and respond to emotion in other people.

ACTIVITY **3.4**

The eye test
Because the right brain is involved in producing emotion, and in governing the left side of the body, the display of emotion in the body is sometimes more evident on the left (though spontaneous facial expressions are mostly symmetrical (Ekman, 2003)). Eye contact is a potent way of exchanging emotional information, so test out how looking into one eye or the other affects your perceptions and emotions.

Stage One
When you are talking with other people, give some thought to which eye you tend to look into. Is it the right or the left? Does this change according to circumstances? You may move from one eye to the other, but pay attention to which eye you favour.

Continued

ACTIVITY **3.4** *continued*

Stage Two

Begin to compare what you see when you look into someone's left or right eye. How does it make you feel? If you habitually look into the right eye, pay attention to the signs of emotion you notice when looking into the left, and vice versa. How does this make you feel?

COMMENT

In spot surveys of students, most people favour the right eye first. Choice of eye has no relation to which eye is dominant in either person. As someone who favours the left eye, I notice I feel less connected to the person in right eye contact. Use both to get all the information.

Goal-corrected empathic attunement

The final concept to be discussed is a way of understanding what makes for successful and unsuccessful contacts between professionals and adult clients. Una McCluskey's work is based in part upon Daniel Stern's observations of parents and infants, which she uses to inform observation of adult interaction (McCluskey, 2005). First we need to understand Stern's terminology.

Damasio's (1999) background emotions, such as excitement or fatigue, Stern calls *vitality affects*. (Affect means emotion. The stress is on the first syllable: *af*fect rather than the more common word af*fect*. Linked words such as affective are pronounced as usual.) In his observations of interchanges between parents and babies, Stern sees attunement to affect, where the parent reflects the baby's emotion in their own face and body. Attunement shows matching of emotion and of intensity, in particular, matching of vitality affects. This is not done through exact mirroring or imitation, however; rather the parent responds with the same energy, such as beating out the rhythm of the sounds the baby makes.

Parents also misattune to babies' vitality affects. Misattunement may be unfortunate, accidental or deliberate. Very depressed or preoccupied parents regularly fail to attune to their infants. All parents make mistakes, but these can be remedied or tolerated with adequate experience of accurate attunement. Deliberate, or purposeful misattunement, has the goal of regulating the infant's emotion. Let's say the baby is very excited and the parent's response is somewhat less intense with the goal of reducing the intensity of excitement, which prevents the baby getting overloaded. Or the baby is hungry but quickly gets sleepy, so the mother jiggles it gently to tune its energy up enough to feed. Purposeful misattunement may be effective (it works) or ineffective. Suppose the mother's jiggling stirs the baby and it feeds well enough – that's effective. But if the baby is more fatigued than hungry, it might burst out crying instead. Deliberately cruel misattunement is another matter, and this will be discussed in Chapter 9.

McCluskey has analysed attunement and misattunement in helping relationships between adults. She also builds on Bowlby's and Heard and Lake's ideas about care-seeking and care-giving, and believes that in all helping relationships, care-seeking behaviours emerge in clients, which stimulate care-giving responses in the professional (social worker, doctor, psychotherapist and others). The main goal of the encounter is to explore a matter of concern to the client, so social work examples are: *How to manage at home now that I am frailer;* or *What to do about my son who refuses to go to school.* In the course of exploration, emotions are stirred up which give rise to care-seeking behaviours, visible in the face and body, which call a halt to exploration. The professional needs to respond sensitively enough so that their respective care-seeking and care-giving systems meet their goals, relief and satisfaction are experienced, and exploration can resume. These brief careseeking–caregiving exchanges occur regularly where one adult seeks the help of another to work on problems.

In McCluskey's view, the care-giving response involves both attunement and empathy. Empathy involves attuning to emotion, combined with the cognitive ability to observe the other person and recognise your own responses, in order to communicate understanding in words as well as non-verbally. She calls this process goal-corrected empathic attunement (GCEA). GCEA may involve purposeful misattunement which is effective in regulating the other person's emotion. So the professional may show more sadness in their face than the client, which enables the client to 'see' their own emotion more clearly; or there may be less intense fear in the face of the worker than that of the client, which helps the client feel contained. Her research suggests that when these moments of care-seeking arise, responsive care-giving is the bedrock on which the success of the working relationship rests. When this process goes wrong because the care-giver misreads signals, or misattunes ineffectively owing to an inability to manage their own emotional response, there is distress in both people. In these instances, the difference can be seen in the change in vitality affects: adults may slump having been alert, turn away having been seeking eye contact, and otherwise show that they are giving up. They may pretend everything is all right, or start to look after the welfare of the person who is meant to be helping them: *You're looking tired, shall I get a cup of tea?* And they stop being able to undertake the exploration they need to do to solve their problems.

Emotional regulation, GCEA and social work

Neglect, abuse and trauma in early life are known to disrupt emotional development. Emotional self-regulation and the ability to respond to others may not form fully. Although some of this can be made good later on, it depends on many factors and some people will continue to have problems with emotional regulation all their lives (Schore, 2003).

Some service users have considerable difficulty with emotional self-regulation, and are prone to panic, overwhelming depression, or intolerable anxiety (which mainly get them into trouble with themselves), or uncontained anger or impulsivity (which also get them into trouble with other people). Some people use alcohol and other substances to try to achieve equilibrium. We have growing evidence that some of the most troubled adults who come our way were once deprived, neglected or abused infants or children, and attunement to and regulation of emotion is a very real issue, whether we work with adults or children. Although our primary task is not therapy, the way that we approach and respond to people will determine whether we tend to help with emotional regulation or dysregulate people further. McCluskey's work highlights how we can repair the inevitable mistakes we make as we go along, as we learn to attune and purposefully misattune more effectively.

None of us is exempt, as even if we have been very fortunate in childhood, traumatic events can befall us, and stress-inducing life circumstances will have an impact on us. Domestic violence and other physical assaults, multiple bereavements or other losses, war (as a civilian or in combat) and torture are all extreme experiences which may overwhelm a person's capacity for emotional regulation.

It is important to recognise that neglectful or abusive experiences in childhood do not automatically make someone unsuitable to parent. People can and do recover, and the concept of resilience (see Daniel et al., 1999) is one way of understanding how some people who have had much less than optimal experience nonetheless manage themselves and their lives. However, those who are less resilient may need help, and we cannot provide this unless we understand what is lacking and how it affects both the adults in the family and their ability to care for young children. (In a minority of cases, we encounter people who are dangerous care-givers and children have to be found alternative care.)

CASE STUDY

Daniela

Daniela was neglected by her mother and brought up in her grandparents' house, where she was sexually abused by her uncle. This was never discovered. When she was about eight she tried to tell a social worker that she was being abused, by saying she always had tummy ache, but was not understood. She married a man who was violent to her and she is now living alone with her two children, a boy aged 13 and a girl aged nine. When she is under severe pressure (for example, having run out of money and food on Friday, with nothing coming in until Monday), she physically and verbally attacks her son and blames him for things going wrong, simply because he is male and men are to blame for life's miseries. Cognitively, she is well aware that this is unjust, but she cannot manage her own emotional state, and there is no adult around to help. She finds social work help invaluable. If she calls her local team, a social worker brings food and talks to everyone, calming the whole situation down.

How do you think the social worker manages to provide the emotional regulation which calms everyone down?

If the social worker is using goal-corrected empathic attunement, how might she behave?

Could something different have been done when Daniela was a child? What else would help now?

What are the impacts on her children likely to be?

Theory into practice

The value of material in this chapter lies in two domains, in my view. First, it allows us to become aware of and deploy our innate human skills to build rapport and shape good relationships with service users and carers. Second, it has the potential to inform our assessments of their day-to-day functioning and should contribute to our thinking about people's fitness to care for vulnerable children and adults.

In terms of building rapport, we have learnt that imitation creates liking. Much of this happens without effort. Unconscious mirroring of the other person's posture, which happens automatically, *results in smoother interactions and the development of liking* (Lakin, 2006, p.69). It will often arise from genuine attentive engagement, whereas if we focus on how we are conveying emotion, we impair our ability to decode the other person's non-verbal signals (Lakin, 2006). Use context, goal and role to determine whether you need to adjust your automatic way of doing things. and 'If it ain't broke, don't fix it'.

Greater sensitivity is often needed in social work than in friendship, because of the less than optimal relationships service users have experienced. Trevithick (2005) points out that people who have been sexually abused in childhood may find touch or proximity very frightening, and my own practice experience and research bear this out (Hooper et al., 1999). The fact that men tend naturally to take up more physical space may therefore need attention. Expressiveness enhances rapport and very shy people may need to make more eye contact and smile more than they normally would.

There are also circumstances when we feel wary or uncomfortable with a service user, and we need to reflect on our responses. Is this a mirroring of the other person's wariness of us? In this case we try to relax and put them at ease. Or is the other person threatening to us? In this case we need to find ways of leaving, or address the intimidating behaviour. This will come up again in Chapter 9.

In terms of using our knowledge to inform assessments and interventions with service users, here is an example. You are assessing a young mother after a report from a neighbour that the baby is left crying for long periods. During your first visit, you note that although the baby is clean and well-nourished, the mother dresses and feeds him a little roughly, and does not talk much to him or engage in any play. You make some funny faces and the baby beams at you, which surprises the mother. *He never does that with me* she says, forlornly. Your emotional resonance with her and your understanding of imitation lead you to suggest she attend a family centre, since you think she will gain more from *seeing* what other more skilled parents do than from *advice*.

CHAPTER SUMMARY

This chapter has brought together research and theory concerning our native ability to understand other people's actions, intentions and emotions. It spans Darwin's early work on the emotions and recent experimental work on the discovery of mirror neurons and their function in relationships. The innate ability to imitate, mirror and learn from others becomes more sophisticated as we grow, and it can continue to develop in adulthood. Much of our responsiveness to others takes place at an instantaneous, unconscious neuronal level, but this does not mean we are unaware of it or that we cannot reflect upon and improve it. We have some control over the display of our emotions, and we can deliberately use behaviours to enhance the rapport we build with other people. The responses others evoke in us are an important source of information which needs judicious consideration in our assessments and decision-making. The new neuroscience has made little impact yet on social work but in my view it will become an increasingly valuable source of knowledge for the profession.

FURTHER READING

Ekman, P (2003) *Emotions revealed: Understanding faces and feelings*. London: Weidenfeld and Nicholson.

A highly readable book with plenty of photographs (some from real life, others posed). There is a self-test at the end which is fairly useful, but the posed photographs lack the vitality of spontaneous emotion.

Farmer, RL (2009) *Neuroscience and social work practice: The missing link.* London: Sage.
The first book on the subject, this is a very readable book which applies neuroscience to different social work situations, Chapter 2, 'A tour of the brain', explains structures and functions.

Fridlund, AJ and Russell, JA (2006) 'The functions of facial expressions: What's in a face?' In V Manusor and ML Patterson, *The Sage handbook of nonverbal communication*. London: Sage, pp.299–319. A critical look at the relationship between emotion and facial expression.

Gerhard, S (2004) *Why love matters: How affection shapes a baby's brain*. Hove: Brunner-Routledge.

An accessible, well-written book on modern neuroscience which explains all the terminology.

Lishman, J (2009) *Communication in social work*. 2nd edition. Basingstoke: Macmillan.

Chapter 3, 'Types of communication: symbolic, non-verbal and verbal', provides an account of non-verbal communication, among others and, like this book, recognises how context-specific social workers' non-verbal behaviour needs to be.

Chapter 4
Getting started

Introduction

This chapter concentrates on first encounters – in person, on the phone and on paper – initiated by the social worker, or the service user, or other professionals, with the greater focus on planned encounters as these are more common. The influence of the organisational and professional context on the nature of first encounters will be explored. We will look at writing letters, making telephone calls, and making visits to or meeting new service users on agency or neutral premises. We will think about making introductions, explaining purposes and the limits of confidentiality, seeking initial consents and taking notes. The use of questions and key statements will be included in examples. Some reference will be made to similarities and differences in working with people of different ages, abilities and cultures. The chapter expands on the account provided by Parker (2010).

Context, goal and role

The agency context, its goals and your role within it will determine a good deal of what happens in first encounters. Social work takes place in a wide variety of contexts, sometimes staffed exclusively by social work and social care staff, sometimes by a mix of disciplines. The size of the agency, whether it has statutory duties, and whether work is mainly conducted at the agency base, in service users' homes, or elsewhere, all affect how you take up your role. The service user group for whom the service exists, and the way in which their needs are defined, relate to the goals of the context, and also affect role relationships between staff and users. In some agencies, the differentiation between staff and users does not exist in this way, particularly services for disabled people who have adopted a rights model (see Chapter 8). In these instances, the 'users' run the service for themselves, with support from other people with particular abilities on a negotiated basis.

CASE STUDIES

Lara works in an agency which aims to work with very young women who have become involved in the sex industry, working on the streets. She and a qualified member of staff work together. In the early evening they look out for young women in a particular area of town, try to engage them in conversation, and at least to give them a leaflet about the service, and about their rights. Lara has to take a very informal, friendly approach, and she has to make sure that she does not behave like an authority figure in dress or manner. She needs to emphasise giving information, such as about sexual health, rather than on changing lifestyle.

Jeff works in a private medium-secure hospital for people with mental health problems. He has keys to his allocated wards but visits to service users are generally arranged with nursing staff, who will accompany him if there is any risk of violence. Everyone who works at the hospital dresses formally, and his visits usually have a formal purpose related to mental health legislation, family contact, future accommodation needs and so forth.

COMMENT

Dress codes are important in working environments. It is useful not to be too different from other people or your clothing instead of your skills will become a focus.

Your role will also be determined by the organisational culture, which is often more implicit or tacit than spelt out, and is influenced by the attitude and approach of team members.

The chapter is designed to give you a clear idea of the principles which underpin good practice whatever the context, as well as some of the pitfalls to avoid.

As we saw in Chapter 1, the ways we think, feel and communicate are mostly taken for granted, they are our habitus (Bourdieu, cited in Thompson, 2003). When we enter new contexts, the rules by which we naturally do things are challenged, and we have to reconsider our assumptions and ways of relating. The challenge may come from organisational habitus, or from working with people from cultures other than our own, including the different cultural norms of different professions, so we have to understand new rules.

Attention to context is therefore essential. Understanding the conventions (and their rationale) in your agency during practice learning, and following them yourself, are part of acculturating yourself to the organisation. Of course you may also form a critique of the conventions if they deserve it; if you do, seek ways of explaining your critique to colleagues.

First impressions count

Human beings make very rapid appraisals of information from other humans, and quickly form judgements. This is an important survival strategy – in situations of threat, people need to know who is friend and who is foe. Given that first encounters are often a little threatening, it is important to make the right kind of impact on service users. We may have additional obstacles to overcome. Some people, before we meet them, will already have positive or negative expectations of social workers, based on past experience, the experience of friends or relatives, or more general public influences such as the media. We often encounter people when they are facing special difficulties in their lives. This means their self-esteem may be low, or they may be angry at the world, or sad and despairing. They may have high hopes of what we can offer, or be dismissive. Their antennae are likely to be in a state of heightened alertness, especially if the encounter has high stakes. We need to be sensitive to these possibilities without being thrown off balance, and work to make a good impression that will help the person to engage with us and the services we represent or can access.

So how do we make the right kind of impression? Since social work aims wherever possible to make a partnership with service users which is empowering and constructive for them, the more skilfully you handle making contact, the more likely this is to happen as you begin to form the working alliance needed for effective work. In seeking to achieve this, you will do well to follow four principles: be clear, concise, comprehensive and courteous. Together these will help you to convey your reliability and trustworthiness, which are essential elements of the GSCC Codes of Practice.

1. Be clear: use simple, direct language, free from jargon and pompous phraseology.

2. Be concise: prepare yourself so you know the key issues in any situation, and can communicate them succinctly.

3. Be comprehensive: keep in mind all the key issues, and watch out for sidelining information that makes you uncomfortable.

4. Be courteous: courtesy is much more than good manners, though these are essential, and a certain level of polite formality is important when communicating with people new to us. Courtesy is also the way in which the underpinning values of social work are communicated – our respect for individuals and their uniqueness, and our commitment to anti-discriminatory and anti-racist practices and hence our respect for diversity.

These four principles will be explored from different angles as the various means of communication come under the spotlight.

Very often, letters or phone calls are the initial means of making contact, rather than face-to-face encounters. A letter or phone call is therefore your first chance to introduce yourself (and perhaps the service) and to make arrangements to meet. On the phone, you may also begin to discuss the issues which have led the person to make use of the service. In some situations (working as duty officer, or in a crisis service, or a drop-in, for example), a face-to-face encounter is the first contact. Another circumstance where a meeting is the first form of contact occurs when a colleague from your own or another agency who knows the service user makes the arrangements and introduces you. At present, since first contacts with service users are rarely if ever made by text or email, I will not deal with those means of communication here.

The first face-to-face meeting you have with a service user, whether or not it is the first point of contact, is of particular importance in building a working relationship. This is dealt with in the section 'Meeting people' later in this chapter. However, the power of letters and phone calls to make a significant first impression should not be underestimated, and these will be discussed first.

Making contact by letter

Before writing to a service user, you will need to know the answers to the following questions:

- Is there a standard way of formulating letters in your agency?

- To what extent can you use your own ideas about how to make a first contact by letter?

- Does your letter have to be seen and approved by someone else before it is sent out?

- Are all letters word-processed? Who does that and how long does it take? What if it's urgent?

- Is it ever okay or preferable to write your letter by hand (on the agency's headed paper)?

- What do you know about the recipient's ability to manage written communication? For example, do you have doubts about whether the person can read? Do they have a visual impairment or other need such as dyslexia so that braille, or a particular font is required? Can you provide this, or would a phone call be better?

- What are the norms in your agency about where you see service users? Is it usual to make a home visit, or invite them to your office, or meet in some other place, e.g. in a school or community centre? Can you be flexible about this and offer a choice, or not? (See Chapter 9 on safety.)

- Have you chosen a time of day, day of week or date which might be unacceptable to the service user? For example, Orthodox Jews will observe the Sabbath from dusk on a Friday, and will not engage with work or use transport. Practising Muslims will want to take Eid as a holiday, rather than attend appointments. If your diary doesn't give you this information, find one that does or check the internet.

- Taking into account the date you are writing the letter, the date it will be posted (which may be quite a bit later if letters are word-processed by a hard-pressed administrator), whether it goes first- or second-class post, the vagaries of the postal system, and adequate warning for the service user, are you suggesting a realistic date for meeting?

Once you have this information to hand, you can set about your task. If you are writing a letter from scratch (and this applies to all written communication, not just introductory letters), consider the four principles above: be clear, concise, comprehensive and courteous.

- Be clear: as noted above, use simple, direct language. If proposing a meeting, put day of week, date, time and place all together, perhaps in bold or on a separate line. Check day and date match. It isn't commonly done, but it can be helpful to indicate how long you expect the meeting to last.

- Be concise: even quite complex letters can usually be completed on one side of standard paper – say things once, and think about the sequence in which they appear so the letter is logical.

- Be comprehensive: include everything that ought to go in. This is likely to include who you are, why you are getting in touch, and what you are proposing. It may also include information about the service or about confidentiality, or leaflets about these may be enclosed as a matter of course and you just need to say so. If you are inviting someone to meet you in a place they might not know, say how to get there or enclose a map and directions. If in doubt, include this information, prefaced politely, e.g.: 'Just in case you don't know where our office is, it is the two-storey brick building next to the doctor's surgery in the High Street'.

- Be courteous: it is safest to use a formal title if the person has one, or first and last names if you don't know what title they use. Check cultural norms as far as possible. Chinese people put their family name first and personal name second. However, Chinese people in Britain often reverse this to conform to British norms. You may not be able to tell which is which until you meet the person and you may need to apologise if you have addressed them incorrectly. For many people of foreign origin this sort of error is an everyday occurrence and is often quickly forgiven. Complete lack of awareness, however, can be offensive.

- Always offer the opportunity to make a different arrangement if the one you are suggesting is not convenient, and say who they should contact and how. Sign off with the conventional 'Yours sincerely' and make sure your own name appears legibly or in type at the foot of the letter under your signature.

ACTIVITY **4.1**

The Birches Centre – introductory letters

A service providing community support to people with mental health problems offers day care, groups and individual sessions at the centre. Service users frequently do not attend the Centre for initial appointments, and staff waste a good deal of time waiting for people who never arrive. They assume this is because the person does not need the service after all, and anyway, people have the right to choose.

The centre has three standard letters on which handwritten additions are made. The introductory letter reads:

> Dear..............
>
> I am writing because you have been referred to our service by ....
> [name of referrer]. You have an appointment at the Birches Centre on
> .... [date] at .... [time].

Continued

I look forward to seeing you.

Yours sincerely

[name of worker]

The follow-up letter says:

Dear..............

I am writing because you did not attend the session recently offered you at the Birches Centre. This letter is to invite you to a further appointment on .... [date] at .... [time].

Yours sincerely

[name of worker]

The final letter runs:

Dear ....

I have invited you to two appointments at the Birches Centre which you failed to attend. I am therefore closing your case. If you decide you would like to see somebody at the Centre in the future, please telephone the number above.

Yours sincerely

[name of worker]

First, put yourself in the service user's shoes. Consider how you would feel as the recipient of these letters and write down your feelings. Now look at the introductory letter as a social worker, compile a list of its limitations and rewrite it. Don't feel you have to invite the person to the Centre. Go back into the recipient's shoes and test your letter out on yourself, or ask another student to read it, and see what feelings it arouses. Make improvements if necessary until you get the effect you want.

Making contact by phone

The first telephone call I made early in my first placement as a social work student was something of a challenge. It was to an electricity supplier, to negotiate repayments for a service user whose bill had mounted up. I was 26 years old; I knew perfectly well how to use the phone; I had been working for three years in a residential home where I regularly made telephone calls in the presence of colleagues; and I was petrified. My perceptive, not to say telepathic, practice teacher, having helped me to rehearse my argument, led me to an empty office and gently closed the door behind her to leave me alone with my phone call. I've rarely felt such gratitude.

Why was this everyday experience so frightening? I think there were three factors:

- I'd never made a call about this specific issue – an unpaid electricity bill – before.

- I was afraid I would fail my client – that I would mishandle the situation and she would have her electricity supply cut off.

- I was afraid of being found wanting by someone who was in an assessment role.

I was lucky. Not only did my practice teacher provide me with the physical and psychological space I needed to do the job adequately, she had given me a task which I had a reasonable chance of accomplishing. So I was successful, and felt relieved and jubilant. I could telephone my client with good news, and I don't remember any stage fright about making that second call.

Making telephone calls is not so difficult for everyone. Now that mobile phones are commonplace, and people are accustomed to talking on the phone in public places, it may be that you have more confidence about this than I had. The other factors – fear of being judged, and of letting someone down – may still affect you.

Until recently, the telephone has involved the voice alone (or the written word, for people with hearing impairments), although video phones may become the norm before long. However, the usual system relies on verbal communication. It appears that the absence of non-verbal cues does not affect people's ability to take turns (Bull, 1983). However, an unfamiliar accent, idiosyncratic English, or unclear speech may cause difficulty; if you can't understand, say so and ask them to say it again. There may be background noise (colleagues talking at your end, a television at the other) which makes it difficult to focus. It is in any case good manners to ask if it is convenient for the person to speak to you right now, but sometimes this is compelling – if there is noise at the other end that you think the person needs to attend to, such as a baby crying, you should check this out and offer to call back. If you are calling a service user's mobile, the person may be in a public place, so you may need to arrange to call again when they have more privacy.

Verbal content

It is important to start phone calls to strangers with an orienting statement which conveys the vital information the other person needs to respond helpfully (without sounding as though you are trying to sell them something). The 'vital information' will be affected by your role, the goal of making the call, and the context in which you are working.

Usually, you should

- Introduce yourself by your title and last name, or, more commonly, your first and last names. You may be used to introducing yourself by your first name only and this is fine in social situations. In social work, though, people need to feel confident about who you are and need to know who to ask for if they want to contact you again, although they will probably not remember it from your saying it just this once.

- Ask for the person you are calling. As with letters, use the person's formal title if you know it, or both their names, unless you only know their first name. Provided you have the right person, you can go on.

- Tell people your role and agency: *I'm a student social worker based in* [name of agency].

- Explain briefly and clearly why you are calling.

Examples

I'm ringing because your GP, Dr Robinson, wrote to us to say that you haven't been very well recently, and you haven't been able to get about as much as usual. Is that right?

I'm calling because you left a message for us at the weekend saying you wanted to speak to someone about your daughter.

I'm phoning to introduce myself, as the Health Visitor said you've been finding it a bit of a struggle since you had your new baby. I was wondering if I could arrange to visit you at home sometime tomorrow, if that suited.

As discussed in Chapter 2, there are often occasions in social work where ordinary social forms of communication are not appropriate, and you may have to inhibit a natural impulse to explain why you are ringing, unless you know for sure that it will not be a breach of confidentiality or create unnecessary risk to do so.

ACTIVITY **4.2**

Making initial phone calls

Compare the following scenarios, and before reading the Discussion, consider what you would say to the person who answers the phone in each instance.

Patrick Fitzgerald is a married man of 68 who was admitted to hospital after a stroke; he has been discharged home and you are following him up to assess whether he and his wife need home care services. When you ring, his wife answers the phone and says he is resting.

Janette Lawrence is in her early twenties bringing up three small children on her own. She has been referred by her Health Visitor. The last child is six weeks old and has not been feeding well or sleeping. Janette is getting exhausted, and losing her temper with the older ones, aged two and three. When you telephone, a woman answers who says Janette is asleep. She is her mother and is helping to look after the children today.

Helen Brown came into Accident and Emergency with injuries caused by her husband on Saturday night. He was arrested and then released on bail with an injunction to prevent him from returning to their house. Helen asked to see a social worker and on Monday you phone her at home. A man answers who says he is her brother, and that she is out.

> ## COMMENT
>
> *Patrick Fitzgerald: it is more or less a certainty that you can talk openly with Mrs Fitzgerald about your reasons for ringing. She must be aware of her husband's stroke and his current limitations, but she may not be aware that they have been referred to you, so tact is needed. Some people are offended if you imply that they are not coping; some people fear they are being offered charity, or alternatively, a service they cannot afford, and find either possibility humiliating. In all these instances, people may reject help they are entitled to. A safe bet, after explaining who you are and where you come from, is to say something like,* I understand your husband has recently been in hospital. I'm ringing to see if I can make a visit, and discuss with the two of you whether there are any services we can arrange which might make things a little easier for you right now.
>
> *Janette Lawrence: this one is a little more difficult. Does Janette's mother know she has been referred to you? If you aren't sure, it is better not to say so. Janette may feel ashamed about being referred to a social worker and may not want her mother to know. It is safest simply to ask when Janette might be available to talk to and ring her back. If you know (or discover from something her mother says) that she has talked with her mother, then you could leave a message asking her to ring you back.*
>
> *Helen Brown: again, all you can do here is ask when she is likely to be around and offer to contact her again. The man may be her brother, in which case the situation is similar to Janette's, but you can't be sure of this. It could be her husband, breaking the terms of the injunction, and posing as her brother to obtain information he can later use against her. It could be dangerous for her if he knows that she has asked to see a social worker. In the longer run, you may end up working with both of them, but you need to speak with Helen first.*

Non-verbal content

So far, we have considered the words you say and some limits on what you would say if the referred person was not available to speak to you. Clarity, and paralanguage (tone, pitch, volume and speed) are just as important as the words you use. Paralanguage conveys the emotional content of a message, so this is where the emotional impact will be made on the person you are calling. Just think of your own name, and the many tones of voice in which it can be said. What meanings do they have and how do they affect your emotional response? Try out this list of possible meanings:

- concern for your welfare;

- a command;

- flirtatiousness;

- irritation;

- anger;

- teasing;

- sarcasm;

- panic;

- reproach;

- calling you from a distance – think about how voice tone is affected if the person knows you are within earshot, or isn't sure.

Remembering the context, the goal of making contact and your role will help you determine the kind of paralanguage you need. In general, you will do fine with voice tone that is neutral to warm, friendly and interested but not matey; medium to low pitch, which carries more authority than high pitch; medium volume unless you know the person has a hearing impairment; and a pace that demonstrates a good level of energy without being pressured. As you listen to the other person, you may deliberately or spontaneously alter your speech. With a timid person, you are likely to drop your voice, and speak more gently, but try to misattune purposefully – don't let your voice become as small as theirs. If they sound agitated, purposefully misattune by slowing down. You can of course ask people to speak up or slow down, as well. *I can't hear you very well, can you speak up a bit?* Speaking clearly always helps. Being prepared and having a good idea of what you are going to say will help you avoid rushing, or getting tongue-tied.

Flexibility

A phone call may not turn out the way you expected. Let's say the person starts to talk about their concerns there and then, while you were expecting to make a visit. Or they are upset or angry. Stay curious about why the person is behaving unexpectedly. Were you under-prepared or did you inadvertently upset them? Are they in more of a crisis than it seemed from the referral? While you might have a good contextual sense of what 'belongs' in the phone call and what you would leave for a meeting, the service user might not – perhaps this person pours out their heart to strangers fairly frequently, and if so, why might that be? Is it a problem? You need to be responsive, as if you stick to your agenda too rigidly, you may alienate them, but keep your goals in mind. Unless it is a crisis which needs immediate attention, then your goal becomes containment. Don't get impatient. A useful pattern is an empathic recognition of the person's state, followed by a question which confirms your commitment to work with them.

Mrs Evans, it sounds as though there's a lot going on for you right now, and there'll be a lot to talk about when we meet. When might be a good time?

Mr MacDonald, thank you for being so forthcoming about your concerns. We'll be able to go over all this in more detail when we meet. Shall I visit or would you prefer to come here?

Melissa, I'm sorry to hear you so upset. Do you want to talk about this now or would it be better to meet face-to-face?

In Chapter 9 there is more about responding to hostility. Stopping the hostile behaviour becomes your priority (Braithwaite, 2001):

Jack, stop shouting at me so that we can talk about what the matter is.

Being on duty: expect the unexpected

This section serves as the transition between telephone contact and meeting people in person, since both happen when you are on duty. Some aspects of meeting face-to-face are discussed here, others in the following sections 'Meeting people'.

Duty sessions involve dealing with service users for the first time at the agency base, and taking phone calls from service users or other referrers. Not all agencies organise duty sessions, but only see people by arrangement. Some local authorities organise out-of-hours duty service, but the discussion here relates to services provided within office hours. Duty sessions are usually organised in agencies where members of the public can refer themselves for a service, sometimes for matters which can be dealt with fairly promptly during a one-off visit. Applications for disabled car badges are one example. Duty sessions in a service for people with problems with substance use may have another name, such as 'drop-in session', aiming to draw in people who would not easily access the service otherwise. In either case, duty sessions are by their nature unpredictable. Students sit in on duty until they have a good idea of how to handle matters themselves, but even then there will be surprises. If you are stumped by a request, seek help.

The skills involved are somewhat different from those employed in initiating contact. You have to disentangle the essential elements of the other person's communication so that you can respond helpfully, as you do when you meet people face-to-face in planned encounters. Some people will communicate their concerns in a straightforward fashion, others won't.

Some people behave as though you know everyone they know, and don't explain who anyone is. In some parts of the country referring with emphasis to a nameless *he* or *she* almost always indicates the person's partner, but if this is not your cultural norm, you could feel bewildered. Some people are very involved in their story and tell it at length, even though much of it may not seem to be of immediate relevance. When any of us is upset about something, our communication tends to get disorganised. Professionals are not immune to these habits or forces, so you might need to organise the information being put across by them, too. Your goal is to provide focus and to shape the encounter so that you can organise the material presented to you.

Stay courteous, be patient, and try to unravel what they are talking about. In Chapter 5, we will learn more about different kinds of questions and statements, drawing on a System for Analyzing Verbal Communication (SAVI™) (Simon and Agazarian, 2005).

Narrow questions (Simon and Agazarian, 2005) are helpful in obtaining facts: *How many children do you have? How old are they? Does anyone else live with you?* Less skilled workers tend to fire off narrow questions like this, and it can begin to feel like an interrogation. More skilled workers use a range of verbal behaviours. For example, preceding a narrow question by explaining what you are doing, and why, avoids abruptness and orientates the other person:

It would help me to understand your situation better if I knew who was in your household. Can I ask you a few questions before we go any further?

Or:

I'm sorry, I want to understand what you are telling me but I've missed a few things. Can we go back a bit? Thank you. Now, I gather that Harry is bothering you quite a bit – could you tell me who he is and how he's involved in your life?

This intervention acknowledges the muddle without blaming the person for their communication style.

Duty sessions usually involve taking down some details in writing, on a standard referral form. This will be filled in with the service user present, or during the telephone call. On the phone, it helps to tell people what is happening at your end, especially if you fall silent. *I'm just writing down the details here. Is that okay? Could you spell that person's name for me, please?*; or *I'm just thinking about what you've said.* An interesting exercise is to compare the referral forms used by a range of agencies – the items they include or exclude tell you quite a bit about the value base of the agency.

Key points to remember are:

- you may be the first representative of the agency the service user has ever encountered, so make the most of the chance to engage with them;

- be prepared for a jumbled story which needs clarifying and ordering, especially if someone is distressed;

- explain what you are doing as you go along, such as why you want to know certain information or why you are completing a form.

Meeting people

This section deals with planned interviews. It will be apparent that much of what has already been said about making contact by letter and phone, and in relation to being on duty, will apply equally when meeting someone in a planned way for the first time, so it will not be repeated here. A planned interview is often a more complex experience, usually lasting considerably longer than a phone call (typically anything from half an hour to an hour, though some contacts are much briefer and occasionally they are much longer). Meeting face-to-face, whether on duty or by design, gives you the opportunity to read non-verbal communication and use your own to good effect. It is usually your first serious opportunity to discuss issues such as the limits of confidentiality, and to negotiate what kind of service is to be provided. You are also likely to hear in some detail about the issues that have brought the service user into contact with the service. Social work students sometimes believe that they should avoid 'going too deep' in a first encounter. This is to muddle personal first encounters with professional ones, where the rules of engagement are different. Service users are often ready to get to the nub of the matter, and want to get started as soon as they can see you can be trusted. The place in which you meet will have considerable impact on how you go about the encounter, and this is discussed first.

Where are you meeting, why, and what is the impact?

Sometimes this will have been agreed jointly between you, and sometimes circumstances, agency norms or service provision make the decision for you. Safety considerations will also play a part. Possibilities are:

- the service user's home;

- a room in your agency building;

- a room in another agency, including residential homes, hostels, day centres, schools;

- a hospital bedside;

- a public place such as a café, or even the street (outreach work with roofless people).

The degree of privacy and, therefore, confidentiality, you can offer varies considerably in these different circumstances, as does the control you have over the atmosphere generated by the environment.

Home visits

Service users sometimes prefer to be seen at home, feeling more comfortable on their own territory. There may be other considerations – if someone is agoraphobic, or has mobility problems, or the journey from their home to your workplace is arduous – their home is probably the best choice. It also gives you an opportunity to see their home circumstances first-hand. If their problems arise from or are exacerbated by dilapidated housing, crowded conditions, housing unsuited to their current needs, troublesome neighbours, lack of adequate furniture or other possessions, or shortage of food, having seen the problem for yourself is likely to make you a more powerful advocate for them.

Does a person's home reach acceptable levels of tidiness and hygiene for safety? If not, how does this affect them and their social interaction? How has it come about? I once shared a house so extravagantly untidy that when it was ransacked by burglars it took a while for us to notice. But the owner was not depressed or defeated and friends visited despite the chaos. It's very different for a child living with a disabled parent where neither can cope with animal faeces and mountains of laundry. Which school friends will visit then?

Home visits also allow you to observe relationships in their natural environment. Where relationships are part of the difficulty, your first-hand experience will inform your analysis and helping strategy. You will of course affect the dynamics to some degree by your presence, and it is perhaps impossible to get an absolutely true picture of relationships, except with a concealed video camera, but your observations are valuable nonetheless.

Sometimes home visits are made even where there is a risk of violence. Investigating child protection concerns, domestic violence and abuse of vulnerable adults, and some visits to people with substance misuse or mental health problems may all carry this risk, though it is by no means the norm. In the past, social workers often went unaccompanied but this is less usual now. Student involvement in such cases is generally as a co-worker. If you ever make a visit where you fear violence, go with a colleague, another professional or the police. There is more about managing hostility in Chapter 9.

Being invited into someone's home is a privilege, and should be undertaken with respect, while keeping the goals of the meeting in mind. If the television is on and you can't concentrate, say, *I really want to hear what you have to say, and I'd find it easier with the TV off. Is that okay?* If the service user seats you somewhere from where it is difficult to talk with them, say how important it is that you can communicate easily and ask if you can move a chair. You might expect a high level of privacy in someone's home, only to discover that friends, neighbours or relatives are present, or come and go during the interview. Ask if the person is happy to talk in the presence of the visitors; sometimes you can suggest retreating to another part of the house for privacy. As you are in someone's home, this might seem impolite. Remember Fisher et al.'s (1984) social workers who were unable to develop rewarding and purposeful working alliances with some service users. Your goal is to build a working alliance, and your role is to ensure that happens, which means taking some control of the context (with the service user's consent). For the duration of your visit, the service user's home becomes your work place. Distractions and interruptions can be serious impediments. Having said that, you may have to give up on the ideal of quiet, focused, uninterrupted time, and just get on with it.

Agency-based meetings

Not all agencies have provision for meetings, but where they do, some service users will prefer this to your visiting their home. Here are some reasons:

- home is a private place;

- they live with other people and can't guarantee privacy;

- they live with an abuser and need to talk away from the situation;

- they get upset when discussing difficulties and want this to be separate from home, which is a refuge;

- they are depressed and find going out hard, so it's an opportunity to practise;

- they live in a hostel or bed-and-breakfast accommodation and can only see you in their bedroom – this feels too intimate or cramped;

- they are ashamed of their home and fear you will make them leave (try to discuss this, as you may be able to help with furniture or cleaning services).

You may prefer to meet at your agency because:

- you have impaired mobility and cannot access the service user's home;

- you have information to hand;

- there are childcare facilities on site;

- there are colleagues to turn to;

- the service user may be violent so you want to see them with a colleague at a time when other staff are about.

Rooms in other agencies

Using rooms in other agencies is sometimes necessary because your agency only makes provision for offices. Sometimes there is less control over the environment – you may find people interrupt because they didn't know you were there, or want to know who you are. Good preparation can reduce the risk of this happening.

Other agencies are sometimes preferred by service users. A voluntary organisation for people with mental health problems might be less threatening than a community mental health team base. A family centre might be more welcoming than the children and families' team office if there are toys for children to play with and a cheerful environment. Sometimes the other agency is the person's home, if they are in residential care or living in a hostel. A private day room is the ideal choice, but you may have to make do with meeting in someone's bedroom, or a sitting room occupied by other people. A bedroom will afford privacy but may feel uncomfortable. You may find you look around less than usual, or sit straighter, as ways of compensating for the intimacy of the space. A communal sitting room offers the same problems as the hospital bedside – discussed in the next paragraph.

Hospital bedside

A person who is confined to a hospital bed has little choice but to be seen in the presence of other patients and their visitors. You may feel awkward about conversing with an audience of strangers, and of course you will have to check out whether the person is willing to discuss matters with you in these circumstances. If there is no other choice, you have to make the best of it. Lowering your own voice can help the other person lower theirs, but paper and pen may be needed if someone has hearing loss (see Chapter 8).

Remember to wear layers going to a hospital – the wards are often quite warm.

Public places

Occasionally, social workers meet service users in places such as cafés. Some of the same considerations pertain as in hospital visits, though other customers in a café usually have more to keep them occupied than hospital patients. Your problem might be that the service user doesn't mind discussing private matters, but you do. This may be a subject for discussion between you. If the service user is putting themselves at risk, say of being robbed, then you have a duty to talk about the risks with them. If it is simply that they are less inhibited about mentioning their problems in public than you are, overcome your embarrassment and meet them halfway.

Starting interviews

Be there on time. Punctuality is quite hard to achieve. It depends upon a realistic assessment of the time needed for appointments and work arising from them, and a good estimate of any travelling time required. It amazes me that I was qualified for quite a while before I began to schedule travelling time into my diary – requiring abject apologies from me and a great deal of patience on the part of my clients, for whom I was often late.

Being punctual is not only desirable at a practical level, it is a courtesy which communicates respect. Arriving at someone's house early runs the risk of embarrassing someone who is not ready – still in the bath, for example, or of wasting your time because they are at the shops. Keeping someone waiting in their own home or elsewhere is also disrespectful, as the person may be getting edgy, or have another commitment later on, or they may have made special arrangements, say for childcare, which are time-limited. From time to time, punctuality has to be sacrificed to unforeseen circumstances which take precedence over plans. If this happens, make every effort to let the person know, and arrange to be late or to see them at another time.

RESEARCH SUMMARY

Phatic communication

Neil Thompson (2003) helpfully discusses what is known in linguistics as phatic communication (p.86). The term refers to the small talk we all engage in with strangers and acquaintances, and at the start and end of contacts, including those with people we know well. Thompson points out that comments about the weather fall into this category of communication, at least in England. In Italy, I have often been given free advice about how to prepare food by shopkeepers; in England, I've only come across this form of phatic offering from fishmongers. Phatic communication is bound to vary in content across cultures, but the style and function are the same. It consists of safe, impersonal, common topics which give people something to talk about, either when they are engaged in another activity, such as shopping, or when they are approaching and completing more in-depth communication. I think of it as an animal behaviour which says, I'm here, I'm not dangerous, I'm being friendly but I'm not going to get too close. *When phatic communication is required, but we or the other person can't think of anything to say, it makes us feel uncomfortable and shifty. Skilled social workers often employ phatic communication to ease the beginning of interviews and draw them to a close. Visually, the shape of an interview, then, is starting in the shallows, going deeper, and coming up again to end on exchanges which take place in the shallows. This is probably a means of regulating emotion, as discussed in Chapter 3.*

Social work interviews start with some phatic exchanges – niceties about the weather, about finding the location, whether a cup of tea or glass of water would be appreciated, and so forth. It is a cultural norm in England to accompany these exchanges with smiling, and a certain amount of eye contact. You will notice that in these circumstances, eye contact tends to be fleeting rather than prolonged, and people do a lot of 'settling down' activities, such as taking off coats, deciding where to sit, rummaging in bags for pen and paper, disappearing to make tea, shutting the dog in the kitchen, and so forth. These behaviours are perhaps the non-verbal equivalent of phatic verbal communication: they create a space in which people make the transition from what they were doing previously to this particular encounter, and they are an opportunity for humans to show each other that they are safe to be around. These activities may all be completed in two minutes, but they have set the scene. It is important to be reasonably at ease in this transitional space – diving in to 'the business' too quickly or refusing to engage with social niceties may well arouse distrust and discomfort in the service user.

Service users of course have a choice about whether they accept a drink of tea, coffee or water if we offer one when they come to our office. We too, have a choice about accepting one from them in their home. Offering a drink is a social norm within the reach of most service users, even those with low incomes and low self-regard. Offering you a drink puts them on an even footing with you in a small but important way. By implication, your acceptance of a drink acknowledges their social standing, and also communicates acceptance of the person. Occasionally you will have reason to feel cautious. Many social workers have a story of the cup of tea they had doubts about. Even then, the information gleaned from this could be useful. I once visited someone depressed, on home leave from a mental health unit, and desperate to impress that all was well. My coffee, with one sugar, also contained powdered soup which had presumably been spooned in earlier and abandoned. Or at least I hoped so. I drank what I could, and came to no harm. If you have worries about this, ask around for survival rates!

Occasionally you may be offered something to eat. Some people who live alone and have few social contacts welcome the chance to share a modest meal with someone else. And in some cultures, offering food is an essential means of showing respect to a visitor to the house. Accepting the food equally indicates respect, but it can be difficult to know what to do, especially when you are visiting a family with very little money. I have certainly occasionally accepted such offers, but this is not something much discussed in social work, so ask your colleagues.

Forms of address

There is only one rule about how to address the other person – that it should be in the form they prefer, which may change over time. The norm in our society of calling children by their first names has become common in many forms of relationship. To some people this feels too intimate, or seems impertinent. Some older people find it demeaning to be called by their first name, but it is dangerous to assume that all older people feel this way. So you need to find out from each individual how they would like you to address them. This is especially important when we are unfamiliar with the service user's language and culture. As noted earlier, if you do not know which is a Chinese person's first or last name, you will need to ask. On a different note, all Sikh men are called Singh and all Sikh women are called Kaur, which denote gender, while other names are used both for men and women. Kaur and Singh should be used in formal communications, but are not needed face to face.

Occasionally, service users may address you in a way you would not normally choose. Again, this may a cultural issue, in relation to respect for professionals, or a more personal feeling about distance and closeness. In Sheffield, bus drivers used to call everyone 'Flower', men and women alike. Consider the following suggestion: if clients want to use a more formal mode of address, accept it, e.g. being called Mr Simpson instead of Michael; if they want to use a more informal mode, e.g. calling you Mick, and it makes you uncomfortable, move it back to a more formal mode. In both instances, try to understand the meaning of the communication.

Essential preliminaries

Once you and the service user have settled down, you will need to outline the following:

- how you see the purpose of the interview;
- how long you expect it to last;
- something about your student status;
- confidentiality and its limits.

These need to be addressed separately and some agreement sought from the service user. Addressing confidentiality is especially important. First, service users have a right to know who will have access to information about them. Second, they need to know that generally social workers are members of teams, and confidentiality is maintained within a particular professional circle. In other words, you can rarely if ever tell someone that confidentiality stops with you. Third, you need to alert them to the fact that in exceptional circumstances, you may have to share information about them when they would prefer this not to happen – in cases of suspected child abuse, for instance. But unless suspected child abuse is the main reason for the referral, in which case this should be explicit between you, you need to be careful how you frame this. The last thing you want at an initial meeting is to worry the person that information about them will be passed on without their consent, or that they are under suspicion. The following example follows the clear, concise, comprehensive and courteous principles.

Example

I've come today to hear more from you about the difficulties you've been having with your little boy, so that we can see if there's anything we can do to help. You may have other concerns, and I'll come back to that in a moment. (If you check out at this point whether they see things this way, or have other concerns, you are inviting them to embark on telling you their story, and your chance of setting out the context for the work will disappear.)

I expect to be here this first time for about an hour – is that all right with you? If we haven't managed to discuss everything, I'll arrange to come back.

Before we actually get going, I want to make sure you have a good understanding of what will happen to the personal information we talk about. As I said in my letter, I'm a student social worker. I'm working at the Family Centre for six months, and all my work is supervised by a qualified social worker. I'll need to talk with that person about all my work, to make sure that you are getting a good service. Does that make sense to you, or do you have any questions?

Also, in terms of confidentiality, I want to explain how things work at the Family Centre. All of us are bound by rules about confidentiality to protect the people we work with, so we are very careful with your personal information. We have team meetings where we talk about the work we are doing. This helps us share ideas and learn more about how to help people. It also means that if I were off sick for a time, other people would know a bit about you and you wouldn't have to start from scratch. I might also need to talk with other professionals, like your little boy's nursery teacher, but I will tell you if I think I should do that, and I'll tell you why and what I'll be saying.

How does that sound so far?

I'll also make notes about our meetings which I can bring and show you if you'd like to see them. They'll be kept under lock and key at the Family Centre, and the only other person who will look at them regularly will be my supervisor. Other people might look at them if the need arose, say if you rang up on my day off and needed to speak to someone urgently. Is there anything you want to ask about that?

Finally, I want to underline that the only reason I would ever pass information on to another professional without discussing it with you first is if it were an emergency, and there was no other choice.

So, can you tell me a bit more about the difficulties you're having?

Some agencies also introduce their complaints procedures at this point. Check with your agency about what is expected.

Making notes

The final matter to be settled before you and the service user begin the main business of the contact is to decide about note-taking. Practice varies widely. Because it is impossible to write without losing eye contact and missing some non-verbal information, some social workers prefer to concentrate on the person, and have all their observational skills available. However, because it is nearly, though not quite, impossible to remember everything from an interview lasting half an hour or more, some social workers prefer to take notes. While some service users may have strong views one way or the other, seeing note-taking either as an obstacle to communication, or conversely as a sign that they are being taken seriously, mostly, how they feel will depend on how you manage the process. It's worth experimenting with both taking notes and not taking notes, and see how you fare. If you take notes, explain what you are doing, check that the user is okay with it, and offer to show them the notes. You can also suggest that if either of you finds it more of a nuisance than you anticipated, you can say so, and change tack.

ACTIVITY **4.3**

Analysing the early elements of a first contact

Think of a first contact with a service user you have observed when shadowing, or one where you have been the interviewer. Write down what you remember of the first ten minutes. Then consider the following questions.

Did the meeting start on time, if it was planned one?

What do you remember of phatic communication?

Were there any distractions (television, dog) and, if so, how were these managed?

Was the story told in a straightforward way or did the social worker (or you) have to unravel it?

If the same piece of work were to happen tomorrow, would you change anything?

What would you change and why?

CHAPTER SUMMARY

In this chapter we have incorporated learning from previous chapters to understand the importance of initial contacts in developing respectful and productive working relationships with people. We have thought about how clarity, conciseness, comprehensiveness and courtesy enable us to put the social work ideal of respect into practice from the beginning. Some issues of diversity and differing needs have been touched upon. We have considered whether to initiate contact by letter and phone and how to do this, and thought about first encounters in planned and unplanned situations. We have seen that the settings in which we work influence how we conduct ourselves – the context thus affects the role we take up. This refers both to the agency we work in, and the immediate physical surroundings. The more personal, informal environment of the service user's home needs to be respected, but not at the expense of losing sight of our goals and role. In this sense, the service user's home becomes the workplace, and we can, with their consent, take charge of the context to facilitate our work in a way we would not do if visiting a friend.

FURTHER READING

Coulshed, V and Orme, J (1998) *Social work practice: An introduction*. 3rd edition. Basingstoke: Palgrave Macmillan.
Chapter 4, 'Interviewing and counselling', pp 69–94, explains different models, describes approaches and provides case examples.

Trevithick, P (2005) *Social work skills: A practice handbook*. 2nd edition. Buckingham: Open University Press.
Chapter 4, 'Basic interviewing skills', provides plenty of practice examples and takes the reader through a range of possible interventions and responses through the whole interviewing process.

Chapter 5
Making progress and managing endings

This chapter will begin to help you to meet the following National Occupational Standards:

Key Role 1: Prepare for, and work with individuals, families, carers, groups and communities to assess their needs and circumstances.

- Prepare for social work contact and involvement.

Key Role 2: Plan, carry out, review and evaluate social work practice, with individuals, families, carers, groups, communities and other professionals.

- Interact with individuals, families, carers, groups and communities to achieve change and development and to improve life opportunities.

Key Role 5: Manage and be accountable, with supervision and support, for your own social work practice within your organisation.

- Manage and be accountable for your own work.

It will also introduce you to the following academic standards as set out in the 2008 social work subject benchmark statement:

5.1.5 The nature of social work practice.

5.5.1 Managing problem-solving activities.

5.5.4 Intervention and evaluation.

5.6 Communication skills.

5.7 Skills in working with others.

Introduction

This chapter will bring together what we have learnt so far to identify the interpersonal and communication skills which underlie models for social work assessment and intervention. The models themselves are not discussed here (Milner and O'Byrne, 2002; and Parker and Bradley, 2007, are good starting points). In Chapter 2 we learnt about the importance of making a goal-directed collaborative working alliance with service users, and the weight service users place on our being approachable, warm, attentive, respectful, interested and understanding. They also want us to share information, offer choices, be reliable, and give them time. In Chapter 3 we learnt about emotional communication and body language, and Chapter 4 took us through the skills needed to make initial contacts. So where do we go from there?

The chapter is organised under the following headings:

- Introducing SAVI™;
- Getting to know SAVI™;
- Collaboration and empowerment;
- Listening;
- Providing information – orienting and responding;
- Gathering information – asking and answering questions;
- Paraphrasing and summarising;
- Using commands and corrective feedback;
- Bringing working relationships to an end.

Introducing SAVI™

First, note that SAVI (System for Analyzing Verbal Interaction) (Simon and Agazarian, 2003, 2005) was originally developed as a research tool, and has only been tested in the US. It is used by mental health practitioners and organisational developers in the US, UK and Sweden. Care needs to be taken in applying its communicative styles in different cultures or non-verbal media.

Taking these reservations into account, it is nonetheless a strength of SAVI (pronounced 'savvy') that, like the working alliance, it is independent of any particular approach, and is useful in a wide range of contexts. It is a metacommunicative tool enabling you to use your second-order skills to think about any interaction in which you are participant or observer. The prevailing communicative norms in relationships tell us a great deal about underlying attitudes to self and others, and about emotion and its regulation. SAVI can therefore also be used to listen to service users' verbal interactions with each other, in families and groups, and to consider the climate of relationships in teams, as well as exchanges between you and service users. You can check letters, case recordings and reports, to see say, whether opinions are presented as though they were facts.

SAVI categorises verbal exchanges, but takes emotional content into account through paralanguage, (voice tone, speed, etc.) which trumps verbal content if it contradicts it. All hostile threatening statements are classed in the same way, whatever grammatical form they take. Remember that service users who are not fluent in English may not speak with the emotional expressiveness they have in their primary language.

A copy of the SAVI grid is included here on page 74. We are not going to explore all the elements of the grid, as there is not the space to explain them all, but we will look at the categorisation into red, yellow and green light behaviours.

Getting to know SAVI™

Initially, trying to make sense of the SAVI™ grid is somewhat daunting. It takes time to understand the meaning of all the categories. Once you have grasped it, you can move about the grid rather like a chessboard.

Look at the SAVI™ grid and read the description in the box. The grid is spelt in US English. Where SAVI terms appear later in the text, they are italicised, and may be in US and UK spellings. Further explanations and definitions of the categories can be found in Simon and Agazarian (2003) and on the SAVI website.

SAVI™ Grid
System for Analyzing Verbal Interaction

	PERSON	TOPIC	
	Person	Factual	Orienting
RED Light	1 FIGHT Attack/Blame Righteous question Self defense Complaints Sarcasm	2 DATA-VOID Mind-reading Negative prediction Gossip Joking around Thinking out loud	3 COMPETE Yes/Buts Discounts Leading question Oughtitudes Interrupts
YELLOW Light	4 SOCIAL SELF Personal information (current) Personal information (past) Personal explanations	5 PUBLIC DATA Facts & figures General information Narrow question Broad question	6 INFLUENCE Opinion Proposal Command Impersonal reinforcement
GREEN Light	7 EMPATHIZE Tells own feeling Asks or Answers (inner-person) question Mirrors others' (inner-person) experience Affectionate joke Self assertion	8 DATA PROCESS Answers question Paraphrase Summarize Clarifies own answer (with data) Corrective feedback	9 INTEGRATE Agreement/Positives Building on others' ideas or experiences Work joke

Silence, Laughter, Noise

SAVI™ is a trademark of Anita Simon and Yvonne Agazarian. Copyright© 2005 Simon and Agazarian. Reproduced with permission.

In SAVI, behaviours are always context-related, and no one behaviour takes moral precedence over another. Asking leading questions, interrupting, and 'yes/butting' are typical behaviours used by UK journalists interviewing politicians, for example. Gossiping and joking around are informal behaviours most people engage in with friends. Red-light behaviours are rarely helpful in your social work role, though inevitably they will be kindled in you at times. Generally speaking, relationships in which red-light behaviours predominate are not happy ones.

SAVI™

The three columns differentiate between Person, Factual and Orienting utterances as follows.

Person

- *In red light, I am in an unregulated angry state, using Attack/Blame, Righteous question, and Sarcasm to express hostility towards the other. Alternatively, I am victim, using Self defense* to blame or justify myself (I'm no good, I'm stupid; it wasn't my fault), or Complaints (The weather's always awful when we go away; you never get an answer when you ring the help line; nobody cares);*

- *In yellow light, I report on my factual and internal current and past states, and offer explanations for them (I've got a headache; I went to school in Lagos; I can't hear you because of the traffic; I felt inferior growing up – my parents favoured my sister);*

- *In green light, I use both emotional and cognitive information to talk about my emotions, see and respond to emotion in others, ask and answer emotional questions (Are you as angry as when you arrived?), make affectionate jokes, and draw boundaries (I'm leaving now).*

Factual

- *In red light, there are no facts. I know what people are thinking without finding out, I know what will happen in the future, I gossip and spread rumours, jokes are a similar distraction, and I um and ah and interrupt myself and go off at tangents and never finish a sentence;*

- *In yellow light I can provide specific and general information about the world, and ask Narrow questions for specific information and Broad questions which invite someone to share their views, ideas, story etc.;*

- *In green light, I organise and reflect back factual information, expand on answers with additional information, and put misapprehensions right.*

Orienting

- *In red, I compete for power; my statements distance me from others. I appear to agree but quickly disagree (Yes/but), demean others' statements, try to force agreement through Leading questions, moralise, and interrupt;*

- *In yellow, I seek to influence others without hostility, and am open to alternatives;*

- *In green, I co-operate with others, support them wholeheartedly, and have fun with them.*

*Self defense combines self-defence and self-attack; it is different in meaning from self-defence as used by Heard and Lake (1997), discussed in Chapter 3.

Collaboration and empowerment

Working collaboratively with service users in an empowering way is a hallmark of social work practice, but what do these efforts on our part look like in action? Given that we have considerable power to make decisions which affect service users' lives, such as judging whether they are eligible for a service, or, usually with others, whether they should live in their own home, or live with their children, can we ever truly be partners in collaboration? Wherever we have statutory powers, service users will rightly regard us as powerful. We can partially empower them by sharing information they need – in SAVI™ terms, yellow lights such as giving facts, sharing opinions, offering explanations for the thinking behind the opinion, making proposals where choices are available; and green lights, such as answering questions, building on others' ideas, mirroring inner-person feelings. These are all discussed in more detail later in the chapter.

In other circumstances, we are freer to help service users determine their own goals. Here our skills lie not in trying to give them 'better' goals that we prefer, but to work with them to ensure their goals are specific and achievable.

For example:

Goal: To stop using street drugs

Your first task is to see if this goal is specific enough: should a target date be set?

You then help the service user to identify as many means of reaching the goal as possible.

Means

- attend sessions with a drugs worker;

- stop seeing my drug friends;

- break up with my partner who uses drugs;

- reconnect with old friends from before I got into drugs;

- move back to my mum's for a while to get out of the area;

- ask my mum to look after my money for a while;

- start going to the gym twice a week to get a natural high, improve my health and give me something to do.

They may need to make choices among these; they may not all be achievable. Is there an affordable gym locally, or would the GP prescribe exercise? Is breaking up with their partner what they want to do? Encouraging the service user to find out about these for themselves, rather than doing it for them, is likely to lead to a greater sense of competence.

A useful concept here is the zone of proximal development (Vygotsky, 1986). This refers to what a person is nearly able to do, but cannot do yet, without assistance. If our expectations are beyond the zone of proximal development, the person will fail; if we do something for them which lies within their capability, they may lose confidence and skills. If we help them to make that next step, they have genuinely extended their capabilities. We can only develop an understanding of the person's zone of proximal development through collaborative discourse. We need to be alert to having misjudged matters; if they agree to do something (e.g. visit the local college to find about computing courses) and week after week they do not do it, then the task needs to be reviewed. Is it too difficult? Are they really interested or not? Did they agree just to please you?

Apparently esteem-building comments based on assumptions should be avoided: *I'm sure you're a good mother; Obviously you've always been very independent.* In SAVI™, these are a red-light behaviour, mind-reading, rather than statements based on knowledge. If we cannot support what we say, but simply want to make the person feel better, this will not convince. A greater risk is that the person who knows they are not being a good mother in some ways will be dissuaded from discussing their anxieties.

Although we spend a good deal of time with people when they are sad, frustrated and trying to cope with complex problems, there are often moments of humour to be shared as well. Laughter does actually make people feel better and those moments should be appreciated.

CASE STUDY

Liam and Becky have mild learning disabilities; Becky also has a hearing impairment. They are in their 20s, living together, and have a baby, Evie, who is seven months old. Evie was accommodated with their consent when she was five months old as she was gradually slipping down the developmental charts after an average start, and because she was frequently found dressed in dirty clothes, with an unchanged nappy and with sores. She was very quiet and didn't respond much to adult invitations to play. Liam and Becky lack knowledge and skills, rather than motivation. The goal is for their parenting skills to reach reasonable levels and for Evie to be returned to them as soon as possible.

There is a plan in place with the family centre, where they will have three sessions a week with Evie for the next six weeks. They are expected to attend separate sessions about child development and childcare, and they can visit Evie at the foster carers' home in between times. The expectations about how they treat Evie, how much weight, approximately, she needs to gain, how to play with her, and so forth, are clearly written up in the plan. Liam can read quite well but Becky finds reading hard. The family centre staff are working on a pack with Becky which uses pictures and the minimum of words and figures, so she can have this available to her.

Think about how you might try to explain what is required of them.

Listening

Listening attentively conveys interest and respect, and is an essential part of the turn-taking that characterises human interaction, starting with pre-verbal 'conversations' between adults and infants involving vocalisation, gesture and gaze (e.g. Trevarthen, 1977, cited in Bull, 1983). Listening usually involves some form of gaze in adult relationships, too, if we are sighted, but this will vary according to individual, gender and cultural differences. It is common when listening to make noises (*Mm, Yes, Right*), often talking simultaneously, but these are not interruptions or efforts to take a turn, rather they encourage the other person to continue. These are a SAVI™ yellow light: *impersonal reinforcements*.

We listen more intently in social work conversations than in everyday ones, as we strive to understand the person's point of view, to piece together the current and past elements of their story, to understand relationships, and to consider our responses. If we rehearse our next response too much, we inevitably stop listening. *I missed that, I'm sorry. Could you say it again?* Our own conversational responses are a mixture of spontaneous interaction and more measured and deliberate utterances as we use our verbal behaviour to make a purposeful impact. We need to think carefully about how we structure what we say. There is considerable evidence that when working with children, and with people with learning disabilities and other communicative difficulties, we use vocabulary and grammar that is too complex. Many of the children we work with have language impairments which are not evident or identified (Cross, 2004), and this may well be true for adult service users too. In many situations, simple straightforward language presented in short sentences is helpful. There will be more about this in Chapters 6 and 8.

It is important to remember details, so that we do not keep asking the same questions; this irritates people and conveys a lack of interest. When we work with people over a period of time, being able to recall what they told us weeks or months ago serves a number of functions. First, it gives value to what they say. Second, it holds their story together in our mind and theirs, which is particularly significant for people who have had fragmented experiences of care-giving, where their story is fragmented. Third, it allows us to identify changes with them. *You used to talk a lot about how bad your childhood was. I notice that you talk more about the present and the future now.* In SAVI™, these are yellow light: *personal information past and current*, stemming from your own knowledge of the service user.

We are listening to the content of the information, and also its form and pattern.

Congruence

Are words and non-verbal signals congruent with each other? When a person talks about a sad subject, do they look sad?

CASE STUDY

Bev was in her mid-twenties, with a mild learning disability and depression. Work with her focused on improving her social network and expanding her interests. She asked for some sessions to talk about sexual abuse she had experienced when she was younger. In the second session, the social worker said, I've noticed that when you talk about the bad things that happened at home, you often smile. Have you noticed that? This led to the realisation that Bev smiled to deflect criticism and rejection, key elements of her experience in her family. The smile also interfered with her experiencing the depth of her sadness and anger. Having her feelings without smiling them away helped her to manage them better.

When communication contains this kind of ambiguity, the person is usually unaware of it. If Bev's social worker had said, *Well, you say it was bad at home, so why are you smiling?*, this would have implied Bev was lying. (In SAVI™, a red-light *Yes/But*.) A neutral description of both elements, conveyed with interest, is much safer. If you and the service user agree that one part is a mask, as the smile was, then it can be used as a point of reference between you. *Did you notice – there was that smile again? If you don't do the smile, how do you feel?* These are *inner-person questions*, SAVI green-light behaviour. Often the non-verbal communication carries the genuine emotion. People who are depressed are often unaware of their anger, but their clenched jaw and fist tell a different story. *You said it was all right that your mother comes round every day. Do you feel how tense your jaw is, though? What does the tension tell you?* Drawing attention to non-verbal clues needs to be done without making the person self-conscious.

Coherence

Is the story told in a coherent way, or is it hard to follow? Lack of coherence has many causes: confusional states caused by alcohol, drugs, physical illness; mental illness; emotional dysregulation and language impairments. Some may require medical or psychiatric attention. Coherence is also used in a very specific way in researching and classifying adult attachment security, but that is too large a subject to discuss here.

Changes in coherence within a single conversation may indicate the advent of difficult topics, and the person will need encouragement and patience to say what they need. When people are very excited, angry or distressed, their speech becomes less coherent.

Although interrupting (SAVI red light) is generally disrespectful and loses information, there are times when interruption is needed. *Geoff, I can't keep up with you. Can we slow down so I can understand?* If you habitually interrupt, try to hold back.

Silence

Allowing silence gives space for people to reflect, and keeping our attention focused on them conveys our continued interest. If a silence feels awkward to you, it may be tempting to fill it, but instead use your second-order skills. You feel awkward, but does the service user? Are they are just thinking? In this case, keep focused and wait. If you both appear awkward, you need to consider how this happened. Have you or they posed a difficult question? Have they just revealed something shameful and need a response? If you cannot see what the problem is, try to remember what happened before the silence and go back to it. *You were just saying* . . . (see Trevithick (2005) for a further discussion on silence).

Providing information – orienting and responding

Providing information that is clear and context-related underpins social work practice. You will need to turn to the SAVI™ grid for the categories mentioned in italics. Here we will look at five kinds of information we give to service users:

- factual information;

- information about boundaries;

- explanations;

- opinions and proposals;

- emotional information – responding with empathy.

Factual information

Let's go back to the first contact discussed in Chapter 4. After a presumed minute or two of phatic communication, the student social worker provides information. Here is an extract:

> *I'm a student social worker. I'm working at the Family Centre for six months, and all my work is supervised by a qualified social worker. I'll need to talk with that person about all my work, to make sure that you are getting a good service.*

This is information about you. It is therefore a SAVI™ yellow light, personal information (current). Much of the information we pass on to service users is of this type, or square 5 facts and figures. We tell them about services, or about charges for services; we explain entitlements and their legal position. We often have information which they need in order to make choices. It should be provided at a pace the person can manage, giving them time to ask for clarification. Sometimes we give written information to support what we have said, which should be in a format they can access. Some service users have poor literacy skills, and these may not be evident. People are usually ashamed of poor literacy and develop ingenious ways of concealing it: *I haven't got my glasses, could you read it for me?* It is tactful always to offer choices: *Do you want to read this yourself, or shall I read it out?* You may also have the opportunity to discuss literacy with them and find out whether they want to improve their skills. When working with anyone who has been in care for long periods or who has attended a special school, bear this in mind, as both groups of people may have had too little educational input to achieve literacy or numeracy, whatever their ability.

Information about boundaries

The second kind of information provided early on relates to boundaries. *I'll be here for about 45 minutes. Is that okay?* Or, *I'll work with you until the end of May, when I'll be leaving. If you still have a need for a social worker, I will arrange that for you.* This is SAVI green-light behaviour, making a *self assertion* without hostility. Some service users have had fragmented care-giving throughout their lives, with little continuity, and the ending of work with you may awaken old losses. Being clear at the outset is a way of engaging their cognitive understanding that this relationship is going to end, but not without warning, and not as a rejection of them. Boundaries are a different kind of information from facts. Factual information is often one thing or another: you have an entitlement, or you don't; there is a choice of respite carers, or there isn't. Boundaries can sometimes be moved – you might expect to stay 45 minutes but the business is done in 30, or the service user tires and you have to return to complete the task.

Explanations

The third kind of information relates to the private thoughts underlying your work. This information is internal to you, and is not evident to other people unless you tell them, yet they need to hear about it to understand what you are doing. It is therefore classed as *personal explanations* in SAVI™, a yellow-light behaviour.

> *I am going to ask you a lot of questions about yourself. If you don't understand something, will you tell me? If you don't want to answer, will you say?*

> *Before I can answer your questions about how long you will be in hospital, I will have to talk to your doctor. Is that all right with you?*

Opinions and proposals

The fourth kind are the thoughts and ideas you have which are SAVI yellow lights, *opinions* and *proposals* – also internal information. We often need to couple the provision of factual information with these other elements, to help people to make decisions. *Proposals* may be about immediate issues: *Let's ring the electricity company right now and see if we can get this sorted out; Let's look at our action plan and see where we've got to.* Sometimes they relate to possibilities external to the immediate session.

> *There is a local group for parents of autistic children [facts and figures] and I wondered if you would be interested in going along [proposal]. I thought it might provide some support and company, from people in similar circumstances [opinion]. What do you think [broad question]?*

It is helpful to frame proposals as possibilities and choices, not as something they ought to do. If you think it will help, say so, and explain why, but look out for any impulses to coerce, however subtly. If the person complies without really being interested, it will fail, and they may be embarrassed about telling you.

Distinguishing between opinions and facts is important in personal encounters, and also in written communications and contacts with other professionals. I once phoned a psychologist for information about a young man whom she had seen in his home town. All the information she could provide was that he was *odd*, and that his brother was *odd*, too. This is an opinion without any facts to support it, explain it, or enable you to refute it. Given we're all a bit odd, it says nothing.

Professional shorthand often takes the form of an opinion: *his health is deteriorating; her parenting skills are improving.* Such statements need to be accompanied by factual information: *he has lost weight, his lungs are congested and he is finding it hard to breathe; she is giving the children a hot meal every day, and gets them to school on time more than three times a week.*

Emotional information – responding with empathy

Empathy is widely recognised as a core skill. More than any other, it communicates that we understand service users' concerns and know how they feel. Empathy, like the other kinds of information in this section, has cognitive elements, since it involves using words to name feelings, but its cognitive expression has to be anchored in a genuine understanding of the person's emotional state. Emotional information is conveyed in facial expression and vitality affects which you notice, and respond to, so your information about the emotional state comes from both observation and self-awareness. Empathy in social workers has been shown to be of particular importance in creating *less resistance*, stimulating *more disclosure of information from clients*, and reaching *greater clarity about what should happen next* (Forrester et al., 2007, p.48). SAVI™ describes empathy as *mirroring the other's inner-person experience*, a green-light behaviour. Our mirror neuron responses are likely to be active here too.

People may not recognise their own emotional states, or have many words to describe them, especially if their early upbringing did not provide them with the responsive care and emotional regulation they needed. The exclusive use of slang words for feelings may be cultural, but may also point to a paucity of feeling words. (*It does my head in* and *Gutted* are two such expressions.) Cross (2004) suggests that naming feelings for children can help develop the private speech we use to talk about our feelings to ourselves, and which help us to regulate them. This may be the case for adults, too.

McCluskey (2005) indicates that there is a close matching of energy levels in vitality affect when you are empathically attuned. This is where congruence between your verbal and non-verbal behaviour really counts. Empathic statements can be about primary, secondary and background emotions (Damasio, 2000). So what form do empathic statements take?

> SU: *I've decided – I'm going to go to college.*
> SW: *That's wonderful – you look really lit up!*
>
> SU: *I went to the housing, and the man asked me all sorts of personal questions, in front of all these people, like why I couldn't live with my mum any more.*
> SW: *It sounds very embarrassing, and you look kind of disgusted and angry about how you were treated.*
>
> SU: *And then they told me that they don't think the baby will see, and she won't be able to hear, and she'll never walk.*
> SW: *That's devastating news; it must be overwhelming to think of her like that.*
>
> SU: *It's so difficult, just watching him get weaker and more confused, and less able to do the things he used to enjoy. I wish I could make the world stop so that he didn't get any worse.*
> SW: *You love him so much, and yet you can't stop this happening to him. It's so sad.*

There are some statements that look a bit like empathy but make no real emotional connection, such as *That must be very difficult for you*, or *I understand how you feel*. The clue is in your energy level as much as the words; you will sound much flatter than the service user. It is better to try to match your energy and if you can't think of the right emotional word, say something a bit vaguer, but with feeling: *I can see this has really affected you*. Our knowledge about mirror responses triggers our own irritation, so look out for this.

Sometimes you will not be sure about the intensity of emotion – is someone sad or despairing, nervous or really frightened? The service user will often let you know if you have it wrong. Beware though if someone appears angry, as it is better to acknowledge the more intense emotion. If you tell them they seem annoyed, the mismatch is likely to stoke their anger. If you suggest they are angry when they are only annoyed, they will simply correct you. Our knowledge about mirror neuron responses suggests that when someone is angry, this will trigger our own irritation, so look out for this.

Goal-corrected empathic attunement (McCluskey, 2005) involves purposeful misattunement. So when responding to someone in a very intense emotional state, your energy level should be somewhat lower than theirs; when they are flat and not fully in touch with emotion, we misattune purposefully with higher energy.

Through observation and growing awareness of how emotions manifest themselves in your own body, it is possible to improve your capacity to attune empathically.

At the end of the next section we will return to information you provide when service users ask you questions.

ACTIVITY **5.1**

Empathic responses

Look at the following statements and think of an empathic response. Test your ideas out with other people, if you can.

- *I've tried everything, but she just won't go to school. I don't know what to do any more.*

- *First there was the graffiti, saying Gyppos out, and now there's been a brick through the window. I'm not sleeping at night, I can't settle in the house, but I'm scared to go out.*

- *Why did I stay with him for four years? Why did I put up with the violence for all that time?*

- *I've got a flat! I can move in next week. Out of bed and breakfast at last!*

COMMENT

Look inside yourself for the feeling generated in you, and try to match it with your words.

Gathering information – asking and answering questions

We gather information through asking three different kinds of question:

- *narrow questions;*

- *broad questions;*

- *inner-person questions.*

(Simon and Agazarian, 2005)

All three are needed for their particular purposes at all stages of work; the first two are yellow-light behaviours, the third is green light. We will also consider leading questions – a SAVI™ red light.

Narrow questions

Narrow questions are invaluable in obtaining factual information and yes/no answers. They also allow you to offer alternatives. Simple narrow questions are easy to understand.

> *SW: How long have you lived here?*
>
> *SU: Three years.*
>
> *SW: Do you like living here?*
>
> *SU: It's okay.*
>
> *SW: Do you prefer living alone or would you rather share?*
>
> *SU: I prefer living alone.*

Paper and electronic forms often contain a series of narrow questions (sometimes called closed questions). On paper, these are easy to answer, but in person, three or more together feel like an interrogation, though this can be alleviated with friendly non-verbal behaviour, and an explanation about why you are asking the questions, e.g. *I need to ask you a few questions now to make sure we have your details correct. Is that okay?*

Narrow questions should be limited when discussing personal topics, as they discourage the service user from expanding on their story. Look at this conversation.

> *SW: When did you realise you were gay?*
>
> *SU: When I was 13.*
>
> *SW: Are you comfortable with your orientation?*
>
> *SU: I am, now.*
>
> *SW: Do you mix mainly with gay or straight people?*
>
> *SU: Oh, both.*

Given that social workers rarely spend an entire session on fact-finding, broad questions should usually be used to lighten the effect of narrow ones.

Broad questions

Broad questions (sometimes called open questions) help you to learn more about the person; they elicit more expansive answers. They invite explanations, ideas, opinions and proposals or suggestions. They may take the apparent form of an imperative, or command, but the tone shows that they are not.

* *How are you managing your finances now?*

* *What would improve your situation?*

* *Tell me about what made you get in touch with us.*

* *How can I help?*

As you begin to understand the person's situation, both broad and narrow questions will enable you to work towards an agreed goal.

- *When would you like to start looking for voluntary work?* (Narrow)

- *What kind of voluntary work interests you?* (Broad)

- *Is that type of work available locally?* (Narrow)

Inner-person questions

The narrow and broad questions above seek facts and ideas, but when they are used to elicit feelings, they become green-light inner-person questions.

- *Are you as sad as you were last time we met?*

- *Are you angry with me right now?*

- *When you think about leaving your partner, how do you feel?*

- *How are you feeling now about living alone?*

Wait for one question to be answered before asking another. A common mistake is to ask a broad question and immediately close it off with a narrow one. *What was it like growing up in your family? Was it tough?*

Hargie and Dickson (2004) cite research suggesting that it is helpful either to start with closed questions and then move to open questions to expand on the story, or to start with open questions and move to closed for more specificity. Moving erratically between the two is less effective.

ACTIVITY *5.2*

Using broad, narrow and inner-person questions
Take the question and answer below as your starting point, and then generate some broad questions and inner-person questions to ask the service user. Either imagine the answers, or work with someone else to develop them through role play. If you work with someone else, discuss the impact the different questions have on you.

　SW　*When did you realise you were gay?*

　SU　*When I was 13.*

COMMENT

Practising different kinds of questions will extend your skills.

Leading questions

Leading questions are extremely useful in certain contexts, but social work is not one of them. Journalists frequently use them with politicians: *You are going to raise taxes, aren't you? Don't you think it would be better just to admit it?*

By their nature, leading questions indicate the answer the speaker wants to hear, and try to coerce the other person into agreement. They are a red-light behaviour which impedes communication, and for all these reasons, should be avoided in social work. The main temptations are when you have a good idea and want the service use to take it up, or when you have made an assumption, signalled by *So. . .* and ending with *won't you, do you*, etc.

- *Don't you think it would be a good idea to go to the family centre?*

- *You'd feel safer, wouldn't you, if we gave you one of these alarms.*

- *So you'll be all right now, won't you?*

ACTIVITY **5.3**

Identifying verbal interactions

Here are the interactions we looked at in Chapter 1 to illustrate feedback. Now consider each of them again, and identify the different verbal interactions the SW uses. Categorise them as red, yellow or green light.

Interaction 1

SW: *Do you live on your own?*

SU: *I do now; ever since my wife died. The house –*

SW: *When did she die?*

SU: *It's only six months ago. It feels like yester-*

SW: *Do you have any children?*

SU: *Yes, one daughter. She's very good to me but it's just not the same without her mother.*

SW: *So your daughter helps out with things, does she?*

SU: *She does, she does her best, but –*

SW: *So you probably won't need much help at home when you get back. What do you think?*

SU: *Well, I don't know really.*

Interaction 2

SW: *Do you live on your own?*

SU: *I do now; ever since my wife died. The house feels ever so empty without her.*

SW: *It sounds very lonely. Were you a close couple?*

SU: *We were – been together since I was 16 and she was 15. We were always together, when we had our shop, you know, and then we gave that up and retired out in this direction.*

SW: *When did that happen, then?*

SU: *Only two years ago – it was always her dream to have a place with a bit of land, and 18 months later, she was dead. I can't believe it. She was only 63.*

SW: *That's young these days, isn't it? How did it all happen?*

SU: *It was a Friday she took ill . . .*

If you feel the impulse, turn it around so that you are offering choice, and be honest if you have an opinion or proposal.

- *I think you might enjoy going to the family centre [opinion]. There are lots of activities for the children and for the parents too [facts and figures]. It's very friendly [opinion]. I could go with you and you could see for yourself before deciding [proposal].*

- *Some people feel safer with these alarms [facts and figures]. What about you [broad question]?*

- *Do you think you'll be all right now [narrow question]?*

Service users' questions

Service users often ask us questions. In some instances, direct answers can be given, but more often we have to think about the concerns that underlie the questions. This sometimes means avoiding a direct reply while ensuring we do not seem evasive. Explaining why we are not giving a direct answer will help.

Information-seeking broad and narrow questions are generally straightforward, and give rise to green-light *answers*.

- *How does the respite care service work?*

- *Are there any services for people who speak Cantonese?*

Questions about what will happen in the future are more difficult, and require more complex replies, though they are still classed as *answers* in SAVI™.

> SU: *Will I get my child back?*
>
> SW: *I can't answer that right now. We have to wait for the medical reports and the case conference.*

Questions about our thoughts and opinions also come up.

- *What do you think? Do you think I'm a looney?*

- *Should I move into sheltered housing?*

These require an exploration of what the service user means, and how they are thinking about matters for themselves.

- *What makes you ask the question [broad question]? Has anyone called you a looney [narrow question]?*

- *Shall we try and work out the pros and cons from your point of view [proposal]?*

We may be asked questions about ourselves that take us by surprise.

- *How will you be able to help me if you're only a student?*

- *Do you have children? I think you need to be a mother to understand these problems.*

Direct answers such as, *I've been worrying about that myself,* or *No I haven't,* overlook the fact that the question is being asked in a professional context. The person is trying to discover whether you can be trusted, and whether you have the knowledge and experience needed to work with them. You need to manage your own anxieties, and then find out more about theirs, ask broad questions and make proposals. For example:

- *Rather than answering that directly, let's talk about what's worrying you.*

- *What kind of help do you think you need?*

- *If I don't understand your problems, will you tell me?*

Sometimes we are asked questions which no one can answer, where an empathic *mirroring of inner-person feeling* is needed rather than an answer:

- *Why did my baby have to die?*

Paraphrasing and summarising

Interviews involve more than questions, answers and empathic responses. We need to shape and organise the information which emerges, and the skills discussed here help us to manage the flow of information. These are both green-light behaviours.

Paraphrasing

Paraphrasing helps us check our understanding. It involves repeating back the essence of what a person has said, generally using some of the same words, but also some of your own. Sometimes exact repetition is required, in order to be sure you do not distort the information, or where adding your own words makes your response too complex for the other person. In other circumstances, exact repetitions can feel parrot-like. Follow up with a question: *Is that right? Have I missed anything?*

Summarising

Summarising is not commonly used in everyday encounters so you might feel awkward when you first try it out. Persevere! Reflective summaries are not used very much in social work but seem to encourage service user disclosure (Forrester et al., 2007). *Summarising* can be used at the start of sessions in ongoing work, during sessions and at the end. At the start, the aim is to keep your shared goals in mind. *Last time we . . . and we agreed to . . . And today we planned to . . . Is that still all right with you?* During sessions summarising gathers together certain types of information before moving on, and helps ensure you have a shared understanding. Because summarising creates a pause, there is also the chance to remind the service user of the time boundary for the session, and to decide how you will spend the remainder. At the end of sessions, summaries enable you to collect up and agree key points, determine whether there are tasks for each of you to complete before the next session, and to confirm arrangements for next time. They help to round off what you are doing.

> *Today we've talked about a number of issues, and we've agreed the following. You're going to contact the dementia care service to tell them your concerns about your mum. You're going to see the GP about your arthritis. I'm going to contact the gas company on your behalf to see if anything can be done about the bill. I'll ring you when I've*

spoken to them, definitely by Friday, and hear how you've got on with the other issues. We didn't get round to talking about your worries about your son. Let's make sure we talk about that next time.

Getting into the habit of summarising key points with service users makes it easier to write succinct case notes, which then makes reports or letters easier to write as you have the vital information to hand.

Using commands and corrective feedback

Commands

Commands (yellow light) are designed to influence behaviour, often in the moment, and are a succinct means of conveying what needs to be done. They can be polite in form or more assertive, but if delivered with an authoritarian tone, they will evoke hostility.

- *Come in.*

- *Ring the doctor – don't forget.*

- *Slow down – I can't follow what you're saying.*

In situations where people are hostile, commands delivered without hostility are useful, as detailed in Chapter 9.

- *Put that down.*

- *Stop pointing at me.*

In family and other groups, they can be used to address everyone together.

- *Everybody quiet now so we can hear what Tina has to say.*

- *Everybody leave – that's the fire alarm.*

- *When I say start, turn your card over and start the quiz. Start!*

Service users may give us commands, certainly of the polite kind. If we think they are getting aggressive, then follow the suggestions in Chapter 9. If you need to leave, do so.

- *Stop writing in that silly notebook and look at me.*

- *Tell your boss I'm taking this to the top.*

- *Get out of my house.*

Corrective feedback

Corrective feedback (green light) means providing information correcting something said previously. It is factual information, not an alternative opinion, and it has to be said without demeaning the other person, or it will be rejected. It can be used to provide supporting information for an opinion.

SU: *You said you were visiting on Tuesday, and then you never turned up.*

SW: *It's true I was going to visit on Tuesday. I rang you on Monday to change it. At the time you said it would be okay; I'm sorry I couldn't come till today.*

SU: *You promised me I'd get a grant for a new washer.*

SW: *I said I'd do my best to get you a grant. I didn't promise, because you can't predict the decisions they make.*

SU: *I just don't have the confidence to go to the school and tell them Celine's being bullied. I've never had any confidence with people like that – people in charge.*

SW: *I know it's scary. I think you've got a lot better with people in charge than you used to be. Remember how you dealt with the council about the drains?*

SU: *I just don't think these Muslims should be moving into the area. They should go back to their own country.*

SW: *This is their own country; everyone in the UK came from somewhere else originally, if you go back far enough.*

Bringing working relationships to an end

As noted earlier, the ending of a working relationship can be difficult for service users. Apart from evoking past losses, there may be apprehension about losing the support and contact we have offered. It is important that you do not take flight from endings, that you set dates for the last few meetings, and keep gently reminding the service user how many sessions remain. Sometimes a celebration or special event is appropriate, particularly when working with children. There are three kinds of ending:

- planned endings where work is deemed to be complete, at least for now;

- planned endings involving transfer to another colleague or agency;

- unplanned endings.

Planned endings which bring work to a close

Planned endings allow you to review the work you have done, and to highlight accomplishments. You discuss how the person is going to consolidate their gains, and plan next steps. In terms of the working alliance, these are your efforts to ensure *The incorporation of the gains of treatment so that they are maintained after its termination* (Luborsky, 1994, p.47).

The completion of a period of work where goals have been met is satisfying, and a source of pride for both service user and social worker. Some planned endings are less satisfying, as the service user may still have difficulties, but not at a level which justifies our involvement. This can be hard for both parties to come to terms with, particularly where service users have very limited social networks, despite our efforts, and are lonely (seemingly part of the social worker's predicament reported by Fisher et al., 1984). Highlighting what has been achieved takes on a new importance. Often we get attached to the people we work with, and are sad to say goodbye, though it can be a relief and we may be ready for something new.

Planned endings involving transfer to another colleague or agency

There are many reasons for transferring work. Here are some:

- the service user moves to another area;

- their needs indicate referral to another service;

- service provision is age-related and they reach the age boundary;

- you leave your post;

- your agency is reorganised, along with the remit of your post.

In an ideal world, the same work is done as with planned endings which bring work to a close. The achievements of the work, and planning next steps, are equally important. It is good practice to have a joint meeting between you, the new worker, and the service user, to make introductions, and to share the review and plans. This is not always practicable, and your contact with the new provider may be limited to phone calls, emails and paperwork.

Where the reasons for transfer do not relate to the service user's perception of their needs, they can be puzzled, disappointed or resentful. If we are confident that the transfer makes sense, we can remind them of the goals. Where it seems arbitrary and senseless, it is much more difficult. Take adult mental health services. In area A, everyone with a functional mental health problem such as schizophrenia (see Golightley, 2008) has one service, while everyone with dementia, such as Alzheimer's disease, has another. In area B, everyone aged 18–64 has one service, and everyone 65 and over has another. There are arguments in favour of both arrangements. When someone has to transfer, your role is to acknowledge the service user's difficulty in accepting the change and help them to manage it. Take your doubts about the system to your management; do likewise when facing reorganisation. If you have evidence that the current or new system causes harm, you need to take a vigorous approach to challenging it, and will need allies.

Unplanned endings

Unplanned endings occur for a variety of reasons, and in some cases, there are warning signs. Here are some examples.

- The service user moves, or disappears, without warning. Where service users are at risk or constitute a risk to others we will need to take action.

- They decide not to use the service and do not wish to discuss it. This happens often with people using substance misuse services.

- The relationship breaks down and they refuse to see you. If your working relationships break down much sooner or more often than those of colleagues, take this to supervision.

- The relationship becomes unsafe for you and someone else is allocated. If safety permits, this is handled as a planned transfer.

- You are unexpectedly off work for a long period.

- The service user dies. This can be expected in work with older people and in hospices, but can still take place much sooner than anticipated. Otherwise, sudden death is a rare experience, but can have a major impact, especially if the cause is suicide or murder. Agencies need to take care of staff when these events occur.

By their nature, unplanned endings leave an unsatisfactory feeling in their wake, especially if we feel responsible in some way, even where those feelings are unfounded. This also is a subject for supervision.

ACTIVITY **5.4**

Analysing an encounter

This could be done when you are undertaking preparation for practice, shadowing a social worker, or when you are in practice learning. You can use a session of your own work, or one which you observe. If you are able to record it on audio or video/DVD, this will make it much easier. Otherwise, try to use an observed session and take detailed notes.

Which kinds of information were provided by you or the social worker?

Were narrow, broad and inner-person questions all used? What did you think of the way they were used? How did the service user respond?

Did the service user ask any questions? What kinds of questions were they?

What about paraphrasing, summarising and commands?

Did you notice any red-light behaviours? What was the effect of them?

If you were in the social work role, what was easiest and what was most difficult? Why do think this was so?

If you were observing, what would you have done differently, and why?

COMMENT

This activity is designed to use your observational and reflective skills.

CHAPTER SUMMARY

In this chapter we have learnt about how to develop and maintain relationships with service users over time. We have seen that our overall approach is based on collaboration and empowerment, although these are not always easy to achieve. Listening and responding, with our cognitive and emotional capabilities working in harness, enables us to organise complex information. We need sensitivity in our delivery to service users so that the pace at which they can absorb facts, suggestions and emotional information is respected. By learning about the components of verbal interaction, we have begun to understand how our verbal behaviours affect service users and their responses. We have seen that skilled and flexible use of the different elements enhances the quality of the information we exchange, the working relationship between us, and the likelihood of identifying and achieving agreed goals. We have looked at the impact of endings, and how to manage them, in good and less than optimal circumstances.

FURTHER READING

Hargie, O and Dickson, D (2004) *Skilled Interpersonal communication: Research, theory and practice.* 4th edition. Abingdon: Routledge.
A UK text which brings together a wealth of information and evidence-based guidance covering a wider field than social work. Chapter 5, 'Questioning,' pp.115–46 provides a very useful account of the value of different kinds of questions in different contexts.

Kadushin A and Kadushin, G (1997) *The social work Interview: A guide for human service professionals.* 4th edition. New York: Columbia University Press.
Written from a US perspective, this is a useful text with plenty of practice examples. It discusses transcultural work, which is significantly different in the USA, but nonetheless provides food for thought about the UK context.

Trevithick, P (2005) *Social work skills: A practice handbook.* 2nd edition. Buckingham: Open University Press. There is a good discussion on endings.

Chapter 6

Communicating with children

Introduction

The welfare of children and young people is of paramount concern to social workers (Children Act 1989). This is self-evident to social workers providing services for children, but it also matters in fields where the presence of children is less apparent. Adult service users with mental health or substance use problems, with physical impairments or learning disabilities, may also be parents or carers of children; older people too care for children. While some social workers choose these fields because they prefer working with adults, the potential needs of children should be held in mind and referral to other services made if necessary.

In much childcare provision, work is directed at the adults in a family, particularly mothers, and while we work for and on behalf of children, we need also to work with them (Brandon et al., 1998, p.1), principally for three reasons. The first concerns children's rights to have their voice heard, and to participate in decisions affecting them. The second relates to concerns that if we overlook or misinterpret communication with children, we are led into erroneous decisions (Jones, 2003). Finally, a focus on parents at the expense of communicating with children has been implicated in failures to protect children from serious harm (Simmonds, 2008).

It is inevitable that mistakes will sometimes be made, but minimising their frequency and impact is a central aim of good practice. For these reasons, the Department of Health has put heightened emphasis on the need for social work students to acquire skills in communicating with children. This chapter invites you to consider the skills needed to engage with children at different stages of development, and for a range of purposes. The chapter focuses more on children than adolescents.

We need to engage with children and young people who:

- require assessment to establish if they are in need or at risk of significant harm;
- may be adopted by a step-parent or by a new family;
- are looked after by the local authority, either accommodated on a voluntary basis or subject to a care order;
- have disabilities and health problems;
- have emotional and behavioural problems, also referred to as mental health problems;
- have educational problems;
- are carers;
- offend;
- are leaving care;
- have substance misuse problems;
- are roofless.

Many children that social workers see have more than one kind of difficulty. Children with disabilities are more likely to be abused, more likely to be in care, and yet are *seriously under-represented in our child protection systems* (Marchant, 2008, p.162). Looked after children are of particular concern, as they have higher rates of mental health problems, perform less well at school, have poorer health, and are more likely to smoke, drink alcohol and use drugs than their contemporaries living in private households (Meltzer et al., 2003). Early intervention is needed to prevent lifelong problems (Walker, 2003). Looked after children may face changes and disruptions about which they have little choice, such as where they live, who they live with, and the nature of contact with family members. Continuity of a good relationship with a social worker, being told the truth, being given explanations in terms they can understand, and having their feelings acknowledged and understood, can all help with these difficult life events (Luckock, 2008).

ACTIVITY *6.1*

Think back to a time as a child or young person where you have faced difficulties. How did you cope with them? Did you turn to anyone for help? How did the other person or people respond? Did you feel understood and supported? What kind of help would you have liked, ideally?

Key issues

Child development

A sound grasp of child development is needed before we can communicate successfully with children. A brief account is provided here, with emphasis on language acquisition, so refer to Aldgate et al. (2006), or Smith et al. (2003); to Chapter 3, where emotional development was discussed; and the recommended reading at the end of this chapter.

Communication difficulties and differences

A significant number of children have communication difficulties, perhaps 6 per cent (NHS Centre for Reviews and Dissemination, cited in Buckley, 2003). In children with emotional and behavioural problems, the proportion rises to 50–90 per cent, and where the communication difficulty goes unrecognised, the child's behaviour may simply be seen as immature or inappropriate (Cross, 2004).

Some children use sign languages such as British Sign Language or Makaton, or speak another language but not English. If we do not understand the child's means of communication, then we will need the aid of a colleague who does, or an interpreter. When children have hearing or visual impairments, learning or physical disabilities or chronic illnesses which limit movement or speech production, their needs have to be taken into account in advance, where possible, so that the possibility of creating a trusting relationship is maximised. They and their carers will usually help with this. See Chapter 8 on special communication needs.

Play

Language alone is rarely an adequate means of communicating with children before adolescence, and not always then; children do not enjoy sitting and talking face-to-face for any length of time. You need to be comfortable with using age-appropriate toys and games, and creative activities such as drawing and making things, as these are more likely to engage a child successfully. There is cultural variation in time spent playing with parents and other adults or with peers; in playing alone, in pairs, or groups; in levels of adult supervision; and in access to found objects, commercially produced toys, television and so on. Nonetheless, playing with objects, engaging in games, and organising 'pretend' activities, such as making 'journeys' in cars, boats, etc. are spontaneous and universal in children (Roopnarine et el., 1994).

Power

Adults are inherently more powerful than children, and Jones (2003) explains that vulnerable and disadvantaged children, especially younger ones, are highly susceptible to adult influence. They defer to adults, are sensitised to verbal and non-verbal cues and comply. We have to take care not to cue them into telling us what they think we want to hear.

Vigilance is called for when exploring possible abuse or other serious concerns such as domestic violence. Inadvertently leading children into making statements which distort the truth could prejudice criminal proceedings. It could result in unnecessary action, such as separating a child from carers, which may harm the child and jeopardise working relations with the adults. A decision not to take action and leave a child in a damaging or dangerous situation is also harmful and may jeopardise their trust in us and other adults. Errors such as these may even result in a child's death (Jones, 2003).

Impact on the social worker

Working with distressed children is distressing. It may stir up painful memories, or fill us with sadness and anger about the harm children suffer and adults' capacity to inflict such harm. Good preparation, careful reflection and skilful supervision are needed to enable you to manage your own feelings (Aldgate and Simmonds, 1988; Colton et al., 2001). Working with children can also be great fun, and we can make a real difference. See Cook (2008), for example.

Communication with adults, consent and confidentiality

Finally, work with children depends on maintaining good communication with the adults and other agencies in their lives. Consent to work with children needs to be given by those with parental responsibility and by the child, too, especially when they are older. Unless a child divulges information about abuse, what they tell us can usually be kept confidential from their carers, teachers and so forth, or shared if the child agrees, which may be helpful. Carers may need to be given general information, such as the fact that work is going well.

ACTIVITY **6.2**

Think back to your experiences at school. Did you or any of your peers find it hard to mix? Looking back, why might this have been the case? Did anyone help? If so, what did they do?

Were you or any of your contemporaries looked after by people other than your immediate family at any time? What were the reasons for this? Did adults talk to you or your peers about what was happening and why? Looking back, do you think the right decisions were made? What would you have preferred to happen?

COMMENT

Reflecting on your own experiences as a child may help you to understand children better.

Infants

RESEARCH SUMMARY

The first year

Babies vary considerably in the age at which they reach certain milestones, so this is a rough guide. Infants:

- *show a marked preference for human faces and voices (if they have both sight and hearing);*

- *in the first few days know their mother's voice, face and smell, and usually show a preference for her;*

- *prefer moving objects to fixed ones;*

- *engage in turn-taking 'conversations' from about three months;*

- *follow the adult's gaze to look at the same object in shared or joint attention from four to six months;*

- *begin to make deliberate efforts to reach and grasp, and play interactive games such as 'peek-a-boo' at around six months;*

- *begin to point and wave, and indicate vocally that they want an object, and will look at an object which the carer points to at around nine months;*

- *make communicative sounds from about eight weeks, babble in the sounds of their primary language(s) from around six months, and produce simple words by the end of the first year;*

- *are born with different temperaments, making some easier to care for than others;*

- *do not mind being held by strangers until six to nine months, when fear of strangers develops (Buckley, 2003; Brandon et al., 1998).*

Joint attention marks the start of the baby's understanding that other people have minds and see things from different perspectives. Autistic children do not develop this capacity (Cross, 2004).

Infants with communication difficulties may show some of the following signs:

- *no infant babbling;*

- *no early speech sounds;*

- *not crying;*

- *constant crying;*

- *unusual eye contact;*

- *being withdrawn and silent;*

- *feeding difficulties*

(Buckley, 2003, p.213, citing a survey by AFASIC, 1993).

Working with infants in the first year

Bearing in mind the considerable variation between infants, you will learn most about them through observing them in their home environment with their primary carers. Brandon et al. (1998) propose that the carer introduces you to the infant, and uses your name, so that the baby knows who you are. As you may also play and interact with the baby yourself, this ensures that the baby has the carer's permission to relate to you. Do the baby and carer seem to enjoy communicating with each other? Does the baby seem afraid of or avoidant with its carer? Is the carer clumsy, impatient or insensitive? How does the baby respond to you? Is the carer concerned that the baby is not communicating as well as siblings or friends' babies? Infants who are unusually fretful or listless over time, and those who fail to gain weight or reach other milestones may cause concern (Department of Health et al., 2000; Brandon et al., 1998). Well-founded early interventions may be able to transform behaviour leading to difficulties and an example of this will be discussed in Chapter 7.

Children
Language – a social skill

After infancy, language acquisition gathers pace, though at widely varying rates. A child may use 50 words at 16–22 months, typically comprehending about four times as many. Two-word phrases appear at 18–20 months, and three-word phrases soon after. Children who share extended periods of joint attention with carers (15 minutes) acquire more words. Books and storytelling help children learn about narrative; they start to tell simple stories at three years, with the length and complexity increasing over the following years (Buckley, 2003). By the age of six a child has *a working vocabulary of around 14,000 words* (Jones, 2003, p.22).

It is well reported that children in their second year use words in situations and to refer to the world around them in ways that do not always correspond with adults' use of the same words (Buckley, 2003, p.56). All women may be called 'Mum', or only the child's teddy may be called 'teddy'. Even at six years, the age of the child in the following example, the adult use of the word 'house' to mean 'home' may be understood literally, so a child asked if something happened in his house said *No* because he lived in a flat (Jones, 2003, p.22). Words such as *any, in, on, between, inside, before, after, above, below, always, sometimes* are not fully understood or used with adult meaning.

Children of about three understand *what, who* and *where* questions; by about five, they can answer *when* questions. Before then, their understanding of time and words such as *yesterday, tomorrow, soon, later*, is limited. *How* questions are more complex. A child may be able to answer a question about how to do something at three and a half (Buckley, 2003), but not how often something happened (Jones, 2003). The ability to answer *why* questions is not reliably established until around eight years old or later (Aldridge and Wood, 1998).

Sounds in English tend to be simplified until the child is about four and a half, so adults do not always understand them.

During the second and third years, children find it hard to switch their attention from an activity which absorbs them to something the carer points out. They readily learn novel words related to their chosen activity, but if the carer directs their attention to something different, new words are not learnt so quickly. They engage other people's attention in objects which interest them – the first signs of introducing a conversational topic. They begin to notice communicative failures and attempt to repair them, for example, by making a request again or in a new way when a first attempt fails; this capacity takes many years to develop fully. When children do not understand what we say to them, they are less skilled than adults in asking for clarification, and may say nothing or agree (Jones, 2003).

Imaginative play and language

Imaginative play starts early in the second year, drawing upon the child's experiences, and advances in the third year, with imaginary friends, imaginary objects, and a growing propensity to use objects to represent other things, such as mud to represent food. Play people are given voices, have feelings and wishes, and act out events, with the child providing a commentary on what is happening. It is thought that children consolidate their understanding of the world and of human experiences through imaginative play (Buckley, 2003). Their commentaries are the beginnings of private speech – the means by which we think inside our minds – and are believed to be connected with self-regulation. Put simply, individuals who are able to talk to themselves (in words or sign language) can manage their emotional states better than those who cannot. Evidence from a number of studies suggests that language learning takes place in neutral emotional states; children who are often in aroused, unregulated states will acquire less language. It therefore appears that the children with the most disturbing emotional experiences have the least opportunity to develop the cognitive skills to manage them (Cross, 2004).

Children in their third year begin to show interest in peers and play games such as hide and seek, but the ability to play co-operatively only emerges at four or five. Those with good communication skills who are responsive to others get on better with peers (Buckley, 2003).

Memory

The younger the child, the more quickly events are forgotten. Between about 20 months and four years, children begin to recall past events and tell about them, but their ability to retrieve past events, especially more distant ones, is very limited before the age of three, and recall for specific instances of frequent events is poor, e.g. going to the shops. The importance of this is evident in trying to clarify particular instances of abuse, or family conflict, if these are common occurrences (Jones, 2003).

Stressful events may be remembered quite vividly. Highly negative and personally threatening events may not be recalled in detail at a factual level, while the memory of how the child felt will be more clearly remembered (Jones, 2003, p.16).

Problems in communication

The causes of communication difficulties are many and usually there is no single cause. They can arise from genetic inheritance, impairment, such as learning disability, or disorders such as autism or ADHD. They may also be caused by the neurological and social impacts of neglect, abuse, trauma and deprivation of social contact with peers. Problems with expression are easier to recognise; problems with comprehension are less obvious, as the child may appear bored, frustrated or recalcitrant. Children may find it hard to join in conversations, initiate topics, keep conversations going, or explain when they do not understand, while carers, peers and teachers find it harder to relate to them, thus compounding their problems by reducing their opportunities to engage in and learn from positive interactions (Cross, 2004). Interestingly, *withdrawn children who were physically abused, neglected or at risk* showed improvements in *social adjustment* after mixing with *well-adjusted, socially-skilled peers* (Fantuzzo and colleagues, cited in Edgeworth and Carr, 2000, p.34).

Poor parental care requires help for parents. In other instances, the causes lie in the child, and parents' concerns should be taken seriously. We need to consider the whole picture and involve other professionals, such as health visitors, psychologists and speech and language therapists, as needed. Children with learning disabilities or other communication problems may have the communicative ability of a younger child.

ACTIVITY **6.3**

Think about your own experiences of playing as a child. Did your parents or carers play with you? Did you play mostly with siblings or friends, or alone? Did you have many toys or did you create your own? What were your favourite activities?

Now think about yourself in the present. Do you play with your own children or other people's? How do you feel about playing with babies, toddlers, and older children? If you have worked with children, review how you communicated with them in the light of your learning.

Write a list of your strengths and needs in communicating with children and young people. Think of a way you could improve on one need.

COMMENT

Becoming relaxed at working with children is essential, or they will not feel comfortable in your presence.

Working with children

We start with a list of generic skills, drawn from Wilson et al. (1992), Brandon et al. (1998), Colton et al. (2001), Jones (2003) and Webb (2003). Being friendly, smiling, greeting the child and not just attendant adults, are simple but critical behaviours in showing the child that you are interested in them. Talking about ordinary things, everyday life and interests helps build rapport (Lefevre, 2008).

You will need:

- the capacity to build a relationship with the child, which depends on genuine interest;
- warmth that is not over-involved – you do not have a primary relationship with the child, nor do you want your warmth to influence them (e.g. to say things to please you);
- respect for the child, their experience, and their knowledge of their experience;
- respect for the child's diversity;
- empathy;
- to use clear, simple communication, i.e. words and grammar or signs and pictures that the child can understand;
- to be comfortable with play as a means of communication;
- to build on the child's interests;
- to follow where the child leads;
- to communicate constructively with the people surrounding the child, even if you feel angry with them on the child's behalf;
- to be reliable and take enough time to do the work.

Children do not readily understand what social work is, so you need to explain it to them. Brandon et al. (1998) suggest producing an album of photographs depicting you in your workplace, car, etc., to show to smaller children. They recommend you maintain regular contact with the child, inform them directly if you change arrangements to see them (as well as telling their carers), and provide them with your details so that they can contact you themselves. Children should have timescales and potential outcomes explained to them, taking into account their capacity to understand these.

Using play in social work

Play takes many forms, such as using art materials or making music, play with dolls, puppets, animal figures and building blocks, and indoor and outdoor games. Play can be used to understand how children feel about their present or future circumstances, or how they understand the past. It is also a means of enjoying an activity together to build the relationship and facilitate discussion. *The more approaches you feel confident in using, the more likely it is that you and the child will find a mode of communication which works between you* (Lefevre, 2008, p.135).

Social workers tend to see children in the child's home, or a room in a family centre which may have other purposes. Play work can be carried out in these circumstances, with imagination and care. Travelling play kits can be assembled which you bring with you in a box or a bag, and a cloth or rug can be placed on the floor to create a play space, or a table can be used instead. For younger children, the kit could contain: *some soft toys, some small figures, one or two puppets, two toy telephones (because some children find it difficult to talk about painful issues face to face), some paper and crayons* (Banks and Mumford, 1988, p.103). You could also include a *car, baby doll, piece of cloth for playing peep-bo, washable felt-tip pens and play-dough or similar* (Brandon et al., 1998, p.74). For older children of school age you could add a *simple book*, a *variety of drawing materials, stars, stickers* and a *sticky message pad, modelling clay*, and *cars, fire engines and ambulances* (Brandon et al., 1998, p.75). A doctor's kit is helpful if illness or bereavement are an issue. Some adolescents will use similar materials, but others will regard them as childish and need more sophisticated items such as a better range of drawing materials and coloured paper and collage (Brandon et al., 1998, p.76). Increasingly, computer-based games and activities are available (see Ahmad, Betts and Cowan, 2008).

It is important to start with the child's interests and follow these, rather than determining the focus ourselves. As we saw, younger children find it hard to switch attention from a chosen activity; in addition, if we follow where the child leads, this conveys interest and respect. Occasionally it is wiser to guide them to an activity. For example, where toys for different age groups are available, a child may choose activities beyond their ability, and become bored or frustrated; if there are too many choices, they may never settle (Aldridge and Wood, 1998).

The following sections cannot be comprehensive; they are designed to give you some ideas about how to work with children individually. Whilst these kinds of work with children have not to my knowledge been evaluated with any rigour, relying rather on practitioner accounts, they are widely recognised as useful.

Assessment

You might start an assessment by proposing to the child: *Draw me a picture of your family,* or offering play people and animals: *Show me who's in your family. Which one are you going to choose to be you?* Brandon et al. (1998) suggest using stars or sheets from sticky message pads instead of drawing. You can encourage the child to embellish the result by suggesting the child adds other important figures in their life, or shows visually how close the child feels to members of their informal network. Remember that children may comprehend and use words in different ways from adults, such as the concept of closeness (Jones, 2003). We mean emotional closeness, while a child may take it literally to mean *Who is physically nearest at this moment in time?* A narrow question such as, *Do you like being with X?* or *Which do you like best, being with X or Y?* would clarify matters.

Brandon et al. (1998, p.78) cite an exercise from Borba and Borba (1982) which allows a child to talk about their worries by drawing a stripe for each worry on a picture of a 'worry bee'.

Recognising and talking about emotions

Since recognising and naming feelings is essential to emotional regulation, helping children to develop this ability appears valuable. This can happen in the moment, through accurate mirroring of inner-person feelings (Simon and Agazarian, 2005). It can also be included in imaginative play: *What does the teddy feel now he's in the hospital?* Structured methods such as *Feelings faces* and the *Body map of feelings* can be used as a prompt to talk about emotion (Heegaard, cited in Webb, 2003, p.277). Feelings faces involve the child drawing faces with the emotion which matches them written beneath. Webb (2003) states that the exercise asks the child to draw five faces (angry, sad, afraid, worried and angry), but in bereavement work she uses no more than three. This exercise can be used in other circumstances, such as to raise a child's awareness of what makes them angry, and to notice the early warning signs in their body so that they can manage their feelings better.

Similarly, the body map is an outline drawing of a person on which a child can mark out where they experience a particular emotion, to increase awareness of the sources of feelings, to understand them better, and to learn how to regulate them.

These techniques are not an end in themselves: they must be a starting point for talking with the child, so that the child can reflect on their experience. Remember that the capacity to learn words is greater when the child is not in a state of high emotion.

Life-story work

As noted above, small children forget events very easily, and their conceptual understanding of the world is not fully developed. Ordinarily, children build up a picture of their own story through the consistency of their lives (e.g. sleeping in the same bedroom, playing with a growing collection of toys). In addition, carers and older relatives tell stories about past events, including stories about children when they were younger, which blend with their own memories. Where children have had many changes of home, school and carer, the continuity fragments, and the memories may not hold together as a story.

For these reasons, social workers sometimes engage a child in life-story work which establishes the sequence of events, identifies who peopled the child's world at different stages, and gathers together information that helps to make the story cohere. This could include stories which previous carers tell about the child, or photographs of people, places they have lived, schools. You might accompany children on visits to a former foster carer (who would need adequate preparation), or to see the street where their birth family lived when they were born. You and the child might draw a series of houses, which you then fill with information such as the floor plan of the house, and who lived there. Sometimes the work is done to prepare a child for joining a new family (Cipolla et al., 1992). Ryan and Walker (2007) highlight the value of life-story work in providing children who are to be adopted with *comprehensive information about themselves* (p.1), as required by the Adoption and Children Act 2002.

Life-story work relies upon the worker's ability to go at the child's pace and be led by the child about the elements they wish to explore. They may know more or less than you and others imagine. It is potentially a very intense experience for a child to embark upon. In order to get to know them and enable them to trust you, you may need to share their interests and experiences for some time before starting work (Aldgate and Simmonds, 1988). The goal is not simply to complete the life story book as an object. It is to help the child know and understand their life and their feelings about it better than before. It may also provide the opportunity to correct misperceptions (Fahlberg, cited in Aldgate and Simmons, 1988, p.50), such as *Mummy gave me away because I was bad.*

Verbal communication with children

This section draws on two sources: guidance about work gaining evidence from children in cases of suspected or alleged abuse or other criminal activity (Aldridge and Wood, 1998; Jones, 2003); and the needs of children with communication problems (Cross, 2004). These suggestions are valuable in most work with children since they aim to make communication simple, clear and as free as possible from behaviour which will bias what the child tells you.

ACTIVITY **6.4**

Take a sheet of paper and draw all the places you have lived, who was living with you at which points, and all the schools you attended.

Now think of two or three of your earliest memories. Can you distinguish between what you remember for yourself and what you have been told by other people? How old do you think you were? If you lived in more than one place, where did these early memories take place? What do you think made them memorable?

COMMENT

Practising this yourself will show you how powerful such an activity can be for a child.

Do:

- encourage the child to tell you if you get in a muddle or get things wrong;
- model this for them by saying when you don't understand;
- encourage the child to tell you if they don't know the answer to something you ask;
- slow down;
- use short sentences;
- allow time for your utterance to be processed;
- use simple language;
- give choices;
- be specific about time, e.g. rather than using *later*, say *At 4.00*, or *Next time we meet*, or *On Wednesday*;
- if a child has attention problems, make sure you have their attention before you speak;
- use pictures, diagrams and gesture to illustrate what you mean;
- ask one question at a time;
- ask both broad and narrow questions;
- pay attention if a broad question goes unanswered – it may be too open for the child to comprehend;
- use the active voice rather than passive

  – *Was Mummy hit by the man?*

  – *Did the man hit Mummy?*

  The first question is passive voice, and may be understood to mean its opposite, *Mummy hit the man*? The active voice employs the usual sequence of nouns in English;

- remember that children may use the same name for more than one person (Daddy), or call someone by more than one name (Jim and Granddad). Clarify by asking: *Is that Daddy who lives with Lorna? Or Daddy who lives with Mummy?*;
- offer corrective feedback about misapprehensions or facts.

Don't:

- talk at length – make turns short or the child may lose the thread;

- ask yes/no questions; younger children tend to answer the same way each time (*no* is more common in English);

- ask leading questions;

- ask tag questions (a form of leading question which is also over-complex)

  - *You went to granddad's, did you?*

  - *You used to have a dog, didn't you?*;

- use questions with a negative form

  - *Do you not like school?*;

- use complex sentence structures with extra clauses which obscure the meaning

  - *When the man hit Mummy, and your brother was in bed, where were you?*

  - *We'll go to see your first foster mother, and while we're on the train, we'll have a sandwich and a drink, and we'll stick these photographs in your book;*

- ask *why* questions; in discussion of abuse, they imply guilt and can cause defensiveness; and in other circumstances may simply be too difficult;

- correct mistakes in the child's use of language, but respond using the right form:

  - *I teached my brother how to ride a bike*

  - *Did you? That's great. And who taught you?*

ACTIVITY **6.5**

Choose one of the following scenarios. Plan how you would explain your role to the child and the means you would use to communicate with them.

Leanne is six, a black British child accommodated for the last six months with Tanya, a single woman who is an old friend of her mother's. Before she went to live with Tanya, Leanne had never been to school, the initial reason for social services' involvement. Little is known about Leanne's early life, as her mother rarely agreed to speak to anyone; when she was accommodated, Leanne was slightly underweight, and listless, but otherwise in reasonable health. She has begun to settle down at school and recently told Tanya that her mother used to see dragons and other creatures flying in the sky, but Leanne couldn't see them and it was scary. Tanya has asked you to talk with Leanne about this.

Bruce is a white British boy of nine years old who has cerebral palsy which affects his gait, and he has mild learning difficulties. He lives with his parents and two sisters, one older, one younger. He attends a special school and is doing quite well, but has no friends locally. His parents think it would help him to have shared care in a family with boys around his age. You plan to meet Bruce to talk about his views and ideas.

Continued

ACTIVITY **6.5** *continued*

Janey and Sam are white British children aged five and four, living with their mother Denise, who is expecting a baby, and her husband, Raju, a British Asian. She and Raju have been together since Sam was born, and they now want him to adopt the children. The children's birth father is living with a new partner and their baby; he used to see the children once a month but this has tailed off since the baby's birth seven months ago. You expect to spend time with the children to establish whether adoption appears to be in their best interests.

COMMENT

Planning and preparing are usually helpful but do remember to be flexible too.

CHAPTER SUMMARY

In this chapter we have learnt about some of the circumstances in which it is desirable or necessary for social workers to communicate directly with children. Work with children usually takes place within a context where their primary care is the concern of other people, and we need to maintain open communication with parents, carers and other professionals, without prejudicing the child's confidentiality.

We have considered the development of linguistic skills in the first few years, and the importance of play as a medium for communication. We have seen that children who become service users are likely to be those whose development is atypical, for a range of reasons related to genetic endowment, poverty, parental engagement, illness and impairment in the parent or child, and disruptions in care and education. We have begun to think about some of the play techniques which may be helpful in building and sustaining working relationships. We have also learnt that adults frequently use language that is too complex for children to understand, and that younger children especially are unlikely to let us know this. Furthermore, children who have been maltreated defer more than others to adult authority and are highly sensitive to non-verbal cues; children with communication problems such as ADHD may conversely be unable to attend well to verbal or non-verbal input. Consequently, communication should be tailored to the child's capacities, so that they can engage as fully as possible in problem-solving, participation in decisions, and recovery from difficult circumstances.

FURTHER READING

Jones, DPH (2003) *Communicating with vulnerable children: A guide for practitioners.* London: Royal College of Psychiatrists.
Essential reading with an eloquent account of children's communication needs at different stages, and clear guidance on how to simplify adult communication and reduce the risk of influencing what children tell us.

Lefevre, M (2010) *Communicating with children and young people: Making a difference.* Bristol: The Policy Press.

Luckock, B and Lefevre, M (2008) (eds) *Direct Work: Social work with children and young people in care.* London: British Association of Adoption and Fostering.
An excellent collection with many papers written by practitioners, with wide applicability beyond children and young people in care.

Chapter 7

Working with families and groups

Introduction

So far, communication and interpersonal skills have been considered in the context of one-to-one relationships, with little about how to manage the dynamics of working with more than one person at a time. This chapter begins to address that issue, which is the reason for considering both families and groups in one chapter, even though there are important differences between them. Working with family and other groups offers different challenges from individual work, and many people initially find it a more daunting prospect than one-to-one encounters. The section on families will discuss work with the mother–infant dyad, the use of cognitive-behavioural strategies with families, and give a brief account of family group conferencing. The final section presents a group parenting programme and elements of a systemic model for groupwork.

Families

What is a family?

The concept of family is elastic, according to culture and perspective. This chapter takes a broad view, to recognise family diversity. 'Family' is taken to include parents who are married, or not; live together, or not; in heterosexual or lesbian or gay relationships; and single people raising children alone. It encompasses birth, step- and adopted children, and families where several generations or several adult members and partner of a single generation comprise the family group, living in one household or not. It embraces older parents caring for learning disabled, physically impaired or mentally ill adult offspring and older parents who are cared for by their adult children for similar reasons. In some cultures, cousins, aunts, uncles and other adults with no evident blood tie are included. Refugees, asylum seekers and other migrants may bring with them a very different conception of family from the nuclear one supposedly the norm in the UK, but may lack the family support they would have had at home.

Women (and men) who have been sexually abused within their families sometimes raise their own children in isolation, because of the threat abusing relations may pose, or where they have been ostracised by non-abusing members for revealing family secrets (Hooper and Koprowska, 2000). People who make a lesbian or gay relationship, reject an arranged marriage in favour of a love match (exacerbated if the person is from a lower caste), or choose a partner from a different ethnic or religious group may lose family affirmation.

ACTIVITY **7.1**

Maryam is 19 years old and has recently arrived from rural Pakistan with her husband and son, aged nine months. They live in a rented first-floor flat on a busy street and have no family nearby. Her husband works long hours. In Pakistan, the family group comprised adults of different generations, and children of varying ages. Toddlers explored safely outdoors overseen by a group of relatives. Encounters with animals, people and daily objects provided the stimulation for the child's development. Maryam's son has recently started crawling, and she doesn't know what to do to entertain him.

How would you go about helping Maryam to play with her son?

COMMENT

Working with someone from a very different culture is challenging. You may have to explain much more about your view of what is important about play with them with an urban-born British mother.

Genograms, ecomaps and culturagrams are ways of mapping family membership, and are well described by Parker and Bradley (2003). Intergenerational influences too need to be borne in mind, for example, the impact of early parental loss on the parents of the next generation.

Working with families

There are many methods of working with families, some better validated than others. How do we know whether to work with the individual who appears to have the main difficulties, or a subsystem such as the spouses or a parent and child, or the whole family? How do we know which is the most effective approach, or whether different approaches have similar outcomes? The evidence base for different forms of intervention is still being developed and models which have not been validated may nonetheless be effective; they have simply not yet been researched with any rigour. The literature on social work practice with children and families offers a range of approaches, some better evidenced than others. See, for example, Coulshed and Orme, (1998); McMahon and Ward, (2001); Bell and Wilson, (2003).

In this chapter, three well-evidenced approaches will be discussed. The first is an intervention directed at mothers and infants; the second is a cognitive and behavioural approach; and the third is family group conferencing, a relatively new means of working to mobilise the resources of larger family groups. These have been chosen as valuable examples, but the intention is not to decry other methods.

The three examples work with different constellations of family members, yet they have common features which mesh well with the principles underlying this book, as they all expect you to:

- build a working alliance with family members;
- prepare family members for the work they will do;
- respect members' knowledge and expertise about themselves;
- use your observation and understanding of verbal and non-verbal interactions between family members;
- manage structure, not content;
- mobilise the family's resources to help themselves.

Interactions between parents and infants

This example is of a project offering very early intervention with mothers and infants with the aim of promoting attachment security, in the knowledge that secure attachment predicts resilience and resilience predicts emotional health and well-being. The aim was to be cost-effective. Although this is a Sure Start project, health visitors rather than social workers were the frontline personnel. Health visitors provide a universal service free from association with problems, and this was no doubt a strength of the project design. They worked with child–parent psychologists. See the research summary.

RESEARCH SUMMARY

The Sunderland Infant Programme

All women with a new baby were invited to participate. Each participating mother–infant pair was videotaped by the health visitor for three to four minutes, engaging in typical interaction, and the tapes were assessed by the psychologists using measures of attachment behaviour – the CARE-Index – developed by Patricia Crittenden. Some were identified as showing satisfying interaction, and some appeared to need information about child development. Others showed problematic interaction for which an intervention was designed, and a few were deemed to need psychotherapy as well. The tapes were discussed by the psychologist and health visitor, who revisited the mother to view the tape with her.

Continued

Where there was no problem, this was an enjoyable experience which provided positive feedback; the health visitor gave the mother information about child development where this was thought to be a need. Where the interaction was less satisfactory, many mothers were quick to see this, and wanted to change. The intervention focused on enhancing the mothers' understanding of 'babyese', i.e. the baby's communications, and on the elements of the interaction which were going well, with health visitors making between one and four additional visits. A small number of mothers were also referred for psychotherapeutic help.

A control group from another similarly disadvantaged area was used to compare outcomes; while the researchers readily admit that the research design has limitations, and is not the randomly controlled trial which is taken as the gold standard, the results are compelling.

At a six-month follow-up, programme mothers increased significantly in sensitivity to their infants, while the control group mothers' sensitivity diminished; programme infants increased in co-operativeness. At a 12-month follow-up, 55 per cent of the programme infants were secure (close to the average, in the general population, of 60 per cent), compared with only 30 per cent of the control infants; and only 14 per cent of the programme infants showed non-normative, complex, attachment behaviours, in comparison with 43 per cent of the control group.

All staff were trained in the CARE-Index, and health visitors who had received the training accurately assessed mothers' sensitivity when compared with formal rating. Other health visitors who did not receive the training consistently assessed maternal sensitivity inaccurately (Jennings, cited in Svanberg).

(Svanberg 2005, unpublished)

This project depended on thorough training in observing mother–infant interaction. Desirable though it might be for all health visitors, psychologists and social workers to be trained in this way, generally we are not. So what is the purpose of using such an example here? The reasons relate to the skills involved, as it is evident from the outcomes that the mothers were able to make use of the interventions offered.

The project seems to have a number of strengths:

- Observation of interaction between mother and infant, which is more informative than asking how a mother feels towards her baby, or whether she is having difficulties.

- Viewing the video with the mother some time after the event means the mother's cognitive and observational capacities are available.

- Mothers were often able to see for themselves that the interaction was unsatisfying – far preferable to feeling criticised by a professional.

- Interventions were designed on the basis that most mothers are motivated to make a good relationship with their baby, and insensitivity is unintentional.

- Interventions concentrated on the baby's communication to the mother, and on what the mother was already doing well, rather than correcting the mother.

In Chapter 3 we saw that unsuccessful care-giving leaves the care-giver as unsatisfied as the care-seeker; experiencing more satisfying interaction becomes its own reward. In systemic terms, the engagement and interest which health visitors must have communicated to the mothers meant that they were open systems, able to take in information and use it to improve their relationships with their infants.

CASE STUDY

Joe is three, and his parents say he has become destructive. He throws toys around rather than playing with them, he kicks the furniture and his mother's legs. He has been hitting younger children at his play group. He seemed to be all right until three months ago, soon after his older brother started school, and a baby sister was born prematurely. She was in the special baby unit for six weeks. His mother, Miriam, stayed in hospital with her for the first week, and then visited daily. Joe's Dad looked after him for two weeks, and then his grandma after Dad went back to work. The baby is home now, but naturally needs quite a lot of attention.

You notice that Miriam is highly alert to any sounds or movements from the baby, who is often on her lap. Joe tries to get close to his mother but is told to play and not bother the baby; Joe asks for a drink and Miriam seems oblivious to the request until he has asked several times and finally kicks her, at which point she tells him off. You observe similar interactions over the course of a visit lasting an hour. Towards the end of your visit, the baby falls asleep and is put in her pram. Miriam plays a game with Joe on the floor, during which he is contented. Play is broken off by the baby waking.

Next visit, you ask how things are going, and on hearing there is no change, ask Miriam if she would like to hear your observations. She would. Starting with the contented game, you describe what you observed. You say Joe has some good communication skills, as you noticed he asked several times for a drink without getting frustrated, and that he tried to be affectionate towards her. She is reminded of what things were like before the baby was born, and begins to recognise that Joe is missing out on time with her, and has no one to play with now his brother is at school. She also talks about how anxious she is about the new baby, and expects Joe to cope; the two of you begin to think about how to change the pattern of interaction between her, the baby and Joe.

Working with family groups

As discussed in Chapters 4 and 5, explaining the approach you are taking, your rationale, and how the family members are expected to behave, is critical in seeking people's involvement. It may be obvious to you why you wish to see them as a group, but not to them, and it leads to better outcomes if you discuss these matters with them prior to embarking on work. Families are often puzzled by a family approach if they locate the problem in one or two members:

- mother is depressed;
- child is badly behaved;

- adult son diagnosed with schizophrenia spends all day in bed and plays music all night;

- father and teenage daughter don't get on;

- mother is overprotective of learning disabled son.

Common sense might suggest that this or that person or relationship needs 'fixing', rather than the family, and indeed many social workers and agencies operate on this premise.

Taking another angle of vision, however, families are often in the best position to solve their own problems (with some assistance), and marshalling the resources of all the members may be far more effective than working with one or two. Suggesting family work can then be heralded with a simple explanation:

> *Everyone in the family is affected by current circumstances, and everyone can help to change things.*

Explanations for children need to be framed in language they understand, and they should be encouraged to ask for clarification. Younger children will need toys, games and drawing materials to enable them to be involved in the meeting. McCluskey (2003) suggests seating the family in a circle so that everyone can see everyone else, with space in the middle for children to play on the floor. Falloon et al. (1993), whose work forms the main basis for this section, also stress the importance of families being able to organise meetings in their own home where people can make eye contact and attend to each other. You may feel it violates social norms to ask people to rearrange their furniture, so keep the goal in mind, which is to create a working environment in which to respect and enhance family relationships.

A cognitive behavioural approach

Falloon and his colleagues (1993) teach people cognitive and behavioural strategies to enable them to achieve desired goals, reduce stressful communication, create a more positive communicative climate and solve problems. The method takes time and commitment on the part of worker and family, but has explicit goals which prevent drift, and the expectation is that once the family is able to maintain its changes, perhaps with occasional help at difficult times, the therapist will disengage. It therefore meets all the criteria for a successful working alliance.

Changing the emotional climate is a central goal. Research suggests that in non-distressed families the ratio of negative to positive comments is nine to one; in distressed families it is close to 99 to one (Stuart, cited in Falloon et al., 1993, p.79). Juxtapose this depressing finding with the knowledge that long-term low warmth, high criticism households cause the most harm to children (Department of Health, 1995), and we see that this model has value for families of all ages.

Younger children's involvement depends on their abilities, but ten-year-olds can usually be fully involved. Close friends and relatives who do not live in the household may be included, as may anyone involved in caring for a family member, with the optimum number not exceeding six in all. The authors suggest that the model's educative and structured style enables people with illness or impairment that limits concentration to maintain focus. Simple communication, repetition where required, short bursts of work and frequent breaks help. Where someone's concentration is seriously impaired (e.g. by severe depression), it is better to delay sessions until there is improvement.

The starting point is to meet the family as a group to explain the approach, the therapist role, and expectations of the family, giving them the chance to ask questions. Ground rules are established about aggression and intoxication, which would lead to the cessation of a session or the exclusion of the individual. Once they have agreed to the work, each person is seen separately. The purpose is to make a working alliance with each member, identify their personal goals, assess their strengths and deficits in problem-solving, and clarify whether any assistance is needed in managing issues relating to health, impairment or mental health.

Each person chooses two goals, and the worker's role is not to influence the choice, but to ensure that they are specific and sufficiently modest to be attainable. They have to be within the person's control, not reliant on someone else changing, though other people may be recruited, for example, where the goal includes the company of another member or a friend. Goals may take some weeks to formulate as the person researches what is available, for example, whether there is a creative writing class in the locality. Ideally, goals are shared with other members of the household, so that there is support in reaching them. At the same time, obstacles to the accomplishment of goals are identified. A number of detailed assessments are carried out, including observation of the family in problem- solving interactions, and the completion of diaries by family members.

Thereafter, two family meetings take place each week. The first is an opportunity for the family to review progress with goals, problem-solving, skills and the status of specific disorders; to practise skills, learn new ones, and plan how to incorporate them into daily life prior to the next session (Falloon et al., 1993, p.17). The authors argue that working with the family in their own home speeds the learning of new skills, as this is where they will be put into practice, and impediments are readily identifiable, for example, the difficulty of attracting people's attention when they are watching television.

The second meeting is chaired and minuted by household members, to solve shared problems or achieve shared goals. Subjects where considerable conflict and high emotion are likely should be avoided until there is success in solving less taxing problems. The pattern is as follows:

- *Pinpoint the problem or goal*
- *List all possible solutions*
- *Highlight likely consequences*
- *Agree on 'best' strategy*
- *Plan and implement*
- *Review results.*

(Falloon et al., Table 6.1, p.112, reproduced with permission of Routledge.)

The therapist acts as coach to the family's communication. As with the Sunderland Infant Programme, we can see the value of observing and responding to typical interactions. The therapist also teaches specific communication skills which research by Vaughan and Leff shows were *most lacking in families under stress*.

These skills are:

- *expressing pleasant feelings*;

- *making constructive requests*;

- *expressing unpleasant feelings*;

- *active listening.*

(Falloon et al., 1993, p.78)

These relate closely to SAVI™ yellow- and green-light behaviours. Expressing feelings, both pleasant and unpleasant, is *Tells own feeling* in SAVI. Telling pleasant feelings (*I felt grateful that you let me sleep in this morning. Thanks for being quiet*) makes people feel better about themselves and the relationship. Falloon et al. suggest that these statements should be made with eye contact, and a smile, so verbal and non-verbal messages are congruent. We know from SAVI that it is easy to display unpleasant feelings through red-light behaviours such as *attack/blame*, etc., but these usually provoke a defensive or hostile response. Telling someone your feelings without the full emotional charge, accompanied by congruent non-verbal expression, allows them to respond emotionally and cognitively (*I was upset that you forgot our anniversary*).

Making constructive requests relates to SAVI yellow lights *asking narrow and broad questions* and making *proposals*. It is likely to stimulate the sharing of personal information and sometimes further proposals. *Active listening* is a core skill, since expressing feelings and making requests depend upon the other person reciprocating by attending.

The therapist models these communication skills in work with the family, observes their interactions, praises efforts even when achievements are not great, and helps members to structure their communication so that it is clear, without determining its content. For instance, someone might express a pleasant feeling, *I like the way you look today*, and the therapist might encourage expansion: *What do you like exactly?* This could lead to: *You've washed your hair and combed it nicely; your clothes are freshly ironed – and you smell good too!* Communication needs to be directed to the family member in question, not told to the therapist.

Another element of this model is for family members to share and increase their knowledge of any disorder or illness present in the family. The authors suggest that members may be under misapprehensions (often through having been given inadequate information by professionals) which can be put right by up-to-date information. Mutual understanding can be enhanced by the person with the difficulty explaining what it is like, and by family members explaining their perspective. 'Mind-reads' (also a SAVI term) need to be addressed.

CASE STUDY

Jacqui is 41 years old and was diagnosed with manic-depressive disorder in her early thirties. She and her husband, Mike, have two daughters, Annie and Lisa, aged 19 and 15. Annie lives with her boyfriend nearby and is expecting a baby. Jacqui's first serious depression was after Lisa was born. During her last hypomanic episode 18 months ago, she put a down payment on a house in Spain which the family could not afford, and it took several months and legal expenses to have part of the sum returned. It was only after this episode that Jacqui realised she was unwell; previously she had enjoyed the energy and euphoria of hypomania and thought Mike wanted her to be unhappy.

In the family discussion about manic-depressive disorder, the following ideas emerge: Jacqui has vague memories of sexual abuse by her grandma's second husband, and wonders if this could be the cause of her mental health problems. The worker would need to explain that many factors contribute and no one factor is responsible. It might be important to say that if asked, many people with severe mental health problems do report sexual abuse.

She is afraid that if she has another episode, Mike will leave her, because I've put him through so much. This is a red-light negative prediction – she may never have another episode. There is an opportunity here to explore what the family knows about the early signs that she is getting 'high' (or low), and to look at what will help prevent a full-blown episode. It is important not to encourage Mike to speculate about how he might feel in the future, as he cannot know. But he does know if he has ever had thoughts in the past of leaving because of Jacqui's illness, and if she has this mind-read, she could check this out by asking him a Yes/No question. He might say, Yes, and Jacqui might find this upsetting, or quite understandable. She could ask him how close he got to actually going. It is essential here that the worker does not try to sanitise Mike's response, but simply helps keeps the communication straight, encouraging them to tell their feelings.

Mike and Annie are both concerned that manic-depressive disorder can be inherited, and are worried about Annie's unborn baby. Again, inheritance is only one factor. A genogram of family members over several generations, identifying any with mental health problems, compared with data from research, would be useful here.

Lisa reveals that she has always thought she caused her mother's illness, and is relieved to hear that there are other factors. She may also need to check out a mind-read, if she thinks anyone else blames her. The worker could also explore and help put right a mind-read of herself that she is to blame, since even if her birth precipitated a depression, this was not of her volition or within her power to do anything about.

Family group conferences

I now want to turn to family group conferences (FGCs), as they offer a more empowering model than some social work practice, and involve working with larger family groups. They are now used quite extensively in restorative justice, but here I discuss wider applications.

FGCs originate in New Zealand, where they are enshrined in law. They emerged as a means of addressing problems in the Maori community which New Zealand's European models of social welfare and justice were unable to solve. Maori were over-represented in the child welfare, criminal justice and psychiatric systems and the ranks of the unemployed, facts which have been attributed to the deliberate destruction of their cultural ties and relationship to land, tribe and family by the state system itself (Love, 2000).

In Maori culture, problem-solving to address social transgressions traditionally took place at a community, rather than an individual or family, level, and similar processes exist in Native American cultures, where they are referred to as a circle (Ross, 2000). Those whose interests are in conflict (e.g. rejecting parent/rejected child; young offender/older person who has been burgled) each have the support of members of the community, and decisions are made according to the best interests of the community as a whole. The problem itself may be seen as the product of community failure, rather than an individual transgression, for example if someone is so poor they have to steal (Ross, 2000). Social problems were managed without state involvement.

By contrast, FGCs operate as a meeting place between family and professionals such as social workers, health visitors and probation officers. The professionals contribute information about how they see the problem at the start of the conference, after which the family takes private time to arrive at a plan; the plan then has to be agreed with the professional service providers. For example, the plan for a child neglected by its parents might be for the child to live with an aunt and uncle; this proposal would have to be agreed by social services. The plan might recommend specific services, such as therapeutic help for the parents, or financial support for the aunt and uncle, which would also need approval. FGCs may be single events, or can be reconvened as a means of monitoring progress and arriving at new plans.

Love (2000) argues that for Maori, this is at best a poor compromise, and at worst a covert means of continuing to undermine Maori decision-making autonomy. For families in the UK, where such structures are novel, FGCs are seen as providing far greater autonomy for families than well-established methods such as childcare case conferences (although FGCs are not necessarily an alternative – they may take place prior to a case conference for the plan to be agreed, or after a case conference as a means of moving forward). It is likely that FGCs reflect social decision-making for some of the UK community whose origins are abroad.

Two elements of FCGs that I wish to highlight are the skills involved in the role of the co-ordinator; and the impact on social workers of the need to deliver information publicly to a wide family group.

The role of the co-ordinator
In the UK, co-ordinators have been appointed to the role; in other words, it is no one else's job to act as co-ordinator. Many of them have a social work background, but the role is independent of social services, and they play no part in the decision-making process (Marsh and Crow, 1998). These factors are probably essential for families to have confidence in them. The role is to organise and manage the conference by:

- identifying all the possible attendees (both family and professionals);

- inviting everyone;

- preparing them for participation in the conference;

- encouraging them to attend and see their attendance as valuable if they have reservations or objections (e.g. *I'm not going if he's going*);

- ensuring that professionals give their information clearly and substantiate their opinions, and enabling family members to ask for clarification;

- orienting the family to the decisions that need to be made during their private time;

- helping the family clarify the resulting plan so that it is unambiguous and specific.

The co-ordinator also takes on practical tasks such as finding a suitably neutral location with adequate space, and arranges transport, refreshments, provision of toys and play materials for children, and so forth.

The role of the co-ordinator thus seems to exemplify the user-friendly model proposed by Treacher and Carpenter (1993). Particularly interesting is the use of influence to bring people to the conference but not to shape the plan. The plan needs to belong to the family, or its chances of success will be limited. Equally important is preparation to enable people to contribute to the process, and orienting them to the task so that it is accomplished.

Delivering information

Marsh and Crow (1998) found that social workers and other professionals had to change their way of communicating when delivering information to FGCs. They had to write shorter reports than for case conferences, write clearly without jargon, provide substantiation for opinions, and include information about services which might be available, to inform the plan. Some had concerns about sharing confidential information with a wider family group than usual. As they point out, the ideal is that there are no surprises at the meeting, as the professionals are expected to share the information with the family beforehand, but this is not always possible. Careful consideration of what really needs to be shared reduces the problem: Marsh and Crow cite an earlier study by Barker and Barker (1995) which showed that social workers *learnt how to present relevant information clearly, and to omit information not relevant to the concerns* (Marsh and Crow, 1998, p.110). Interestingly, some social workers initially experienced anxiety about ceding power to the family, but for many this was replaced by enthusiasm for the better outcomes.

Groups

This section offers a brief discussion of working with groups which have the goal of benefiting their members. Members usually share some common ground relating to the reason for bringing them together, on the basis that they will gain from exchanging thoughts or feelings, or from engaging in activities together. Group sessions may be formally organised, with a specified membership, taking place at a special time, or be much more loosely structured, for example while using common spaces in drop-in centres, family centres, residential care, supported housing schemes, hospital wards and day centres. (All of these environments may offer structured groups too.) Here we will consider more structured groups.

Groups require careful planning, including the selection and preparation of members. Starting a group only to have people drop out is unsettling for everyone. Research into psychotherapeutic groups (Science to Service Task Force, 2007) shows that *cohesion* is the main *mechanism* leading to *client improvement*. Cohesion arises from a number of factors. First there needs to be clarity for leader and members about group structure, processes, rules, and skills needed for participation. The leader needs to model and facilitate the giving of interpersonal feedback in ways and at stages that can be made use of by members. A good balance needs to be struck between individual and group needs. Finally, there needs to be a climate of openness and responsiveness to emotional expression, with the group leader able to *manage his or her emotional presence* (Science to Service Task Force, 2007, pp.14–16).

There are many different approaches to groupwork, some better suited to particular memberships and goals. They may focus on the past, or on current issues, or on the here-and-now experience in the group. Groups for children will always involve activities, while some for young people and adults consist solely in talk. See Whitaker (2000) for a comprehensive account of planning different groups for different populations. Here are some examples of kinds of group.

1. An ongoing weekly support group with flexible attendance, for carers of people with dementia. Thirty people are members; on each occasion, between three and 14 turn up. They start with refreshments, and mostly engage in informal discussion. Every few months, they invite someone to inform them about a topic, such as social security benefits, or new approaches to working with dementia.

2. A group run six times over three months for eight to ten black people with sickle cell anaemia, with the aim of understanding and managing the disorder more effectively.

3. A group for eight children aged 8–11 with difficulties in managing angry behaviour in school. The group has eight weekly sessions, and members are expected to attend every time. Activities are designed to make the group fun, but also to help the children explore what makes them frustrated, and to look at different strategies for managing their anger.

4. A group run by the user/members of a voluntary mental health organisation. The agency is user-led, and meetings aim to facilitate the involvement of as many members as possible in deciding how the agency is organised, what activities should take place, and what kind of assistance the members require from support staff to enable them to achieve their goals.

5. A group for ten young people with learning disabilities living in supported housing. They join for six months to a year, depending on their needs, and there is a rolling programme of activities which the group plans with the facilitators. New members can join every two months, when a vacancy arises.

RESEARCH SUMMARY

A parenting programme known as the Incredible Years programme developed by a US psychiatrist, Carolyn Webster-Stratton, has taken hold in the UK, and there are quite a number of well-designed US and UK research studies offering testimony to its effectiveness (e.g. Webster-Stratton and Hammond, 1997; Webster-Stratton, 1998; Bell and Fisher, 2003; Gardner et al., 2006; Hutchings et al., 2007). The group programme usually involves parents whose young children are at risk of conduct disorders, though in Bell and Fisher's study the programme was available to all parents within a given locality. The provision of transport, food and crèche facilities all make the programme much more accessible for disadvantaged parents.

The Webster-Stratton ... parenting programme employs a collaborative approach, building on parents' strengths and expertise. The sequence of topics includes parent–child play, praise, incentives, limit-setting, problem-solving and discipline. Video clips are used to illustrate different strategies parents use to manage children. Parents are encouraged to discuss their children's behaviour and role plays are used to find solutions and practise *skills for managing their child.* Each week parents practise tasks at home; telephone calls are made to encourage progress *(Gardner et al., 2006, p.1124). It can quickly be seen that the design of the programme depends on skilled communication and facilitation. Implicitly, it targets the* long-term low warmth, high criticism *climate known to be harmful to children (DoH, 1995). Sessions last for two hours each week, and programmes last 12–14 weeks. Sometimes a group programme for children known as the Dinosaur School is run alongside. Edwards et al. (2007) provide evidence for cost-effectiveness.*

Strong evidence of improvements in parents and children, and in siblings, are reported by Gardner et al. (2006) and Hutchings et al. (2007). Changes were assessed using a range of measures and observation of interaction. At a 6-month follow-up, parents showed significantly increased positive parenting responses, *and some reduction in* parental criticism. *In the children, there was* significantly reduced antisocial and hyperactive behaviour and increased self-control *(Hutchings et al., 2007, p.4). Gardner et al. (2006) found similar results at 6-month and 18-month follow-up. They found a high level of satisfaction with the programme in parents, despite the fact that they experienced no improvement in depressed mood.*

Both studies attest to the value of the 3-day training staff received prior to offering the programme, and the weekly supervision which was provided to support them. Warmth and frankness appear to be essential interpersonal attributes. Communicative skills described are the ability to model the behaviours being taught and the ability to talk about parents' experiences and difficulties while acknowledging their feelings *(Hutchings et al. 2007, p.3). This latter point echoes findings about the effects of social workers'* empathic responses to parents on reducing resistance, increasing *disclosure and leading to* greater agreement about what happens next *(Forrester et al., 2008, p.46).*

Communication and interpersonal skills in leading groups

Most of the skills in this section derive from Agazarian's model for group work (1997, 2006).

Preparation

Before committing themselves, potential members usually have an opportunity to talk about the group. It is helpful to meet potential participants beforehand and discuss what the group will be like, either individually, or through one or two 'taster' sessions, after which people decide whether to continue (Brown, 1992). With some groups (e.g. 1, 2 and 5 on page 118), you solicit ideas for group events they would find valuable. For children's groups, permission from their carers is needed, and you may need to meet them to discuss what is involved, though sometimes an explanatory letter with a consent form for return will suffice. If members have been referred by another professional, the nature of information to be sent back to the referrer will need to be made clear.

Starting off

It is commonly recognised that group members will initially be anxious and that getting off to a good start, with a welcoming emotional climate, is important (e.g. Preston-Shoot, 2007). Most initial sessions start with a brief introduction by the facilitator. This could include expressing pleasure at everyone's presence; naming the main purpose of the group; and providing orienting information, such as the length of the session, whether and when there will be a break, where and when people can smoke, the number of sessions, etc. You need to introduce yourself, and group members are often asked to introduce themselves or each other. The content of these introductions needs to be considered beforehand, as you want to make sure that people disclose only as much as is comfortable for the group as a whole. You need to consider whether anyone will quickly feel like the odd one out. Evaluate the following, and add your own suggestions.

ACTIVITY 7.2

Name – first name only or first and last? title?

Occupation – what if people come from very different backgrounds?

Home circumstances – if most are married, how might single or gay people feel?

Problem – how much information should be given? Do you want the group to be problem-focused?

What they hope to gain from the group.

Whether they have any worries about the group.

Whether they have been in a group before, and what it was like.

The last two present opportunities to stop red-light behaviours and start a yellow- and green-light communication pattern. Worries are negative predictions, e.g. *No one will understand me; I'll be left out; I won't say anything because I'm shy; I'll have a panic attack and will have to leave.* Negative predictions are often based on past experiences, and people may describe bad experiences in groups: *I was scapegoated; the leaders never said anything and I felt lost; I said something to another member and they never came back.* Members often worry about the past and the future at the start of a group, so bringing them into present reality is the first task (Agazarian, 2006).

First you can normalise the worries by saying that it's usual for people to feel anxious in new situations. (Don't forget that you will be anxious, too.)

Don't be tempted to offer reassurance –*That won't happen in this group* – since you do not know what will happen. Instead, ask the following two questions. *Has that happened so far in this group?* This narrow question alerts people to the present, and the new context, and stimulates their cognitive capacities. They will almost invariably say *No*. The follow-up question is:

If that begins to happen, will you tell us about it? This question contains a proposal which empowers people to do something different this time, gives them responsibility for doing it, and indicates that you as group leader take their concern seriously. (It is also a good response if they qualified their answer to the first question by saying, *No, but it might*, and avoids contradicting them.) As you can imagine, your voice tone has to convey warmth and interest – any hint of ridicule and you will lose their confidence, and possibly the group's.

Cohesion can be built by actively encouraging people to connect with others on the basis of similar feelings, a process known as *functional subgrouping* in systems-centered therapy (SCT®) (Agazarian, 1997, p.41) Functional subgrouping occurs when people genuinely feel resonant with the experience of another, at that point in time. This process expands awareness of the range of experiences we all have, and reduces the chance of people getting stuck in their usual, familiar, and often self-defeating ways of experiencing the world. By encouraging people to join others only when they feel similar, and to wait for a change in the group to bring in different experiences (which are equally valid), red-light behaviours of fighting and competing are reduced, and green-light behaviours of building on others' ideas, agreements and positives, and telling own feelings, are promoted. Functional subgrouping behaviours include asking 'Anyone else?' when a member has finished speaking, and by encouraging members to make and maintain eye contact with members of their subgroup (Agazarian, 2006). SCT groups analysed using SAVI™ as a research tool consistently work in yellow and green light (Carter, personal communication).

Patterns of interaction

Allan Brown provides a useful summary of the direction of communication: *worker–member; member–member; worker–group; and worker–external environment. With co-workers there is the fifth direction . . . worker–worker* (Brown, 1992, p.88).

Here we are concerned with the first three. You communicate with the whole group at the beginning of the initial session. There are many other occasions when a statement to the whole group will be useful. Explanations and instructions about activities, educative inputs (e.g. on the nature of stress), and summaries of group themes or process are of this kind:

Today we've explored feelings of anger about having an illness which causes extreme pain, and for which there is no cure.

In the early stages of a group, it is common for members to communicate most with the leader, and they are most preoccupied with what the leader has to say. As the group develops, they will usually communicate more with each other, and contributions are weighed on merit more than on who has made them (Agazarian, 1997). Functional subgrouping enables people to communicate with each other, and once you have established this as norm, you can nudge members in that direction. *Winston, John said he found it difficult to cuddle his children, and you are explaining how you find it difficult too, but are getting better at it, so tell John directly.* (This is worker–member, in the service of member–member communication.) If you make eye contact around the group then you will encourage the members to do likewise rather than looking to you.

Just as with families, we try not to influence the content of what people say, but we influence the structure. Three patterns commonly occur in groups: one person's problems regularly become the focus of group attention; one person becomes a scapegoat and is attacked and blamed; one or two people talk a great deal, and one or two scarcely speak. Subgrouping can help change the first two patterns. Look at these examples.

> *Brenda: I can't sleep at night, I lie awake worrying about my mother all the time, I feel so helpless, I don't know what to do.*
>
> *Janice: Have you tried a hot bath before you go to bed?*
>
> *Brenda: Doesn't work, I just get tensed up as soon as I get out. I don't think anything will help.*
>
> *Kevin: Valerian pillows are supposed to be good.*
>
> *Brenda: I bet they're expensive, I can't afford things like that.*
>
> *Leader: Ok group, you keep trying to help Brenda by making suggestions. Maybe you could subgroup with her instead. Does anyone here know these feelings of helplessness, and feeling nothing will ever make a difference?*
>
> *Janice: Yes! Some days I can hardly get up in the morning I feel so hopeless and helpless. I just lie there thinking things'll never change.*
>
> *Leader: Anyone else?*

In this example, the group tries yellow-light proposals, but Brenda stays firmly in red light, complaining, discounting, making negative predictions, and so on. The leader directs the group to green-light behaviours, of telling own feelings.

> *Dorothy: Jon, I get the feeling you just don't want to be here. You never contribute much.*
>
> *Doug: I agree. You just sit there with that superior look on your face and I don't know what you're thinking.*
>
> *Leader: Sounds like we have some good scapegoating impulses here. If you don't direct them at Jon right now, you can explore them in a subgroup.*
>
> *Doug: OK. Dorothy, when Jon gets that look I just feel he knows something he's not telling us, and I feel like shaking him.*

123

Dorothy: I know, and it's like, I want to shake the words out of him, I want to make him tell us.

Leader: Anyone other than Dorothy and Doug feel like scapegoating anyone?

Jon: Well, as a matter of fact I do. I feel like having a go at Dorothy for always being so icky nice to everyone.

Leader: Anyone else?

Here, Dorothy and Doug use red-light attack/blame, and the leader recognises the underlying feelings of hostility without accepting the behaviour. Subgrouping around the impulse to scapegoat (rather than doing it) is a green-light behaviour, and even the initial scapegoat joins in, taking him out of the scapegoat role. It doesn't matter that his target is different; the feeling is the same.

Teaching people how to subgroup is quite a skill, but once people have grasped it, it enables them to manage conflicts in the group. It helps people to contain and regulate their emotions, rather than putting them into action in red-light behaviours.

Where some people talk a great deal and others are almost silent, you can draw the group's attention to this without making individuals feel at fault by making a worker–group statement:

In any group, there are some people who immediately know what they want to say, and some who take longer, so let's make room for the people who take a bit longer.

Have you noticed that we seem to let Brenda do a lot of the talking for the group? Maybe we could give her a break and see where other people are.

This statement recognises that silence and talking are reciprocal behaviours, and tries to avoid scapegoating too, but this would be risky with a brand new group, as Brenda would feel put down. Timed right, it could become a green-light affectionate joke that Brenda always has something to say.

Sometimes you will notice someone starting to speak who gives up if someone more assertive comes in, and you can make a worker–member statement: *Could you hold back a second there, Kevin, as I think Mandy was about to say something.*

This is the briefest introduction to some of the skills used in SCT®. The challenge, as with families, is to keep both the individuals and the interactions between them in mind, so that you actively decide whether to intervene at the individual or group level. The same principles apply of mobilising the group's own resources, and working with them to a point where you can disengage.

CHAPTER SUMMARY

In this chapter we have learnt about working with two or more people at once, in families and groups. Skills in observation of verbal and non-verbal interaction, and in structuring communication to make it more successful and satisfying without trying to change the content are common to both kinds of work. Our own skills in communication provide a model, exemplified by clear, simple language free from blame. SAVI™ provides a useful means of taking the emotional temperature of an interaction and enabling people to lower the heat. We have seen that enabling people to tap under-utilised resources in themselves and those close to them tends to lead to better outcomes, allowing us to disengage, rather than drifting into becoming unsatisfied and unsatisfying care-givers. We have also identified a need for more robust evaluation of social work practices so that we can have confidence in the methods we employ.

FURTHER READING

Bell, M and Wilson, K (eds) (2003) *The practitioner's guide to working with families*. Basingstoke: Palgrave Macmillan.
This offers a good range of papers tackling subjects from social policy, theory and practice.

Dallos, R and Draper R (2000) *An introduction to family therapy: Systemic theory and practice*. Buckingham: Open University Press.
A book which draws on theory, research and practice to provide an account of the development of family therapy. It describes different ways of working and skills needed.

Preston-Shoot, M (2007) *Effective groupwork*. 2nd edition. Basingstoke: Palgrave Macmillian.
A good introductory guide setting groupwork in a modern context.

Whitaker, DS (2000) *Using groups to help people*. 2nd edition. Hove: Brunner-Routledge.
This book provides a detailed and lucid guide to the whole process of groupwork. Part 2 deals specifically with planning and is invaluable.

Chapter 8

Working with people with 'special communication needs': communicative minorities

Introduction

First we need to consider what is meant by the term 'special communication needs', which comes from the Department of Health requirements for the social work degree. The central questions we have to pose are: *Who has special communication needs? Is it the service users, or the service providers?* What difference does it make to put the problem in the one rather than the other? If we locate it in the service user, there is a risk that this begins to define them, and defines them by what is lacking (they do not speak English, or they do not see), and we overlook who they are and all their capabilities. If we locate it in the service providers, we recognise that, as a profession, we work with a very diverse group of people, and we need to expand our capabilities to meet this challenge, even though we cannot be equally skilled in every area. As we saw in Chapter 5, social work and the wider culture sometimes focus on deficits and problems more than on people's capabilities; in this chapter, we consider some of the skills needed to work effectively with people from what we might call 'communicative minorities'. The first half of this chapter will consider issues in working with people who use minority languages from other countries, or British Sign Language, and the use of interpreters. The second half introduces the social model of disability (Oliver, 1990) and considers the skills needed to communicate with people who have hearing loss, visual impairment, learning disability and permanent or temporary changes in communicative ability.

Minority languages

Speaking a minority language is not an impairment, yet many of the barriers people face when they do not speak much or any English are similar to those faced by people with impairments. They are at risk of being misunderstood, inaccurately assessed and thus disadvantaged. Broadly speaking, in social work you are likely to come across four groups of people who speak little or no English:

- new arrivals;

- longstanding residents who have not learned English or can no longer remember it;

- deaf people (discussed on pages 130–31);

- some people with learning disabilities (discussed on pages 136–37).

Their needs are not all the same, though there may be overlapping areas of skill needed.

New arrivals

New arrivals include many people who will never need a social work service. Those who do are predominantly asylum seekers and refugees who have often had difficult journeys, sometimes traumatic and loss-filled histories of war, political oppression, and torture, and who may also have knowledge, skills and qualifications which are overlooked or discounted when they come to the UK because of political, institutional and personal racism. Not all are literate, and others are unfamiliar with the English alphabet and script. Sometimes 'legitimate' migrants, say from the European Community, also run into serious difficulties and may be homeless, unemployed and 'at sea' in the British system. A grasp of the impact of such experiences is the foundation for any communication skills.

Consider the following voluntary service, which is a real agency, and answer the questions.

ACTIVITY **8.1**

The START project in Plymouth

START (Students and Refugees Together) is an agency set up to provide services to asylum seekers and refugees, and to provide practice learning for students (initially social work students but now including healthcare, psychology, arts and media, business, etc., and taking students from countries outside the UK).

During the year 2003–2004, the service was used by 303 asylum seeker and refugee families and individuals, from 37 nations. Six social work students from UK programmes and two from Germany undertook practice learning.

(START, 2004, and information from personal visit)

English is the common language of the project. On occasion the workers do need to use interpreters, or to draw on the language skills of the students placed there.

Why do you think English is the common language of the project? List as many reasons as you can think of. Now think about any disadvantages there are.

What special communication skills do the social work students need to acquire?

When might it be critical to use an interpreter?

COMMENT

The UK continues to be a multicultural place with incomers from Central and Eastern Europe now settling here. Being able to communicate effectively with them takes time and effort.

Here are some skills to consider:

- To avoid complex grammar and ambiguous terms when working with people whose English is limited. How could you make the following statements simpler and less open to misinterpretation?

    I might as well strike while the iron is hot, so what I'm going to do now is, phone the Housing Office about your application.

    Would you mind – I know it's a bit of a cheek – but could I use your phone to make the call? My mobile seems to have died.

- To be imaginative in describing words or concepts that aren't understood. Think about how to explain the following in simple language:

    Social work student: *I will be doing a needs assessment of you.*
    Service user: *What means needs assessment?*

- To draw pictures, bring in objects such as maps, or magazines, as sources of visual information to aid communication.

- To check out the person's understanding and ensure that decisions are not arrived at without their full involvement. This can be difficult if other professionals are involved and want to rush things.

What other skills did you have on your list?

CASE STUDY

You, Rahid and Asha, a couple from Iraq, are at the housing office. The officer is getting impatient, and wants them to sign for accommodation. You know that neither of them has fully understood what they are signing for. How might you handle the situation?

Longer-standing residents

ACTIVITY 8.2

Consider the following imaginary statutory service.

The Midlands Team for children and families

The Midlands Team serves an area where around 70 per cent of the population speak English as a first language, and 30 per cent speak Urdu or Punjabi or both as their first language(s). Most are Muslim, and represent the range of Muslim practice, from uninvolved through to devout. Women in the community who have come from Pakistan are less likely to learn English than their husbands, brothers and contemporaries born in the UK. For devout Muslims, it is not acceptable for a woman to be alone with a man who is not a relation. Bear in mind that women are far more commonly service users than men across all cultural groups, especially where children are involved; engaging fathers is never easy.

The team structure and personnel look like this:

Manager	*White British man; speaks English*
Reviewing Officer	*White British woman; speaks English*
Senior Practitioner:	*White British woman; speaks English and average French*
Senior Practitioner:	*Black Jamaican man; speaks English*
Social worker 1	*British Pakistani woman, speaks Urdu, Punjabi and English*
Social worker 2	*White Irish woman, speaks English and some Irish*
Social worker 3	*White British man, speaks English*
Social worker 4	*Vacant post – occupied by one agency worker after another*
Social worker 5	*Vacant post*

The team and the manager want to improve the service to their local Urdu/Punjabi-speaking community. In addition, the vacant posts are about to be advertised. A decision has been made at Director level to improve staff morale and promote retention by saving money on expensive, transient, agency staff and put some into training.

Evaluate the following suggestions made by the team after a team-building day.

Continued

> ## ACTIVITY *8.2* *continued*
>
> - *In an ideal world, select two women social workers who already speak Urdu or Punjabi.*
>
> - *In an ideal world, select two social workers who already speak Urdu or Punjabi – one woman and one man.*
>
> - *Select anyone who's good enough regardless of language skills – fill those vacancies!*
>
> - *Send all the team members who don't know Urdu or Punjabi to a class, in work time, funded by the department. No more than two could go each year, so who should go first?*
>
> ## COMMENT
>
> *This would make a good debate if conducted in a group.*

It sometimes seems a good idea to recruit people from the immediate community because of their connections and knowledge, yet, aside from such individuals being in short supply, they may not be acceptable to the community. Although professionals expect to abide by rules of confidentiality, this is not always credible to members of a minority community. Even if they trust the principle, there can be reluctance to divulge information to someone known, or known of, in a private context.

Second, it may appear 'obvious' that people from the same culture should provide a service to one another. The profession has everything to gain from attracting talented people from black and minority ethnic groups, but it remains difficult to match the staff make-up of any team to local demography. And to provide a good accessible service, and for our own development, we all need experience of working with a wide range of service users. We also need people from black and minority ethnic groups to rise through the ranks to manage and design services, and not be held back because of their value at the 'coal face'.

Given the relatively high proportion of potential service users who speak Urdu or Punjabi in this example, I would recommend staff training in language and culture, as well as trying to recruit staff who do.

This example uses a children and families team, but similar situations arise in care management, where in some parts of the country there are small but significant numbers of older people originating from Pakistan, India and mainland China who may never have learnt much English. Some older people with good English may lose some of their vocabulary if they develop Alzheimer's or another form of dementia, and words from their first language may present themselves instead. We will return to this subject when considering interpreter services.

Deafness

There are between 50,000 and 60,000 deaf people in the UK, and about five million with hearing loss. Deaf people use British Sign Language (BSL) as their preferred or only means of communication (or American Sign Language, or Spanish, etc.). Such people are almost always prelingually deaf, i.e. they were born with little or no hearing or lost their hearing through illness or accident before speech was learnt. Most deaf people are born into hearing families. Politically, deaf people regard themselves as a linguistic minority rather than as a group of disabled people. BSL is a distinct language which is visual and spatial and has its own grammar; it is not English translated into BSL. It is a living, changing language, and is the basis for deaf history and culture. Some deaf people have speech, and some of these will use it, but their English may not be as fluent or as expressive as their use of BSL; others have no speech. Deaf people generally read and write English but, just as hearing people prefer to talk than write notes, deaf people prefer to sign. (Summarised from Young et al., 1998.)

Not all deaf people are politicised. They may have internalised the idea that they are disabled (see the 'Social model of disability' later in this chapter), in some way 'inferior' and unable to act in their own right. Working towards greater autonomy and self-worth needs to be taken slowly.

Deaf people may use hearing aids, but for some they serve no purpose and others reject them on political grounds that they aim to make people 'hearing', and suppress deaf culture.

Since BSL is a visual language using sign and gesture, signers need to be able to see each other. Where hearing people often use voice to attract attention, deaf people use *waving, tapping on the shoulder, flicking lights on and off* (Williams and Abeles, 2004, p.645). Facial expression is even more important than between hearing people, and eye contact tends to be held for longer. Physical closeness accompanies discussion of personal matters, distance when *processing stories or learning new concepts* (Glickman, cited in Williams and Abeles, 2004, p.645).

When a hearing and a deaf person meet, their cultural norms differ, and both are vulnerable to misinterpreting the other and feeling uncomfortable or offended.

Except where hearing people use BSL, there are real risks that deaf people are excluded from discussion and decision-making, as service users and as colleagues. One-to-one communication, using lip-reading or notes, can work. Group discussion becomes impossible: hearing people talk too quickly, talk over each other, turn away, hide their mouths. Deaf people find they are presented with a summary of the discussion, but their contribution and participation in any decision have been lost (highly oppressive where decisions affect them personally), and they have become bored and alienated. Even signing hearing people slip into these behaviours when other hearing people are present (Harris, 1997; Young et al., 1998).

Some deaf people are angry and despairing about making good contacts with hearing people. I believe that some hearing people who don't sign feel uncomfortable about their inability to communicate competently, but don't know what to do.

Harris (1997) argues that all social workers should learn to sign. One of her interviewees puts it well: *I can't learn to hear, but Hearing people can learn to sign* (Harris, 1997, p.36). Where social workers cannot sign, Harris suggests that modest changes in practice, such as resorting to paper and pencil, overcome many obstacles.

Working with deaf people (after Harris (1997); Williams and Hewitt (2004), and Young et al. (1998)):

- respect deafness as a difference, just as we do gender, sexual orientation, etc;

- respect BSL as a full and complex language;

- be anti-discriminatory through creativity with pen and paper, gesture, drawing;

- be patient;

- allow more time for meetings;

- meet in uncluttered environments with few visual distractions;

- speak more slowly;

- form words more clearly (but not exaggeratedly);

- don't turn away or cover your mouth when speaking;

- if you don't understand, ask;

- use interpreters, especially for critical meetings;

- communicate by letter, fax or email in preference to phone;

- learn BSL – even a little shows respect and interest;

- become fluent in BSL if you work with deaf people regularly.

Working with interpreters

Serious misunderstandings can occur where we share no common language with service users. Misjudging a person's mental health or misconstruing an explanation for injuries to a vulnerable child or adult can have grave, even fatal outcomes. Problems arise in both underestimating or exaggerating the problem, so it is sometimes best to use interpreters. This does not mean just *anyone* who knows the language. Guidance such as the Code of Practice to the Mental Health Act 1983 (DoH, 1999) warns against using family members or other informal networks. This is because the translator may:

- have no specialist knowledge of the problem;

- hide the problem because of shame;

- be a child who should be protected from the problem;

- be someone who has no right to know the problem;

- be an abuser who causes the problem.

In practice, this guidance is often dispensed with, since professional interpreter services are scarce and can take too long to arrange. They are also expensive – an unwelcome reality. Relative risks need to be weighed so that you can make the best use of available candidates.

It takes some skill to make good use of interpreters, either in the room, or at the end of a telephone. Telephone interpreting goes like this: social worker or service user talks to interpreter; hands phone to the other; interpreter translates what has been said and listens to response; phone goes back to first person, who hears translation and responds. And so on. Using such a service efficiently means being well prepared and having your questions and possible responses to service-user queries organised in advance.

An interpreter in the room is needed for signing (though video link is a possibility). They act as a conduit for information back and forth between you and a service user. Small chunks of information need to be translated, not long speeches. Both you and the service user may feel drawn to talk to the interpreter rather than each other. Resist this. It has been suggested that worker and interpreter meet beforehand, not to discuss the details but to clarify their roles in relation to the goals of the meeting (Williams and Abeles, 2004). This could be hard to arrange, and in some instances it could be done in the service user's presence just before the meeting, to be less threatening and to help them grasp your different roles.

Though interpreters are professionals, they may be subject to the same doubts as social workers from a minority ethnic community. Service user and interpreter may know each other in other arenas, making disclosure of private details uncomfortable for some. Williams and Abeles (2004) make this point in relation to American sign language; it is equally applicable to BSL or any minority language.

RESEARCH SUMMARY

The medical and social models of disability

The medical model is not a formal model which is taught under that name, and you should not assume that every medical and health professional upholds it. Rather it is tacit, visible through the approach taken in thinking and practice. Here the model has been expanded to include other communicative minorities.

1. *It is a* deficit *model: it highlights what is missing or has been lost (a limb, hearing, intellectual capacity, ability to speak a mainstream language).*

2. *It locates the disability in the person and regards them as suffering a tragedy for which they are to be pitied.*

3. *It therefore seeks solutions which 'fix' the 'broken' (or skill-deprived) person, to make them more like other people or how they were before (e.g. through provision of a prosthetic limb, hearing aids, intensive training).*

4. *It confers a singular, disabled, or otherwise derogated, identity, obscuring the unique, complex, multiple identities of the whole person.*

The social model is usually taught to social work students and sometimes to healthcare students.

1. *It is a* rights *model, and looks towards a* strengths *model. People's fundamental human rights remain the same despite impairment or temporary skills deficits, and it focuses on what people can do rather than on what they can't.*

Continued

2. *It distinguishes* impairment *(the missing or lost part) from* disability, *which is brought about by barriers in the physical and social environment that prevent the person from engaging in mainstream life. Acquired impairment (or transition to a new country and culture) may be a shock but need not be tragic if barriers to ordinary life are removed.*

3. *It therefore seeks solutions which 'fix' the environment. This means, for example, physical access for people with who use wheelchairs; socially it means changing attitudes and behaviours.*

4. *It recognises the complex multiple identities of people with impairments and members of communicative minorities.*

The social model of disability

The social model of disability (Oliver, 1990) occupies an important place in social work thinking, and has begun to influence social work practice, service provision and legislation. The social model of disability takes a different view from the so-called medical model which holds far more sway in everyday thinking and attitudes. Use it to reflect back on what has been said about deaf culture, as well as to throw light on the following sections.

Disabling factors are interpersonal and social as well as physical, and people without impairments can be disabled by the same attitudes. It is disabling to be ignored, talked down to, treated as stupid, have people lose patience with you when you need more time, and be excluded from decision-making – common experiences for all the groups of people discussed in this chapter. People with mobility problems will not be discussed here, although they too are subject to these disparaging attitudes.

The social model of disability makes a better fit with the social work values of empowerment and liberation than the medical model. The argument underpinning this chapter is that putting the social model into interpersonal practice means addressing our own 'special communication needs' in order to meet those of service users. And let's not forget that service users and social workers are sometimes the same individuals. More people with impairments are joining the ranks of social work, and social workers without impairments may acquire them during the course of their careers.

There are potential pitfalls in applying the social model of disability unthinkingly and it has been well critiqued by Shakespeare (2006). Some disabled people are treated as incompetent for so long that they come to regard themselves as such, and work with them needs to progress sensitively and slowly. Also, people vary widely in their responses to acquired impairment, associated physical pain, medication and its risks, and the possibility of a reduced lifespan. When people do feel downcast, depressed, frustrated, furious, we should not demean their feelings in our search for a more positive outlook.

Hearing loss

People usually acquire hearing loss later in life, use spoken English as their preferred language, and will often use hearing aids, distinguishing them from deaf people, but some of the same issues apply. Again you will need patience, more time for meetings, and pen and paper. Written communication may be better than phone. However, most people with hearing loss are older, and some will also have visual impairments, so you will need to experiment with what works. (See below under 'Visual impairment'.)

Many people with hearing loss, unlike deaf people, will welcome you raising your voice and speaking very loudly and clearly. This can create confidentiality problems when visiting people in hospital, or in the lounge of a residential home. If you cannot secure privacy (say because the person is confined to bed), pen and paper will come in handy. A student told me she had done this, rather than broadcast the service user's bank balance to the whole ward.

Social isolation can be an effect of hearing loss, as group activities become a strain, and people become bored and cut off if they cannot join in conversations. Lack of social contact equally has problems, often lowering people's mood and making life feel empty, so it is important to help a person with hearing loss work out ways of engaging in a satisfying way with other people.

People with hearing loss easily lose the thread of group discussions, and this can be alleviated by careful planning and agreeing some 'rules'.

ACTIVITY **8.3**

Think about the following situation.

Ellen is 89 and lives with her daughter, Carol, aged 65. They get on well. Ellen has been in hospital for the last week after an episode of severe confusion and forgetfulness, owing to a urinary tract infection which has been treated. She has severe hearing loss; she uses a hearing aid in a quiet environment talking to one person, but switches it off otherwise, as it amplifies traffic sounds, the clattering of cutlery, etc. Carol has been visiting daily and nursing staff think she is exhausted, and might welcome a break from continuous caring. You are the social worker and have arranged a meeting to discuss this. Invited to the meeting are:

Ellen

Carol

Ellen's named nurse

The doctor (Senior Registrar) looking after Ellen.

How will you ensure that Ellen is able to participate in the discussion and decisions?

COMMENT

It is only too easy to talk with hearing people and let the hearing impaired person drop out of the conversation. Gaining everyone's commitment to involving Ellen may be crucial.

Visual impairment

A small proportion of people with visual impairments are completely blind but the vast majority have sight. There is considerable variation in the kind of vision people have, so someone who cannot see a bus number may be able to recognise you at close quarters. Just as hearing people can 'forget' someone's deafness when they speak, sighted people may forget what service users and colleagues with visual impairments can and can't see, and thus misinterpret their behaviour and exclude them. We need to learn from each individual the kind of vision they have, insofar as it affects our communication skills with them.

French et al. (1997) suggest some practical steps you can take to which I have added some further ideas:

- In an interview, your facial expressions may be visible if you sit in the light.

- Some people see best in sunlight, or indoors, at dusk or in the dark. This will influence the circumstances when it is easiest for you to communicate.

- Many people can read print; it may be legible in an everyday font size or need to be enlarged; it may be clearer on a particular colour of paper; in any event, allow sufficient time for information to be read, and send it out in advance of important meetings.

- If people can't read print, do they read braille and can you produce braille documents for them? Do they use a computer with voice features so you can send email? Is the phone a good means of contacting them? The phone is better for brief information; braille and email allow the person to review information in their own time.

- Recognition of people may be visual for some but many need an aural cue: don't just smile for *Hello*; say something. Remind the person who you are and make sure to introduce anyone else present.

- Deciding when to enter a discussion involving more than one other person is more difficult without access to non-verbal cues, so make sure you check in from time to time, pick up non-verbal messages that the person is wanting to speak, and make space for them to have their say. They may lean forward or draw breath in anticipation, for example.

- If an assistance dog is used, ask the owner how you should behave with it. Remember that the dog is working. Usually, it is important not to distract it with petting, playing or food. The owner will take care of these needs later.

- Some people with visual impairments ride bikes but most are reliant on walking, public transport and taxis, which has implications for the time it takes to get from place to place. Finding unfamiliar places can be time-consuming and this should be taken into consideration when arranging meetings.

Learning disability

It is shocking to discover from the literature on learning disability how little positive inter-personal experience some people have, especially in institutional care. Bradshaw (2001) cites numerous studies showing that staff interact with service users very little of the time (as little as 2 per cent in her own study), that instead of signs, gesture and touch which are recognised, they use complex verbal communication with people whom they know to have little understanding of these utterances, that the majority of communications from staff to service users are to ask or tell them to do something, and that hearing loss often goes undetected.

It is thus a relief to hear that the situation is somewhat less dire in supported housing and in settings which bring staff and service users into more structured encounters with each other (Bradshaw, 2001). There is little room for complacency, though. David Race, who teaches a specialist social care degree in learning disability has compiled, with service users, a list of things staff should and shouldn't do. The should list includes:

- *Spend time getting to know us and any difficulties we might have;*

- *Listen to us and let us finish what we are saying;*

- *Believe us if we say we are ill.*

(Race, 2002, p.18)

The shouldn't list includes:

- *Say things like 'only babies go to bed early';*

- *Block their ears;*

- *Bully us.*

(Race, 2002, p.18)

This small sample speaks volumes about how people are treated. Race says that new students with prior experience with learning disabilities who see these lists often report that such behaviour and attitudes are still prevalent. It seems all too easy to forget that people with learning difficulties are, above all, people, and feel the same way as everyone else. Current policy attempts to recognise this, and once again we see a move away from a medical model of disability to a rights framework.

> *People with learning disabilities have the right to a decent education, to grow up to vote, to marry and have a family, and to express their opinions, with help and support to do so where necessary . . . Like other people, people with LD want a real say in where they live, what work they should do and who looks after them.* (Department of Health, 2001, pp.23–4)

How does this assertion of rights translate into interpersonal practice? Bradshaw (2001) suggests that words, gesture, pointing, using objects and touch all have a place, and may support each other. She notes that context helps make sense of some communication. This is well illustrated by Kelly (2000), who describes a situation which sounds like a workplace or day centre. Every day, regularly, everyone gets their coats and gets on the bus to go home. A staff member asking someone to do these things may be confident they understand what to do from the words alone. But when the same words are used at the wrong time of day, and only this one person is going (to the dentist), it becomes apparent that she does not understand the words and doesn't know what to do.

If we work frequently with non-verbal people with learning disabilities, we need to learn skills in pictorial communication such as Rebus or Makaton. Individualised communication books or boards can be made with people which use the signs of value to them, organised in a way that makes sense to them. They allow a person to build up a sentence in pictures, such as *I am feeling tired and I want to go to bed*. Their way of indicating them (e.g. pointing with finger, fist, eye) needs to be clear so that they can communicate with new people (Kelly, 2000).

Permanent or temporary changes in communicative ability

Finally, we need briefly to consider a diverse group of people whose ability to process communication is altered temporarily, and sometimes permanently, because of illness or injury, resulting in a need for us to adapt our usual approach. They are listed here mostly for reference so that you can find out more about them for yourselves. The themes and principles which have emerged in this chapter will stand you in good stead, but you will need to acquire more specialised knowledge as it becomes pertinent for your work.

Aphasia

After stroke, people's ability to understand language, formulate their thoughts, and express them can be affected. The medical term for this condition is aphasia, and it has also been described as language impairment (Pound and Hewitt, 2004). Both written and spoken communication is hard to decipher and produce. Some people make a full recovery from aphasia and others are permanently affected, to different degrees.

Dementia

Dementia has many causes, the commonest of which are Alzheimer's disease, cerebro-vascular accidents (minor strokes) and atherosclerosis (hardening of the major blood vessels) in the brain. Although dementia can take different forms in these conditions, typically people lose memory for words and events, and may fail to recognise faces. The problem worsens over time. Kitwood (1997) advocates a person-centred approach which keeps the person's experience and needs in view.

Severe mental health problems

People who are diagnosed with any form of psychosis, such as schizophrenia or manic-depressive disorder, will, by definition, have altered perceptions of the world and altered communication patterns. Mental health problems of these kinds are not always present; they come and go, and are frequently treated with medication which often reduces the symptoms. See Golightley (2004) for further information.

CHAPTER SUMMARY

In this chapter we have learnt about the social model of disability and its value in approaching people whose communication varies from the mainstream. Each area we have considered demands specialist skills from social workers who frequently encounter members of particular groups. There are nonetheless common themes which can be relied upon in most situations:

- Get to know what suits the individual.

- Adjust your pace to that of the service user.

- Give time to people.

- In group discussions, ensure people don't talk over each other, and make sure the service user's voice is heard.

- Be patient – with yourself and your learning, as well as with the service user.

- Be imaginative and creative with words, pictures, objects and gestures.

- Try not to get embarrassed when you feel awkward.

A final point: ask people who use assistance dogs how to behave with theirs.

FURTHER READING

Hayes, D and Humphries, B (2004) *Social work, immigration and asylum debates, dilemmas and ethical issues for social work and social care practice*. New York: Jessica Kingsley.
A good reader covering broad ground.

Morris, J (2002) *A lot to say: A guide for social workers, personal advisers and others working with disabled children and young people with communication impairments*. London: Scope.
This valuable guide starts from a human rights perspective and offers clear direction, a useful list of resources and information about legislation

Oliver, M (1990) *The politics of disablement*. Basingstoke: Macmillan.
A classic work on the social model of disability.

Shakespeare, T (2006) *Disability rights and wrongs*. Abingdon, Routledge.
A trenchant critique of the social model of disability.

Chapter 9

Safety and risk: working with hostility and deception

Introduction

This chapter will consider frightening and potentially dangerous situations and how to employ communication skills to reduce risk. Aggression may be directed towards family members, other service users, social workers or other professionals. The importance of planning and anticipation, and the use of effective interpersonal skills for reducing risk will be discussed. Situations where service users try to deceive us will also be discussed. The chapter draws on a number of sources, building particularly on the ideas and models provided by Ray Braithwaite (2001), whose book is recommended at the end of the chapter. Concepts and models from other chapters are used to examine the effectiveness of his approach.

It is vital to remember that generally, encounters between social workers and service users are not characterised by hostility. Many service users in all fields engage with services on a voluntary basis, are honest in their dealings and get on well with their workers. However, some service users, particularly those with whom we have a statutory duty to intervene, are 'involuntary' clients and resent our involvement. They may not be trustworthy in their dealings with us, and they may seek to intimidate us. We need to strike a balance between underestimating risk through having an idealised approach to service users, and being overly focused on risk and living with unnecessarily high levels of anxiety (see Denney, 2010).

In previous chapters we have seen how staff can, often unwittingly, stir up feelings of hostility through poor communication. Mostly this damages trust rather than leading to acts of aggression (Mayer and Timms, 1971; Fisher et al., 1984; Harris, 1997; Young et al., 1998). Bradshaw (2001), however, speculates that poor communication skills with service users with learning disabilities contribute to 'challenging behaviour', i.e. aggressive acts. I am not defending service user aggression, but I believe that good communication skills can often avoid creating a problem in the first place.

A few staff act aggressively towards service users. Owing to a number of scandals about the treatment of vulnerable people, there are many more safeguards in place than before. Whistle-blowers, who at one time risked losing their job if they spoke out, are now protected in the growing number of organisations with whistle-blowing policies. Even where an organisation has no policy of its own, thanks to the General Social Care Council (GSCC), every university accredited to provide a social work degree now has one to safeguard students who report bad practice. Read yours and make use of it.

What counts as hostility and aggression?

Hostile and aggressive acts include:

- shouting;
- swearing;
- using abusive language;
- taking up a threatening stance, e.g. jabbing a finger in the face;
- making verbal threats in person or in writing;
- spitting;
- invasion of personal space;
- unwanted touching;

- throwing objects;

- brandishing a weapon;

- hitting;

- other physical or sexual attacks;

- preventing someone from leaving;

- damaging property.

In some circumstances, such incidents are so regular that staff become inured to them. However, the impact of such behaviour can be far-reaching, undermining your confidence in yourself and your judgement, diminishing your enjoyment of work and everyday life, and leaving you with an underlying anxiety that it will happen again. This is aside from situations where physical injury is sustained, which has its own complications, especially if recovery is only partial. Some people have to take extended periods of time off work for physical or psychological reasons, and some are driven out of the profession. A small number of social workers and social care staff have been killed by service users. We and our agencies should therefore do our utmost to avoid and avert hostility, and take care of each other when it does take place.

Before looking in more detail at the workplace, let's look at ourselves. We are nearly all frightened of violence, with good reason; and we all have aggressive impulses. We have all had a taste of aggression, giving it out and receiving it, through childhood bullying, quarrelling and spite; quarrels with our partners or families; anger between car drivers; scapegoating dynamics in groups; and frustration with people in shops, call centres and so on. Often we feel embarrassed or ashamed once we have calmed down, and want to make reparation. For lucky people, this is the sum total of violent experience, other than seeing it in the media, or perhaps on the street.

Some of us, though, have grown up in abusive homes, or had a violent partner, or been raped, or subjected to racist or homophobic attack. People respond to and recover from such events in different ways over different periods of time. If you feel you have not resolved past issues of violence well enough yet, give some thought to what might help you to reduce the impact on you and your work.

Some of us may have been violent to other people, and not always through self-defence. If you have a history of physical violence, you will know that, not surprisingly, this is more problematic in social work than having been subjected to it. Turning to social work may be part of a transformation in your life, and you have been successful either because any incident(s) happened some time ago and you have resolved the issues well enough, or because there is no record. If you have not resolved past issues yet, think about how you might and take steps to do so. If you are currently physically violent, get help. If you think your violence isn't a problem, please leave social work.

Now let's return to the workplace.

ACTIVITY *9.1*

Look at the list of hostile and aggressive acts. Those of you who have been working in social care may already have experienced hostility or aggression from service users, or seen it directed at other staff. If you have no social care experience, think of any work situation you know, in a call centre, shop or cafe, for example. Think about what happened.

What sort of hostility or violence have you experienced? (Make a list.)

Taking each in turn:

How often did each kind happen?

How did it make you feel?

Were you able to stop it from happening again or reduce the frequency? How did this come about?

Did anyone help you, during the incident(s), or afterwards?

What happened to the person who did it?

(Adapted from Braithwaite, 2001, Activity 1.3, pp.7–8, with permission from Routledge.)

COMMENT

This activity will heighten your awareness of experiences you have had in the past. If done in pairs or groups, it will provide an opportunity to compare notes.

Denney (2010) offers a more fine-grained approach to thinking about violence, citing research with GPs from 2001 which he conducted with Gabe and other colleagues. They arrived at two ways of thinking about violence in the workplace: as *rational* or *irrational*. *Rational violence . . . was usually verbal, unplanned, undirected at any particular individual and predictable*, and was attributed by GPs to *minor mental illnesses in patients and culminations in stressful social circumstances such as marital breakdown and debt*. GPs had some understanding and acceptance of this form of violence as an occupational hazard (Denney, 2010, pp.5–6).

He continues

In contrast, 'irrational violence' was associated with more severe symptoms of mental illness and personality disorder, substance misuse and, in some cases, malevolence on the part of service users. Irrational violence appeared to lack any coherent motivating force and, consequently, was more difficult to manage than 'rational violence'. GPs considered this form of violence to be unacceptable, since it was more likely to result in physical injury, was more personally directed at the professional, planned by the perpetrator and unpredictable (Gabe et al., 2001).

(Denney, 2010, p.6)

Braithwaite (2001) sets out a position of zero tolerance to replace the culture of inevitability and belief that it is just 'part of the job' prevalent in many social service agencies (pp.5–15). In such a culture, excuses are made for service users, and staff expect themselves (and each other) to cope. Staff who get upset can feel weak and unsuited to the work, when the problem lies in the cultural acceptance of aggression. Braithwaite points out that sanctions are rarely introduced for aggressors, and often their behaviour is rewarded, to the detriment of other service users. Examples of such perverse incentives are seeing someone ahead of those who have been waiting uncomplainingly, and giving something for which they don't qualify. There is also the risk of 'contagion': that others will resort to aggression when they observe its benefits.

Denney (2010) offers a contrast to zero tolerance in considering the effect on workers of the culture of risk within which they work. Where risk is viewed *positively* then service user aggression is regarded as *rational*, resulting from *impossible situations and directed more towards systems* than personally against the worker. In this climate, precautions are put in place, and social workers are not afraid of service users, but are optimistic that they can understand and help (pp.11–12). In workplaces with a *negative view of risk [this] can lead to a more pessimistic view of personal safety*. The social worker feels more personally targeted and less confident and hopeful about managing behaviour which is regarded as *unpredictable* (Denney, 2010, p.12).

ACTIVITY 9.2

Go back to the list you drew up for Activity 9.1.

Was the violence rational or irrational?

Do you think the culture of risk was positive or negative?

Were there sanctions or rewards for aggression in your setting?

Do you think there were perverse incentives for aggression?

Were you optimistic or pessimistic about bringing about change?

COMMENT

When we understand other people's motivation and do not think they are directing hostility at us personally so much as venting frustration it is easier to be helpful. However, optimism can be naïve and risk be underestimated.

Working with people to change their aggressive behaviour is part of our work. In terms of the working alliance, aggression can be seen as the common enemy. You and the service user make a collaborative agreement with the goal of reducing the number and intensity of outbursts. This may involve the support of other people too, if the service user lives in a family, in supported housing or in residential care. For example, going for walk, having some calm company watching television, or being able to talk things over may be part of the aggression-reduction plan, requiring co-operation from others. The effect is for service users to develop an early warning system for themselves, and to enhance their capacity for emotional regulation and control of action. This work needs to be done in between aggressive episodes when the person has their full cognitive and reflective capacities available, using SAVI™ (Simon and Agazarian, 2005) yellow- and green-light behaviours to discuss what happens during red-light outbursts. In the early stages of a fresh outburst, these techniques can be called upon, and may help the person to calm down. If someone is really in a rage, they may just fan the flames, and would be best discussed later.

This work is important for people they might target and for service users themselves, who are not always 'rewarded' for aggression, but may pay a high price. The experience of being overwhelmed by aggressive feelings can be unpleasant in itself, and a source of shame; the person may, as a consequence of their behaviour, be considered 'too difficult' to go on trips or holidays, or have a minimal chance of living with their children, or even spend years in a psychiatric hospital away from mainstream life. Some of the questions designed to help you prepare yourself for encountering aggression could also be the basis for questions you and the service user answer together, so you both gain a better understanding of their risk factors and triggers.

Why are people aggressive?

There are a number of theories which attempt to account for people's aggression, and there is probably something useful in each of them, though none is sufficient on its own. Human behaviour tends to have multiple causes.

RESEARCH SUMMARY

Explanations for human aggression

1. *It is an innate capacity, needed for self-protection (nature, evolution).*

2. *It is behaviour learnt in our culture where it is the norm, and where it may confer status (sociological).*

3. *It is behaviour learnt from experience: aggression gets us what we want (behavioural).*

4. *It is a behaviour learnt from observing other people's experience: aggression gets them what they want (social cognitive).*

5. *It is a consequence of early relationships, such as unresolved conflicts, fulfilling expectations that we are as bad as they say, or as a means of gaining power where we once had none (psychodynamic).*

6. *It is caused by frustration at not getting what we want (frustration-aggression hypothesis).*

7. *It arises in pressured environments with scarce resources (space, food) where people have to compete (ecological).*

8. *I'm aggressive, you're aggressive, that makes me more aggressive (interactive).*

9. *It is caused by altered chemistry or the pleasurable feelings which aggression can produce (in primates, successful aggressors have high serotonin levels while the loser,*

Continued

---

who may have been a former leader with high levels, develops low levels; these are associated with depression in humans) (chemical).

10. *It is activated by people coming too close (proxemic).*

11. *It is a response to being hurt, physically or emotionally (retaliatory).*

Adapted from Braithwaite (2001, pp.23–4); Mason and Chandley (1999, pp.21–2); Gilbert (1992).

It seems to me that fear has been left out of the picture. Although aggression makes us frightened, aggressive people are sometimes frightened too. They may be afraid of us, want to escape from the situation, and can only imagine fighting their way out. This can be literally true, so it is important not to block the exit. (There are cases where you may be entitled to detain them and the resources of other skilled staff are available to help, but you need to take great care that you act within the law. This area is too specialised to address here.)

What enables people not to be aggressive? People brought up in violent families or neighbourhoods do not inevitably become violent – some determinedly raise their families without violence, or become campaigners against it. Where resources are scarce, some compete while others share. Everyone experiences frustration; not everyone lashes out. I suggest it relates to emotional regulation. While acting aggressively can be cold-blooded and deliberate, often it is an intense emotional response, usually of anger, and the person cannot regulate it. After a certain point, the feelings have to run their course. Braithwaite (2001, p.49) tells us that it takes about 90 minutes for most people's physiological arousal to return to normal, longer for some people.

Planning and anticipation

In this section we will give thought to factors relating to the service user, the context and the social worker which need consideration when we are able to plan. They should increase safety. Although incidents arise where nothing is known of the service user, such as on duty or in some drop-in centres, factors relating to the context and the social worker will have relevance. In the next section we will look at recognising the signs of aggression, and how to respond.

Service user factors

Past violence is the best predictor of future violence. This dictum is found in everything written on risk assessment for violence. You have a right to know if a service user has a history of violence, and a duty to inform other staff who will be involved. It is essential for their safety, and overrides the usual rules of confidentiality, including the duties laid down in the Data Protection Act 1984 (Braithwaite, 2001).

Simply knowing someone has a history of violence is not enough, and runs the risk of turning them into an object of fear. Only a small number of people, who tend to end up in high-security prisons and hospitals, are aggressive most of the time. For most people, there is likely to be a pattern which will inform our planning, so we should try to get answers to the following questions. They differ somewhat across service user groups; the first are general.

1. What do we know about the service user's history of violence?
Is the information sound? Neither referrals nor files are always accurate, and can overstate or understate the case. Who has made the referral and where does the information come from? Is it one person's perception or substantiated by someone else?

2. What form does the aggressive behaviour take? For instance, is it shouting, or has the person kept someone hostage at knife point?

3. Who has been the target: staff, fellow service users, family members, members of the public? Are particular individuals targeted and why do people think this is so? (Racism, sexism, homophobia, religious bigotry, ageism and class need to be considered here, as particular staff may be at risk and should be protected.)

4. Where have incidents taken place? In public places, hospital, own home, day centre?

5. Is it, so far, a one-off or rare occurrence, or more frequent and regular? How long is it since the last incident?

6. What was the outcome for the service user (and was this sanction or reward)?

7. Is physical aggression preceded by other behaviours, such as issuing threats in person or in writing (take these seriously), or changing their style of dress or appearance? (Braithwaite, 2001)

8. Does the person have serious mental health problems? The majority of such people are not aggressive, but there are three risk factors which should be taken seriously even without a history of violence:

- delusions (unfounded beliefs) which involve you or others directly (e.g. you are against them), or indirectly, e.g. they believe blue cars are driven by aliens who should be eradicated, and you drive a blue car;

- auditory hallucinations (hearing voices) if these reduce their control over actions, especially 'command' hallucinations ordering them to harm someone;

- personality disorders which show a reduced concern for the feelings of others.

9. Have alcohol or substance use been a factor and are they now? Again, the association with violence is not clear (Mason and Chandley, 1999), but alcohol and some other drugs lower inhibitions and may be used deliberately to embolden or to provide an 'excuse' after the event.

10. Is anyone working with the service user on their aggressive behaviour? Who is it and how is it going?

11. What do we know about triggers caused by us or our colleagues in the moment? Here are some examples:

- loss or threatened loss of something of value (dignity, liberty, a child);

- being kept waiting, exacerbated if no explanation is offered;

- discourteous behaviour, e.g. ignoring, excluding, patronising, criticising, also clumsiness, say in getting someone dressed;

- not being given alternatives;

- invasion of territory;

- not being given information;

- unreliability and inefficiency, failure to keep promises.

(Braithwaite, 2001, pp.28–49)

'Bad news' may be a trigger, such as the refusal of a service for which they do not qualify, or a long delay before they can access a service they need (such as an anger management group).

12. Were there (and are there now) additional stressors in the person's life? These could include: relationship break-up; fostering breakdown; undetected physical pain, e.g. toothache or a broken hip in someone with learning disabilities or dementia. Intense emotion may be generated by 'big moments' (often threatening loss), e.g. going to court over childcare; seeing the psychiatrist or Mental Health Review Tribunal; anticipation of a family visit, anger and sadness in its wake, or frustration and despair if it is cancelled at short notice.

CASE STUDIES

Elsie, aged 88, lives in a residential care home for people with dementia. She is a happy person whom all the staff like. One morning, she hits the member of staff who is helping her to get up. It emerges that she has fractured her hip.

Brian and Della met four months ago and live together. Della is pregnant, and Brian is delighted about being a father. Brian has a diagnosis of manic-depressive disorder, and Della had severe post-natal depression after her first child was born seven years ago. This child lives with his father. Della's community mental health nurse thinks Della looks about seven months pregnant (so the baby cannot be Brian's), but the couple insist she is only 16 weeks. You are Brian's social worker and visit with the nurse to discuss this. Everything is fine until you ask if they are sure Della is only 16 weeks pregnant. They both jump out of their chairs and start shouting at you to stop interfering with their lives.

Danny is 13 and in foster care. You take him to visit his mother, leaving him there for two hours. When you collect him he is sitting on the wall outside his mother's flat. He starts shouting at you that his mother is useless, she only spent half an hour with him and then went out to see her boyfriend, she never gave him any tea, he hates her, you should never have brought him, you should have come back earlier, and so on.

Go back to the list you generated for Activity 9.1. Given what you have been reading, what do you know of the history, triggers and additional stressors for the incidents you identified?

Context factors

As we know, context determines behaviour to a significant extent, so think about where you will meet a person and the impact of the environment on them, as well as its safety features or lack of them.

- Are you seeing the person at your office base, in their own private home, in a residential, day care or hospital setting, or public place such as a café? Are you at the *end of a long corridor*? (Braithwaite, 2001, p.61)

- Where are the exits? Is there only one? If possible, ensure both you and the service user have *equal accessibility* to it (Braithwaite, 2001, p.65).

- Will you be alone with the person? Do other people (your colleagues, the residential care staff) know where you are?

- Will other family members, staff, service users, visitors, be around? Will they help if needed, or become victims, or be an audience in front of whom the aggressor will be afraid to lose face?

- Is there a lone working policy? In other words, do you sign in and out at work, and leave details of where you are? Do you have to check in with someone once you have completed your last visit? What happens if you don't?

- Can you contact your colleagues if you need to, or can they contact you? Is there a plan to do so? For instance, a colleague could ring at an appointed time to check you are OK, and if you are not, this could be your excuse to leave, saying you have been called away. (Deception is acceptable in the circumstances.) Have your phone handy.

- What is the space like? Is it *shoddy* and *run down*, or cheerful and welcoming? Is there a better place to meet? (Braithwaite, 2001, p.51)

- Can furniture or other objects be turned into weapons, or be used as *missiles* and *thrown*? (Braithwaite, 2001, p.65)

- Are there alarms? How are they activated and what happens if they are? (Braithwaite, 2001, p.65)

- If you are visiting a new place, particularly the person's home, do you know how to get there and how to get away? Will it be dark?

- Where is your car or bike? Are they parked so that you can get away easily? Don't lose your keys in the depths of a large bag.

- Are you on foot? Or in a wheelchair? How should this influence the location you choose for the meeting? Is there a choice?

Social worker factors

- Have you done your homework on the client and context factors above, and any others you have thought of? Have you planned your encounter?

- If you use an assistance dog, what will it do if you are threatened?

- Should you see the person alone or with a colleague? If it is usual practice to see people alone, but you have doubts, ask for a co-worker.

- Dress code: review your clothing, jewellery and footwear in the light of your plan. Could anything you usually wear be used to harm you? Can you run in your shoes? (I never wore my customary scarves or long earrings on Approved Social Work duties. I also dressed carefully for visits to a client who had made a sexual assault on a woman. Judge my success for yourself. He said he'd been puzzling over who I reminded him of in my red jacket and yellow scarf, and he'd got it – it was Rupert Bear . . .)

- Are you bringing bad news (see triggers above)?

- If the meeting is planned, arrive on time or let them know you are late and check it is still acceptable for you to visit.

- If it is an unscheduled visit, what are the implications?

- Finally, in any situation, use your instincts – don't override them. We often know when something isn't right and it is far better to be safe than sorry.

Recognising and responding to aggression

This section will focus mainly on aggressive behaviour where interpersonal skills may make a difference, rather than where you need breakaway techniques or restraint, which can only be learnt through physical training. We will look at non-verbal and verbal behaviour. There is isomorphy between non-verbal and verbal responses in the social worker, in that the goal of both is emotional regulation, and both involve effective purposeful misattunement. This means that your interventions must not be too different from the aggressor's or they will be rejected (e.g. *Calm down*), nor so similar that they stimulate further aggression (*Just shut up!*). Someone in a heightened state of aggression is a closed system: whatever you do will only confirm their own perspective, and there is no route in. You therefore need to act quickly if you are 'lucky' enough to be there when early warning signs are present and before full-blown aggressive behaviour is in train. You need to misattune purposefully to tune down the aggressive behaviour, and then use goal-corrected empathic attunement to enable the person to explore what it was all about (McCluskey, 2005). This exploration may have to happen on another occasion. Aggression cannot always be regulated sufficiently at the time, and even when it is, both parties can be left exhausted.

Noticing non-verbal signs of aggression

The potential for aggression is evident in facial expression and body movement. The primary emotion is likely to be anger, which has the following facial expression: staring or glaring eyes, with lowered brows; lips pressed together, or drawn back to reveal teeth, chin extended forward (Ekman, 2003). Colour will be lighter, redder or darker; veins of the forehead and neck pulsate, and nostrils widen as the person breathes rapidly and shallowly (Braithwaite, 2001, p.46). Darting eye movements indicate agitation; the person may be looking for a way out or for something to use as a weapon (Wilder and Sorensen, 2001).

The background emotion is agitated and restless, reflected in body movement. The person repetitively taps their foot or fingers, or a pen. They cross and uncross arms and legs, or fidget in a chair, get up only to sit down again, or pace around. *Perhaps the most important and* ignored *sign of impending violence is the patient's motor activity. Someone who is unable to sit still, and who paces around, poses the most serious threat of violence* (Mason and Chandley, 1999, p.60, emphasis added). The aggressive person commands more territory – a sign of dominance (Henley, 1995).

We need to be careful not to confuse aggression with the restlessness caused by anti-psychotic medication, often prescribed to people diagnosed with schizophrenia. This indicates a need for a different additional drug to relieve the symptoms (Butterworth, 2004). In such a case, the person would not show anger in the face, though they could get frustrated if no one paid attention to their needs.

Pointing, jabbing with finger or fist, standing with hands on hips, leaning into your space from a chair or from a standing position with one foot forward are gestures accompanying anger. The voice will be raised, and speech may be rapid and repetitive. (*What are you going to do about it? Well? Well? Well? Tell me, just what are you going to do then? Nothing, that's it isn't it? Nothing – as usual.*)

Pay attention to which is the person's strong side – you are more likely to be hit or kicked by the dominant side. The weak side is usually where the hair is parted, the watch is worn, and men carry pens, cigarettes, etc., in the shirt or jacket pocket. Wallets and handbags, phones, keys and pagers are usually carried on the strong side. Men's belt tips point to the weak side, women's to the strong (but the reference is from the US and I am not sure this is the case in the UK). The strong-side shoulder dips lower, and the foot is back, with a locked knee bearing most of the body weight (Wilder and Sorensen, 2001, pp.82–3).

Non-verbal responses to signs of aggression

Most people feel frightened in the presence of aggression, and this will show facially in wide eyes, arched brows, open mouth with teeth hidden, and pallor (Ekman, 2003). As you initially freeze, you will breathe more sharply and deeply, increasing height and chest expansion as your body gets ready for flight or fight. It is important to get these signs of fear under as much control and as quickly as you can, as they convey signals of either victim or aggressor, both of which can cause an escalation in the aggressor's behaviour (Braithwaite, 2001). A pale, fearful face with big eyes looks like victim; breathing sharply increases height and chest size and looks like aggressor. Breathe deeply and slowly (Braithwaite, 2001). Slowing down your voice and gesture may succeed in slowing the other person down and allowing their cognitive capacities to re-emerge from the tumult of emotion (Mason and Chandley, 1999).

Keep the goal of regulating the person's emotion in mind to help you to regulate your own fear responses.

Summary of non-verbal signals for responding

- position yourself at a *slight angle*, whether seated or standing, *without turning away*; being squarely *face-to-face* looks *confrontational*;

- maintain enough distance to be out of arm's reach: *about two arms lengths if standing, perhaps one-and-a-half (at shoulder height) if sitting*;

- *do not touch the aggressor first* – it will evoke a hostile response (initiating touch is a dominant behaviour (Henley, 1995));

- make *occasional nods*;

- *keep your head straight on to the aggressor*; tilting your head back, chin up, is aggressor; looking down with chin tucked in is victim;

- *do not smile* – it will be seen as mocking;

- make eye contact but don't stare;

- try to *relax* as is this is less threatening;

- keep your hands in sight, not in pockets, preferably with relaxed arms;

- *make gentle, free-flowing open hand movements*;

- *use one hand* to indicate *Stop; two hands up* looks like *surrender*;

- holding out an open hand, palm up, indicates negotiation;

- keep your hands away from your hair and face – you could look anxious, impatient, doubting, bored, or seductive;

- self-comforting behaviours like wrapping your arms round your body or holding your forearm are victim; self-stroking is seductive;

- avoid *repetitive movements* like finger drumming;

- avoid conveying *sexual signals* – don't draw attention to *mouth, genital or breast areas* with hand or body movements, or *lick* your *lips* when you can be seen;

- sit down, provided you feel safe enough to do so, as it makes you less of a threat.

(Braithwaite, 2001, pp.77–85, 100)

Verbal signs of aggression

This section uses SAVI™ to identify aggressive verbal signals and as the means for managing that behaviour. Turn back to Chapter 5 to find your SAVI grid. The verbal content of aggressive behaviour is characteristically 'red light', mainly in *Fight* and *Compete*. It consists of accusations, complaints, self-righteous and defensive statements, and sarcastic comments (Square 1). It is argumentative, with apparent agreements followed by a different tack, discounting of what you say, using leading questions to force agreement, shoulds, and interruptions (Square 3). Remember that red-light behaviours avoid authentic contact (*You lot, you're all the same, all liars*). It is much easier to hurt someone with whom you have no connection.

Verbal responses to signs of aggression

An assertive, confident, approach is recommended for responding to aggressive behaviour (Mason and Chandley, 1999; Braithwaite, 2001; Wilder and Sorensen, 2001; Butterworth, 2004).

Use *I* statements and the person's name, if you know it, to help make the personal connection, name the *behaviour* (be specific and descriptive – no euphemisms or vague statements), say what *impact* it has on you, ask the person to *stop* and only then address the *task* or *issue* they are raising – or *change the subject*; only use *please* in the middle of an utterance as it can sound pleading otherwise (Braithwaite, 2001, p.93). I understand this approach to provide effective purposeful misattunement which regulates both the person's behaviour and emotional state.

Compare the following statements:

* *Please don't behave like this, you know I'm only trying to help.*

* *If you don't stop that immediately, you'll be in really serious trouble.*

* *You're pacing around, Alan, and it's making me edgy. Please stop pacing and sit down, and then we can talk about what's bothering you.*

The first is vague and pleading, the second is vague and authoritarian; the third is specific and direct. It may seem counterintuitive to state how we feel, in case the aggressor exploits the knowledge, but we can only name our feelings when we have access to our cognitive abilities, which means we are regulating our own emotion. This is an essential emotional communication which offers regulation, and the naming accesses the person's cognitive understanding and reasoning. It is the non-verbal signs of fear which make us vulnerable.

Braithwaite (2001) counsels against the use of questions until the aggressive behaviour has stopped – statements are safer. Others recommend questions and suggest asking how the person *is feeling*, how *the situation can be resolved*, what is *causing his anger* and how you can *help* (Mason and Chandley, 1999, p.70). In SAVI™ terms, the first of these is green light and would be risky if the person was in a high state of emotion, evoking a red-light response (*Can't you tell how I'm feeling? Thought you were the expert!*) The others are yellow-light broad questions and seem more useful to me. If met with a hostile response, follow with a statement.

SAVI yellow- and green-light behaviours help you to purposefully misattune in order to influence the aggressor towards a calmer, more reasoned, emotionally connected state. Your own red-light behaviours will be stimulated by the aggressor's, but curb the temptation to resort to them as they will inflame the situation.

ACTIVITY **9.4**

Read through the first example, with the different SAVI behaviours named. Notice your immediate responses to the service user statements. Are they red light? Then go through the other examples to practise some responses, using SAVI to eliminate red-light behaviours. (SU = Service User, SW = Social Worker.)

Continued

ACTIVITY 9.4 *continued*

1. Social worker arrives on planned home visit to see mother where children might be in need.

   SU: Just get lost, you're all a load of useless pillocks.

   Attack/Blame, 1.

   SW: There's no need to talk me like that. I haven't done anything.

   Attack/Blame, 1.

   SU: That's the problem, isn't it. You lot never do do anything.

   Attack/Blame, 1

Alternative

   SU: Just get lost, you're all a load of useless pillocks.

   Attack/Blame, 1.

   SW: Stop swearing at me, please, and tell me what the problem is.

   Command, Command, 6.

   SU: Why should I bother? You won't do anything anyway.

   Attack/Blame, 1.

   SW: If you stop shouting, we can talk about it. I can't understand what the matter is if you're shouting.

   Proposal, 6, Personal information (current), 4.

   SU: The matter is – the matter is – just everything. (Bursts into tears.)

   Personal information (current), 6.

   SW: Shall we go inside and sit down? Then maybe you can tell me about it.

   Proposal, Proposal, 6.

   SU   Ok then. Do you want a cup of tea?

   Agreement/Positives, 9, Narrow question, 5.

2. Pathways planning discussion with care leaver about future

   SU: You just don't bloody understand, do you? Are you thick or something? I've had it with social services, all you do-gooders. Never did me any good when I was in care, no bloody use now.

Continued

3. *Service user has previously received S.17 (Children Act 1989) payments to help support children in times of need.*

   SU: *I'm not leaving till you give me some money! Give me my money!*

4. *Older man living in own home, receiving home care. You are care manager visiting to check everything is OK. Home carer lets you in.*

   SU: *(waving walking stick around) Don't you come anywhere near me, young lady! I know what you're after, yes, I do (jabbing towards you with stick).*

COMMENT

Rehearsing possible responses when you are calm may be useful, as in the heat of the moment you may be angry or frightened.

Deception

Deception is typically defined as messages knowingly and intentionally transmitted to mislead another person (Burgoon and Butler, 2010) (Burgoon and Levine, 2010, p.202).

So far in this chapter we have been thinking about violent behaviour which may be a threat to ourselves. This final section looks at some of the means people use to conceal violence by deceiving us. For example, in child and family social work, the 'rule of optimism' requires social care staff to think the best of parents (Denney, 2010, p.12). However, there are times when wariness and suspiciousness are vital. Just as we have to earn the trust of service users and carers, they have to earn ours when vulnerable people are our primary concern. After the death of Peter Connolly (Baby P), it was widely reported that his abusers had smeared his face with chocolate to conceal bruises (e.g. *Guardian*, 2008). This perverse use of a food associated with sweetness and comfort is both poignant and shocking, and it underscores the lengths to which abusers will go to prevent detection.

Detecting deception is not easy, and we are likely to deceive ourselves about how skilled we are in doing so. There is little co-relation between people's confidence in detecting deception and their success, and there is a strong *truth bias* in people's judgements (Burgoon and Levine, 2010, p.203). In other words, we are much more likely to think that people are being honest and truthful than to suspect them. Being aware that people are sometimes powerfully motivated to conceal the truth or tell us lies is an important step to take.

Telling untruths is a form of deception with which everyone is familiar. Even small children quickly deny being the culprit when a transgression is discovered – *It wasn't me*. In our work, we may encounter people struggling with mental health problems who want to appear well, people with substance misuse problems who want to present as drug free, people experiencing domestic abuse who want to conceal it, people with responsibility for others who wish to present themselves as genuinely caring – the list goes on. We may be told outright lies.

- No, I don't hear voices any more.

- I haven't had a drink since February.

- I fell downstairs.

- I don't know why she's lost weight, I give her plenty to eat.

Gambetta (2005) discusses deception as a studied form of imitation, and compares it with the mimicry we see in some animals, for example, insects with colouring that makes them appear toxic to predators. The deceiver imitates the characteristics of someone different from themselves in order to make a gain. For example, people may change accent, posture and clothing to be identified with a higher status group. Gambetta (2005, p.224) reminds us that deception is a two party process requiring a deceiver and *a dupe*, who has to be duped into seeing the similarity between the deceiver and the genuine article. In times of threat, mimicry and deception can be a matter of survival, such as the case of Jews who 'passed' as Aryans or Christians during World War II.

Social workers have statutory powers to intervene in people's lives, and because of this we constitute a threat to some service users and carers. We work with people who sometimes turn out not to be fit parents, yet who do not want to give up their children. They may try to dupe us by mimicking the behaviour of a good enough parent, making sure the house is reasonably clean and tidy when we visit, producing food they claim to be feeding the children, and showing affection to the children when we are present. For these reasons it is sometimes right to make visits unannounced.

Building rapport at the same time as retaining healthy scepticism is no mean feat. The truth bias may make it difficult for us to see that a person we have come to know and like is being duplicitous. We need enough knowledge about ordinary, good enough human behaviour and use observational skills to notice inconsistencies and deficiencies. We need to recognise when something sits uneasily with us and not override this with justifications in the other person's defence. For example, if we feel anxious about challenging a parent about her behaviour, is this a signal that her child could be afraid of her? These situations need careful handling, so supervision with an experienced social worker, as recommended in the Social Work Task Force Report (2009) is invaluable.

CHAPTER SUMMARY

In this chapter we have learnt about why people become aggressive, what can trigger aggressive behaviour, and how to prepare and plan to reduce its emergence. We have also looked at how aggressive behaviour can be recognised through facial expression, body movement and gesture, and the kinds of verbal statements characteristic of aggression. We have looked at ways of reducing aggressive behaviours through the careful use of our own posture and verbal interactions. Building on the model presented by Braithwaite (2001), we have seen that emotionally regulating ourselves and the service user underpins effective interventions, and seen that SAVI™ ensures our verbal interventions are also emotionally regulating. Despite what we have learnt, it needs to be recognised that hostility and violence cannot always be brought under control, and we may need to escape or call in help to restrain someone. We also need to be aware that some service users will try to deceive us.

Myers, S and Milner, J (2007) *Working with violence: Policies and practice in risk assessment and management*. Basingstoke: Palgrave Macmillian.
A very useful book which brings together theory, research and practice. Using a case study of domestic violence, it explores violence within relationships from many perspectives.

Chapter 10

The demands and rewards of interpersonal work

Introduction

In this chapter, we will consider two dimensions of interpersonal work: the impact you make on others, and the impact of the work on you. You will have the chance to think about your own attitudes and assumptions. Prior to learning about how social workers manage to stay on the bright side of a demanding job, we will look at its darker side – both the way in which our own negativity can be stimulated, and how we might become vulnerable to burnout. This chapter is therefore all about second-order skills: the skills needed to be self-aware, reflective, and observe what happens between you and service users so that the chances of harm to either of you are kept to a minimum.

It is designed to stimulate your thinking about some of the more complex and challenging aspects of interpersonal encounters, rather than provide answers.

Who we are

We all bring our individual dynamics into new relationships. It is widely acknowledged that early experience influences the way that we see and relate to the world. Patterns of expectation and relationship are malleable, but new experiences have to persist over time to bring about change. Building awareness of our emotional and physiological states, and developing our cognitive capacities to understand our reactions to others, protect us from plunging headlong into situations on the basis of automatic assumptions and behaviour. Jones (2003), for example, reports that professionals who have themselves been sexually abused may be quicker than others to identify sexual abuse. Their acuity to possible signs leads to higher rates of both accurate and erroneous identifications. Where someone's circumstances echo our own we are likely to see more similarity than may in fact be present. A concern for this kind of self-awareness has been the backbone for this book.

Our individual personal histories usually take place within a family network, and in a cultural context (which may in itself bring together two or more cultural milieus, e.g. ethnic origin, religious belief, social class, deaf and hearing). We therefore bring our cultural assumptions with us.

ACTIVITY **10.1**

Culture

The issue of evaluating cultural norms is a difficult area of social work. Compare the following two statements and discuss your responses to them. The first describes norms in Native American culture; the second is an extract from the report of the inquiry into the death of Victoria Climbié in London in February 2000. She was an eight-year-old African child who was abused and killed by her aunt and aunt's partner. The report's concern is that the public behaviour displayed by Victoria and her aunt was misunderstood; clearly her abuse violated cultural child-rearing norms in Africa as much as the UK.

> *In Native societies interference in someone else's life, even if to prevent him or her from doing something foolish or dangerous, is not tolerated. Confrontation is often considered inappropriate. The value of non-interference also carries over into child rearing practices and is often misinterpreted by non-Native people as neglect or lack of guidance. Modeling is often the preferred method of teaching and guiding children. (Weaver and White, 1997, p.71)*

> *The basic requirement that children are kept safe is universal and cuts across cultural boundaries. Every child living in this country is entitled to be given the protection of the law, regardless of his or her background. Cultural heritage is important to many people, but it cannot take precedence over standards of childcare embodied in law. (Laming, 2003, p.346)*

COMMENT

Debating these kinds of issues with colleagues is part of good principle.

Managing our uncomfortable and negative feelings

The bringing of old patterns into new situations is described in psychodynamic terms as transference, where it refers to the feelings a client has towards the therapist, and also to the propensity to expect the therapist to treat them in the same way as their early care-givers. Countertransference is the term used to describe two related phenomena: the emotional responses of therapist to client, and the feelings the therapist experiences which may mirror, rather than be reactive to, the client's emotions. In some forms of therapy, particularly psychoanalysis, transference is the prime subject for analysis, to enable the individual to come into present-day reality and develop new patterns of relating. There are times when our reactions to service users and to our work will be negative.

Hostile feelings are sometimes provoked in us simply because we are human, as we learn from Chapter 3's discussion of the mirror neuron system, SAVI™ suggests that red-light behaviours provoke red-light behaviours. Donald Winnicott (1958), in a paper entitled *'Hate in the Countertransference'*, described the violence of his feelings towards a child he was psychoanalysing and whom he and his wife fostered. He helpfully liberates us from the notion that we only have 'nice' feelings towards service users, without absolving us from the effort to use self-awareness and supervision to understand what is happening and work for the benefit of service users as far as possible.

Winnicott's compassion for himself in this predicament is crucial to the discussion, since fostering hostility towards ourselves is no more help than directing it at other people. There is some evidence that therapists with hostile and negative attitudes to themselves treat patients similarly (Henry and Strupp, 1994, p.66). The same studies showed other correlations, such that where therapists are hostile and controlling (showing blaming and belittling behaviours), patients tend to be self-blaming and self-critical (Henry and Strupp, 1994, p.65). It is unclear whether these therapists were troubled by their negativity; the researchers noted that they were poor at recognising the process of interaction as it unfolds and needed training to become more aware.

In everyday life there are occasions when people set out to annoy others, wrong-foot them, hurt their feelings, deceive them and use communication to exert power over them. Duck (1994) contends that too much social psychology focuses on positive communica-tion, and too little on understanding why we needle each other, pick fights, say unkind things, identify each other's weak spots – and often enjoy the process. These aspects of communication are referred to as its 'dark side', so called because it is *difficult, problematic, challenging, distressing, and disruptive*, and by its nature is *elusive, enigmatic and inscrutable* (Cupach and Spitzberg, 1994, p.vii).

As we have noted elsewhere, the environment has a large influence on behaviour, and people in groups may act in ways that they would not usually on their own. The Stanford Prison Experiment (Zimbardo, 2008), for example, showed that people are only too ready to treat each other badly, given a modicum of authority. In this experiment, young men were recruited to spend two weeks under observation in an artificial prison environment inside Stanford University. They were assigned to roles as prisoners or guards, and only they occupied the prison. Zimbardo terminated the experiment after one week because the guards were treating the prisoners with escalating brutality. The recruits were ordinary young men with no history of cruelty to others. Imitation may well have played a part in their behaviour, with guards vying with each other to be liked by the guard group.

None of us is free of this dark side. Think about teasing, which exists on the boundary between affection and cruelty. Think about watching someone flounder, as they realise they have made a social error, and try ineffectually to retrieve it.

ACTIVITY **10.2**

Think of the last time you deliberately needled or annoyed someone, or asked an awkward question, or failed to help someone out of an embarrassing situation, or teased someone with a cruel edge.

- *What do you think motivated you to do this?*

- *Were you conscious that you were doing something hurtful or coercive at the time, or did you only realise later?*

- *Was it fun?*

- *Were you influenced by group behaviour?*

- *How do you feel about it now?*

COMMENT

Becoming more aware of how we are triggered into hurting other people offers us more chance to contain the impulse.

Do such behaviours ever have a place in social work? There are certainly times when we have to ask *difficult questions* which service users would prefer not to be asked, for example questioning a parent about possible child abuse (Petrie, 2003 p.177). In these circumstances we have to override the social conventions which discourage us from asking difficult questions; clearly our motivation should not be deliberately to cause discomfort, but to obtain vital information. Explaining why we are asking may ease the process to a degree, but it can probably never be comfortable for either party.

Similarly, difficult subjects have to be tackled in mental health. Service users with severe and enduring mental health problems were dissatisfied when workers – including social workers – were out of touch with their concerns, for example, focusing on the importance of taking medication, when the medication made the service user feel unwell (Watts and Priebe, 2002). Can such inquiries be made in a way which leads to less dissatisfaction? In this case, acknowledging the severity of the unwanted effects and exploring the possibility of alternatives might be helpful.

Managing complex communication

Spitzberg (1994) argues that current ideology favours *clarity, accuracy and understanding, yet ambiguity, deception, equivocation, and tentativeness are often highly competent communicative tactics* (p.33). Although this book has stated the case for clarity unreservedly, Spitzberg's assertion merits exploration and needs to be understood in terms of context, role and goal. It is not difficult to see why politicians rely on being vague, refuse to come to decisions, try to have it both ways, withhold information and use delaying tactics to fend off questions to which they cannot or do not wish to provide answers, but when might these skills be appropriate to social work? In particular, can deception ever be justified? We have considered deception by service users in Chapter 9, but can social workers justify its use?

CASE STUDIES

Think about the following scenarios.

1. *You are a social worker in a team working with young people and their families. Susan is 15 years old and has been in foster care since she was seven, as a consequence of parental neglect. She has maintained some contact with her mother, who had an alcohol problem for a number of years. Over the last two years, her mother, now 32, has stopped drinking, is in a new relationship, and is expecting a baby. Susan has been talking with you about her wish to return home now her mother has settled down. You have discussed this with Susan's mother, and she has told you in no uncertain terms that she regards Susan as the cause of her problems in her earlier life, that she has made a fresh start and is finally happy for the first time in her life. Susan can visit, but she doesn't want her home as she is convinced it would wreck her new life.*

   Susan is coming in to see you to find out how things went with her mother. What do you plan to tell her?

2. *You are a social worker in a health and disability team working with children and families. Helen and Dave's nine-year-old daughter Lou has, after several unexplained falls, been found to have a rare genetic disorder. Few people with this disorder live beyond 30 and, long before that, Lou will need a wheelchair and assistance with all her personal care needs, though her intellectual ability will be unimpaired. Until the diagnosis was made, Helen and Dave were unaware that they both carried the gene for the disorder, and they have been told that the chance for any children they have of developing it is one in four. They have two younger children who seem fine at present. They are coming to discuss whether or not to have them tested for the disorder.*

   How would you take up the discussion with them?

3. *You are a care manager in adult services. Ahmed is 87 and has severe arthritis which causes stiffness and pain. He lives alone, and personal carers help him with bathing and dressing. He has always looked after his own medication, but over the last few months he has become increasingly forgetful, and appears to be showing early signs of Alzheimer's disease. No other cause has been found. The carers have noticed that he is not taking his medication regularly and is suffering as a consequence, but he hotly denies this if they mention it to him. When you conduct a regular review of service provision, one of the carers takes you to one side and asks whether Ahmed's medication is available in a liquid form that they could administer to him without his knowledge in a drink.*

   If there were such a form of medication, how would you go about addressing the proposal?

Emotional labour

In this section we begin to consider the personal costs of care-giving, and its rewards.

RESEARCH SUMMARY

Emotional labour

The term 'emotional labour' was coined by Arlie Russell Hochschild (1983, 2003) to describe two phenomena: first, the way that service workers of all kinds are expected to display emotion; and second, the way they are expected to manage their emotions, as an inherent part of their work and, often, to promote the commercial well-being of their employing organisation rather than for their own benefit. She thus named emotion as isomorphic with physical and mental labour, but recognised that such labour had an even more profound impact on the individual's private world. Emotional labour is something which traditionally female jobs are more likely to demand; social work of course is one of these.

Hochschild studied different occupations, the largest group being flight attendants, predominantly women. An example of the requirement to display emotion is the bright welcoming smile as people board the plane; an example of the requirement to manage emotion is learning not to retaliate when a passenger is insulting. This is achieved not just through self-control, but by using cognitive strategies to alter the spontaneous emotional response, for example by using real or hypothetical information to explain the passenger's rudeness (He's scared; Maybe she's recently bereaved). Emotional labour may also take the form of negative emotions, so people such as bailiffs and bouncers deliberately appear angry and threatening. Hochschild argues that emotional labour is performed by all service providers, such as shop assistants and waiters, social workers and lawyers.

The relationship between how you feel and the feelings you are expected to present in your work is an intriguing one. People working in call centres put on bright, cheery tones for their brief encounters with the public, whether they feel happy, miserable, or bored. How like social work is this? Social workers often willingly take on the emotional labour of caring for others. Many of us are drawn into the work precisely because we enjoy relating emotionally, so are we performing emotional labour, giving freely of ourselves, or both? The rewards of successful care-giving are considerable, and it is often this which gives us a profound sense of meaning and purpose in our work. There are even times when we are relieved to attend to the problems of others, as it diverts our attention from our own, or puts ours in proportion – though there are times when our own difficulties ought to take precedence, and we cannot expect ourselves to attend to others' needs.

When working with disruptive and distressed individuals, we and others such as teachers clearly use our cognitive understanding to explain people's behaviour and manage our feelings. On this basis we are able to attune empathically and offer emotional regulation to the other person. In our work it is important that we base such understanding as far as possible on real knowledge of the individual, their circumstances, or any impairment or communicative disorder they might have. Hypothetical excuses are a different matter; they may have helped flight attendants to live with insult and even assault, but they are condemned as inadequate by Braithwaite (2001) in his zero-tolerance approach to aggression, discussed in Chapter 9.

Potential consequences of some forms of emotional labour are a feeling of falseness in one's emotions. Ashforth and Tomiuk (2000) interviewed a wide range of service agents to explore how much people felt they were acting at work, and how authentic they felt in role. People who did not feel they acted at work also felt they were authentic; surprisingly, some people who felt they did act at work also felt they were authentic.

The authors explain this by suggesting that acting is performed for different reasons, and has a variable relationship with authenticity as a consequence. For example, a medical technologist describes smiling and engaging in expected small talk, even when feelings of concern for clients are absent – this is clearly an uncomfortable chore. By contrast, a dietician puts energy into convincing her clients that they can lose weight because she genuinely cares for their well-being and sees this as a worthwhile effort; nonetheless she has doubts about their capacity to achieve their weight-loss goal. The element of acting is therefore linked with her beliefs about the value of her work and the possibility that she can make a difference, even in unpromising circumstances. This approach resonates with the kind of energy we often deploy in social work.

The study also suggests that initial feelings of putting on a show reduce as sustained relationships develop. When I worked long term with adults with mental health problems, I sometimes started out with reservations about them. I almost invariably developed warmth, concern and genuine interest in them, even when the work was frustrating – but when our work ended, I gradually recalled the less enjoyable aspects, and personal traits which I would never warm to in a friend. I had not had to put these feelings aside; they were simply not salient during my immersion in the work. Do social workers undertaking very brief work, such as organising packages of home care, feel less authentically connected to themselves and service users than their colleagues whose work lasts several months or years? Or are they kept going by a belief in the value of the task, and do their best in the time allotted to make an authentic connection with service users, perhaps like the dietician above?

Service agents mentioned feeling false when they had to defend conventions with which they disagreed (Ashforth and Tomiuk, 2000, p.192). This kind of emotional dissonance is familiar to social workers having to refuse services they personally believe service users should have, but which are unavailable because of resource constraints. It causes considerable disquiet, and can make people question the meaning of their work, the value the organisation places on their judgements, and even their choice of post.

A type of emotional labour not revealed in this study perhaps underlies Fisher et al.'s (2000) findings about foster carers. When complaints had been made by children in their care, foster carers felt that their social workers could have related to them better. We can hypothesise that the social workers experienced emotional dissonance in this situation, so that having suspicions about the foster carers' behaviour made it very difficult for them to engage in authentic positive communication with them. Keeping a truly open mind is a challenge, and one we need to take up in situations such as these, where the facts are unknown.

ACTIVITY 10.3

Think of work you have done in a social work or social care context, or in an informal caring role if you have no social work experience. Think of two contrasting circumstances: one where you enjoyed the emotional labour involved, and one where you didn't, perhaps because you felt false or because it exhausted you.

What do you know now about what made these two experiences different? If you were in the difficult situation again, do you think you could do anything to improve it?

COMMENT

Thinking about these experiences may help you decide whether you or the context you were working in was the main cause of your feelings.

Hope and optimism

In this section we will consider hope and optimism in two ways. First, the role of hope in people who are facing adversity, and second, the role of hope in the well-being of professionals themselves.

RESEARCH SUMMARY

Hope theory

Hope theory is most closely associated with the name of CR Snyder, who is responsible for having synthesised and articulated ideas about hope into a theoretical framework which is used to shape hope-based interventions.

Hope is primarily a way of thinking, with feelings playing an important, albeit contributory role. It involves the identification of concrete goals, a sense of being able to achieve these goals (agency) and the ability to see how to achieve them – to see and use pathways to the goal. People with high hope tend to be better adjusted, and do not give up when their attempts to reach goals are thwarted, but seek and create new pathways. They are not devastated by goal blockages, but instead they seem to thrive in solving the dilemmas produced by these life impediments (Snyder, 2002, pp.249–65).

The meaning, value and effect of hope have been widely researched in the fields of medicine, nursing and psychology – but not in social work. Broadly speaking, hope in both the helper and the person being helped is thought to improve outcomes. In the case of people with cancer, for example, life may be prolonged, even if recovery does not take place. Interventions designed to instil and enhance hope in a wide range of populations have shown to improve health and psychological well-being (Eliott, 2004).

Hope may be a goal in itself, since hope, in contrast to hopelessness, confers a feeling of well-being, and thus aids psychosocial adjustment, relationships and spiritual life. Options are limited by lack of hope, when people cannot imagine goals or how to achieve them, which has important social consequences. Hope and coping appear to be linked, even where hope is unrealistic. Hope theory has not been examined cross-culturally, and is currently only a valid concept for adults, not children or adolescents (Herth, 2004).

It seems to me that hope theory has considerable but relatively unexplored value in social work. Hope certainly underlies the approaches to working with families discussed in Chapter 7, and with people with special communication needs discussed in Chapter 8. We also know a little about the effect of losing hope from Fisher et al.'s (1984) study discussed in Chapter 2, where many of their mental health social workers (and presumably their clients) had given up believing they could make a difference.

A contrast is offered by a small international study taking as its subjects mental health social workers in both adult and child fields who were judged by colleagues to be expert (Ryan et al., 2004). It found that their belief in their assessments, in their own capacity to make a difference, and in service users' ability to recover, combined with optimism and genuine caring, helped them sustain themselves over long periods of time, working with people with enduring difficulties. They believed that their optimism oriented their interdisciplinary colleagues to service users' strengths, and had a beneficial impact on service users. Although their beliefs were not tested against service-user experience or outcomes, there is no doubt that these social workers were able to do their work creatively and courageously for many years, performing their emotional labours without losing heart or becoming burnt out.

Burnout and compassion

Finally, I want to raise the issue of burnout, which can affect all of us who work with people. Burnout describes a state where people can no longer connect authentically to their work, to themselves or to service users. It has three dimensions:

- emotional exhaustion;
- depersonalisation;
- loss of personal accomplishment.

(Maslach et al., 1996)

Emotional exhaustion is self-explanatory. Depersonalisation means becoming unfeeling towards service users, and loss of personal accomplishment entails loss of satisfaction and feeling of competence in working with people. Badly managed, burnout leaves those who experience it with impaired self-esteem; it reduces their effectiveness in their work with service users; it saps the energy and enthusiasm of colleagues and can drive valuable individuals out of the profession.

Some studies show that members of mental health teams, including social workers, are often emotionally exhausted, but nonetheless have high job satisfaction (e.g. Onyett et al., 1997). Therefore the emotional labour involved in social work does not in itself lead to burnout, and it is not known precisely what mechanisms contribute to its emergence. Emotional self-regulation may be implicated. Workers who have strong, emotionally empathic responses to service users' distress may be more vulnerable to depersonalisation, while those who are able to summon the more cognitive elements of empathy such as taking the other person's perspective, appear more resilient (Gross, 1994). This suggests that being able to regulate and manage our emotions rather than be overwhelmed by them is protective.

Gross's study takes an individual view of burnout. A contrasting view is presented by Meyerson (2000), who found burnout carried very different meanings in two social work teams. One saw it as a consequence of individual weakness, a sign of incompetence, and a source of stigma and shame. The other saw it as a consequence of engaging meaningfully with service users, and a sign that a worker needed a break, which was made available by workers covering for each other. These social workers had a strong belief in the value of their work. Their willingness to engage emotionally with distressed service users as fellow human beings clearly mattered to them, and was matched by their compassion for each other when they became depleted. Just as Winnicott (1958) had compassion for himself, these social workers were able to extend it to members of their team.

The interpersonal skills in responding to colleagues who are distressed are identical to those we employ with service users. It requires attunement, empathy and the readiness to put ourselves out for the sake of another. Compassion for colleagues is hard to provide when we are overworked and short of time (Frost et al., 2000), and when it is not formally part of our remit. As students you may have to contend with unfeeling organisations in which your chances of making an impact are at best modest; you can at least decide not to seek permanent employment there. And offering compassion to colleagues too carries risks of emotional exhaustion, so the goal is not to become a sole provider in the workplace, but to help it become a cultural norm. There seems good reason for both seeking out and trying to create compassionate organisations. We do a difficult job, and to do it well we need the mutual support of our colleagues. In benign circumstances we have the opportunity to work together and care for and inspire others.

ACTIVITY **10.4**

Reviewing what you have learnt in this chapter, put together the following information:

- *Your interpersonal strengths in social work.*

- *The strengths that you would like to develop.*

- *The help that you need from others to achieve your goals.*

- *The help you can offer to others to help them achieve theirs.*

- *A plan of action if you find yourself in an organisation which is characterised by unfeeling responses to staff distress. Include the help you would seek from others.*

CHAPTER SUMMARY

In this chapter we began by thinking about the influence of our personal backgrounds on how we approach social work and service users, and we have ended with the effect of the culture of the organisations in which we work. Burnout is an experience where these two ends of the spectrum probably intersect. Along the way we have begun to recognise that communication is not always clear-cut and positive. We have seen the need to watch for everyday impulses to thwart or tease other people, and to notice if we have hostile impulses and guard against giving way to them. We have also learnt that there is sometimes value in ambiguity and tentativeness in dealing with emotionally complex situations. We have begun to

Continued

CHAPTER SUMMARY *continued*

consider the emotional demands of social work, and how important it is to take care of ourselves and our colleagues. The welfare of service users and our own well-being depend upon bringing together our cognitive and emotional capacities, acknowledging both the dark and the bright. The reality of social work practice in pressured times means that it is more important than ever to foster hope and compassion in service users, in our colleagues, and in ourselves. Good luck.

FURTHER READING

Eliott, JA (ed.) (2004) *Interdisciplinary perspectives on hope*. Hauppauge, NY: Nova Science.
A very good collection of papers which presents findings from health care. Social work research needs to start to match some of the accounts here.

Fineman, S (ed.) (2000) *Emotion in organizations*. 2nd edition. London: Sage.
Again, a stimulating collection of papers about organisations and the role of emotional life in the workplace.

Appendix

Subject benchmark for social work

3 Nature and extent of social work.

4 Defining principles.

4.6 Social work is a moral activity that requires practitioners to recognise the dignity of the individual, but also to make and implement difficult decisions (including restriction of liberty) in human situations that involve the potential for benefit or harm. Honours degree programmes in social work therefore involve the study, application of, and critical reflection upon, ethical principles and dilemmas. As reflected by the four care councils' codes of practice, this involves showing respect for persons, honouring the diverse and distinctive organisations and communities that make up contemporary society, promoting social justice and combating processes that lead to discrimination, marginalisation and social exclusion. This means that honours undergraduates must learn to:

- Practise in ways that maximise safety and effectiveness in situations of uncertainty and incomplete information.

4.7 The expectation that social workers will be able to act effectively in such complex circumstances requires that honours degree programmes in social work should be designed to help students learn to become accountable, reflective, critical and evaluative. This involves learning to:

- Work in a transparent and responsible way, balancing autonomy with complex, multiple and sometimes contradictory accountabilities (for example, to different service users, employing agencies, professional bodies and the wider society).

- Acquire and apply the habits of critical reflection, self-evaluation and consultation, and make appropriate use of research in decision-making about practice and in the evaluation of outcomes.

5 Subject knowledge, understanding and skills.

Subject knowledge and understanding

5.1 During their degree studies in social work, honours graduates should acquire, critically evaluate, apply and integrate knowledge and understanding in the following five core areas of study.

5.1.1 Social work services, service users and carers, which include:

- The social processes (associated with, for example, poverty, migration, unemployment, poor health, disablement, lack of education and other sources of disadvantage) that lead to marginalisation, isolation and exclusion, and their impact on the demand for social work services.

- The nature of social work services in a diverse society (with particular reference to concepts such as prejudice, interpersonal, institutional and structural discrimination, empowerment and anti-discriminatory practices).

- The nature and validity of different definitions of, and explanations for, the characteristics and circumstances of service users and the services required by them, drawing on knowledge from research, practice experience, and from service users and carers.

- The focus on outcomes, such as promoting the well-being of young people and their families, and promoting dignity, choice and independence for adults receiving services.

- The relationship between agency policies, legal requirements and professional boundaries in shaping the nature of services provided in interdisciplinary contexts and the issues associated with working across professional boundaries and within different disciplinary groups.

5.1.3 Values and ethics, which include:

- The moral concepts of rights, responsibility, freedom, authority and power inherent in the practice of social workers as moral and statutory agents.

5.1.4 Social work theory, which includes:

- Research-based concepts and critical explanations from social work theory and other disciplines that contribute to the knowledge base of social work, including their distinctive epistemological status and application to practice.

- The relevance of psychological, physical and physiological perspectives to understanding personal and social development and functioning.

- Social science theories explaining group and organisational behaviour, adaptation and change.

- Models and methods of assessment, including factors underpinning the selection and testing of relevant information, the nature of professional judgement and the processes of risk assessment and decision-making.

- Approaches and methods of intervention in a range of settings, including factors guiding the choice and evaluation of these.

- User-led perspectives.

- Knowledge and critical appraisal of relevant social research and evaluation methodologies, and the evidence base for social work.

5.1.5 The nature of social work practice, which includes:

- The characteristics of practice in a range of community-based and organisational settings within statutory, voluntary and private sectors, and the factors influencing changes and developments in practice within these contexts.

- The nature and characteristics of skills associated with effective practice, both direct and indirect, with a range of service-users and in a variety of settings.

- The processes that facilitate and support service user choice and independence.

- The place of theoretical perspectives and evidence from international research in assessment and decision-making processes in social work practice.

- The integration of theoretical perspectives and evidence from international research into the design and implementation of effective social work intervention, with a wide range of service users, carers and others.

- The processes of reflection and evaluation, including familiarity with the range of approaches for evaluating service and welfare outcomes, and their significance for the development of practice and the practitioner.

Subject-specific skills and other skills

5.3 All social work honours graduates should show the ability to reflect on and learn from the exercise of their skills. They should understand the significance of the concepts of continuing professional development and lifelong learning, and accept responsibility for their own continuing development.

5.5.1 Managing problem-solving activities: Honours graduates in social work should be able to plan problem-solving activities, i.e. to:

- Think logically, systematically, critically and reflectively.

- Plan a sequence of actions to achieve specified objectives, making use of research, theory and other forms of evidence.

- Manage processes of change, drawing on research, theory and other forms of evidence.

Problem-solving skills

5.5.4 Intervention and evaluation: Honours graduates in social work should be able to use their knowledge of a range of interventions and evaluation processes selectively to:

- Build and sustain purposeful relationships with people and organisations in community-based, and interprofessional contexts make decisions, set goals and construct specific plans to achieve these, taking into account relevant factors including ethical guidelines.

- Negotiate goals and plans with others, analysing and addressing in a creative manner human, organisational and structural impediments to change.

- Implement plans through a variety of systematic processes that include working in partnership.

- Undertake practice in a manner that promotes the well-being and protects the safety of all parties.

- Engage effectively in conflict resolution.

- Support service users to take decisions and access services, with the social worker as navigator, advocate and supporter.

- Manage the complex dynamics of dependency and, in some settings, provide direct care and personal support in everyday living situations.

- Meet deadlines and comply with external definitions of a task.

- Plan, implement and critically review processes and outcomes.

- Bring work to an effective conclusion, taking into account the implications for all involved.

- Monitor situations, review processes and evaluate outcomes.

- Use and evaluate methods of intervention critically and reflectively.

Communication skills

5.6 Honours graduates in social work should be able to communicate clearly, accurately and precisely (in an appropriate medium) with individuals and groups in a range of formal and informal situations, i.e. to:

- Make effective contact with individuals and organisations for a range of objectives, by verbal, paper-based and electronic means.

- Clarify and negotiate the purpose of such contacts and the boundaries of their involvement.

- Listen actively to others, engage appropriately with the life experiences of service users, understand accurately their viewpoint and overcome personal prejudices to respond appropriately to a range of complex personal and interpersonal situations.

- Use both verbal and non-verbal cues to guide interpretation.

- Identify and use opportunities for purposeful and supportive communication with service users within their everyday living situations.

- Follow and develop an argument and evaluate the viewpoints of, and evidence presented by others.

- Write accurately and clearly in styles adapted to the audience, purpose and context of the communication.

- Use advocacy skills to promote others' rights, interests and needs.

- Present conclusions verbally and on paper, in a structured form, appropriate to the audience for which these have been prepared.

- Make effective preparation for, and lead meetings in a productive way.

- Communicate effectively across potential barriers resulting from differences (for example, in culture, language and age).

Skills in working with others

5.7 Honours graduates in social work should be able to work effectively with others, i.e. to:

- Involve users of social work services in ways that increase their resources, capacity and power to influence factors affecting their lives.

- Consult actively with others, including service users and carers, who hold relevant information or expertise.

- Act cooperatively with others, liaising and negotiating across differences such as organisational and professional boundaries and differences of identity or language.

- Develop effective helping relationships and partnerships with other individuals, groups and organisations that facilitate change.

- Act within a framework of multiple accountability (for example, to agencies, the public, service users, carers and others).

- Challenge others when necessary, in ways that are most likely to produce positive outcomes.

5.8 Honours graduates in social work should be able to:

- Advance their own learning and understanding with a degree of independence.

- Reflect on and modify their behaviour in the light of experience.

- Identify and keep under review their own personal and professional boundaries.

- Manage uncertainty, change and stress in work situations.

- Handle inter- and intrapersonal conflict constructively.

- Understand and manage changing situations and respond in a flexible manner.

- Challenge unacceptable practices in a responsible manner.

- Take responsibility for their own further and continuing acquisition and use of knowledge and skills.

- Use research critically and effectively to sustain and develop their practice.

Glossary

Affect Used in the fields of psychotherapy and neuroscience to mean emotion.

Attunement Accurate reflection of emotion through a spontaneous physical response which matches the other person's energy and rhythm (Stern, in McCluskey, 2005).

Background emotions They shape posture, level of animation and body movement, and are shown in energy levels, such as weariness or excitement; akin to **vitality affects** (Damasio, 2000).

Burnout A syndrome characterised by emotional exhaustion, depersonalisation and loss of personal accomplishment (Maslach et al., 1996).

Countertransference The emotional responses of therapist to client, and the feelings the therapist experiences which may mirror, rather than be reactive to, the client's emotions.

Emotion See **Primary emotions**; **Secondary emotions**; and **Background emotions**.

Emotional labour The display and management of emotion as part of one's employment (Hochschild, 1983, 2003).

Emotional (self-)regulation The ability to manage one's emotional responses so that they are within tolerable rather than overwhelming limits; the ability to respond to others so that their emotional responses are also managed.

First-order change Change that takes place within a system (Watzlawick et al., 1967).

First-order skills The skills required in direct communication itself, with service users, colleagues and others (Koprowska, 2000).

Goal-corrected empathic attunement An attuned response which is expressed empathically in words and which matches the other person's experience; also includes accurate, regulating purposeful **misattunement** (McCluskey, 2005).

Habitus 'Taken for granted' aspects of culture, thinking and feeling (Bourdieu, in Thompson, 2003).

Isomorphy Those aspects of systems which they have in common. Literally it means 'equal in form' (von Bertalanffy, 1971).

Metacommunication Communication about communication (Watzlawick et al., 1967).

Mirror neurons Describes neurons which fire both when we perform an action and when we see someone else perform it. Used to describe actions and intentions and tentatively used to explain our emotional responses.

Misattunement The opposite of attunement – an inaccurate response which can be purposeful and effective as a means of regulating the other person's emotions, or simply out of tune, leaving the other person misunderstood.

Primary emotions Also known as universal emotions, there are said to be six which are expressed in the same way by all human beings: happiness, sadness, fear, anger, surprise and disgust (Darwin, 1998).

SAVI™ System for Analyzing Verbal Interaction originally developed as a research tool but also used in practice (Simon and Agazarian, 2005).

Secondary emotions Also known as social emotions, these include jealousy and embarrassment. They may not be visible to an observer (Damasio, 2000).

Second-order change Change which affects the system itself (Watzlawick et al., 1967).

Second-order skills The skills required in planning our communication strategy, thinking about what we are doing, observing interactions, paying attention to feedback, reviewing what has happened, and modifying our next and future communications accordingly (Koprowska, 2000).

Transference The feelings a client has towards the therapist, and also to the propensity to expect the therapist to treat them in the same way as their early care-givers.

Vitality affects Similar to **background emotions** (Stern, in McCluskey, 2005).

Zone of proximal development This refers to what a person is nearly able to do, but cannot do yet, without assistance (Vygotsky, 1986).

References

Agazarian, YM (1997) *System-Centred Group Psychotherapy.* New York: Guilford Press.

Agazarian, YM (2006) 'Individual and Group Therapy', in SP Gantt and YA, *SCT® in Clinical Practice: Applying the systems-centered approach with individuals, families and groups.* Livermore, CA: Wingspan Press, pp.1–29.

Ahmad, A, Betts, B and Cowan, L (2008) 'Using Interactive Media in Direct Practice', in B Luckock and M Lefevre (eds), *Direct Work: Social work with children and young people in care.* London: British Association of Adoption and Fostering, pp.169–80.

Aldgate, J, Jones, D, Rose, W and Jeffery, C (eds) (2006) *The Developing World of the Child.* London: Jessica Kingsley.

Aldridge, M and Wood, J (1998) *Interviewing Children: A guide for child care and forensic practitioners.* Chichester: John Wiley & Sons.

Ashforth, BE and Tomiuk, MA (2000) 'Emotional Labour and Authenticity: Views from service agents', in S Fineman, (ed), *Emotion in Organizations.* 2nd edition. London: Sage, pp.184–203.

Banks, E and Mumford, S (1988) 'Meeting the Needs of Workers', in J Aldgate and J Simmonds (eds), *Direct Work with Children: A guide for social work practitioners.* London: Batsford/ British Association of Adoption and Fostering, pp.101–10.

Bateson, G (1972) 'The Cybernetics of "Self": A theory of alcoholism', in *Steps to an Ecology of Mind.* Chicago, IL: University of Chicago Press, pp.309–337.

Bell, M and Fisher, T (2003) *The Family Foundations Parenting Project: A study of the implementation and impact.* York: Joseph Rowntree Foundation.

Bell, M and Wilson, K (2003) (eds) *The Practitioner's Guide to Working with Families.* Basingstoke: Palgrave Macmillan.

Bordin, ES (1994) 'Theory and Research on the Therapeutic Working Alliance', in AO Horvath and LS Greenberg (eds), *The Working Alliance: Theory, research and practice.* New York: John Wiley & Sons, pp.13–37.

Bowlby, J (1988) *A Secure Base: Clinical applications of attachment theory.* Abingdon: Routledge.

Bradshaw, J (2001) Complexity of Staff Communication and Reported Level of Understanding Skills in Adults with Intellectual Disabilities. *Journal of Intellectual Disability Research*, 24 (3), pp.233–43.

Braithwaite, R (2001) *Managing Aggression.* Abingdon: Routledge.

Brandon, M, Schofield, G and Trinder, L with Stone, N (1998) *Social Work with Children.* Basingstoke: Macmillan.

Brown, A (1992) *Groupwork.* 3rd edition. Aldershot: Ashgate.

Buckley, B (2003) *Children's Communication Skills: From birth to five years.* Abingdon: Routledge.

Bull, P (1983) *Body Movement and Interpersonal Communication.* Chichester: John Wiley & Sons.

Burgoon, JK and Levine, TR (2010) 'Deception and Detection of Deception', in SW Smith and SR Wilson, *New Directions in Interpersonal Communication Research.* London: Sage, pp.201–20.

Butterworth, R (2004) 'Managing Violence', in T Ryan and J Pritchard (eds) *Good Practice in Adult Mental Health.* Abingdon: Routledge, pp.311–32.

Carter, FB (2005) *Personal communication.*

Cheetham, J, Fuller, R, McIvor, G and Petch, A (1992) *Evaluating Social Work Effectiveness.* Buckingham: Open University Press.

Cipolla, J, McGown, DB and Yanulis, MA (1992) (UK edition) *Communicating Through Play: Techniques for assessing and preparing children for adoption.* London: British Association for Adoption and Fostering.

Colton, M, Sanders, R and Williams, M (2001) *An Introduction to Working with Children: A guide for social workers.* Basingstoke: Palgrave.

Cook, A (2008) 'Knowing the Child: The importance of developing a relationship', in B Luckock and M Lefevre (eds), *Direct Work: Social work with children and young people in care.* London: British Association of Adoption and Fostering, pp.215–22.

Coulshed, V and Orme, J (1998) *Social Work Practice: An introduction.* 3rd edition. Basingstoke: Palgrave.

Crawford, M and Walker, J (2010) *Social Work and Human Development.* 3rd edition. Exeter: Learning Matters.

Cross, M (2004) *Children with Emotional and Behavioural Difficulties and Communication Problems: There is always a reason.* London: Jessica Kingsley.

Cupach, WR and Spiztberg, BH (1994) 'Preface', in WR Cupach and BH Spitzberg (eds), *The Dark Side of Interpersonal Communication.* Hillside, NJ: Lawrence Erlbaum, pp.vii–ix.

Dallos, R and Draper, R (2000) *An Introduction to Family Therapy: Systemic theory and practice.* Buckingham: Open University Press.

Damasio, A (1999) *The Feeling of What Happens: Body and emotion in the making of consciousness.* London: Harcourt.

Daniel, B, Wassell, S and Gilligan, R (1999) *Child Development for Child Care and Protection Workers.* London: Jessica Kingsley.

Darwin, C (1998) *The Expression of the Emotions in Man and Animals.* 3rd edition. London: HarperCollins.

Denney, D (2010) Violence and Social Care Staff: Positive and Negative Approaches to Risk. *British Journal of Social Work.* 1–17. *British Journal of Social Work Advance Access,* March 10.

Department of Health (1995) *Child Protection: Messages from research.* London: The Stationery Office.

Department of Health (1999) *Code of Practice to the Mental Health Act 1983 (revised 1999).* Norwich: Stationery Office.

Department of Health (2001) *Valuing People: A new strategy for Learning Disability for the 21st century.* London: The Stationery Office.

Department of Health, Department for Education and Employment, and Home Office (2000), *Framework for the Assessment of Children in Need and their Families.* London: The Stationery Office.

Department for Children, Schools and Families/Department of Health (2009) *Social Work Task Force Report.* www.publications.dcsf.gov.uk

Dijksterhuis, A (2005) 'Why We Are Social Animals: The high road to imitation as social glue', in S Hurley and N Chater (eds), *Perspectives on Imitation, Volume 2: From neuroscience to social science – imitation, human development and culture.* Cambridge, MA: MIT Press, pp.207–220.

Duck, S (1994) 'Stratagems, Spoils, and a Serpent's Tooth: On the delights and dilemmas of personal relationships', in WR Cupach and BH Spitzberg (eds), *The Dark Side of Interpersonal Communication.* Hillside, NJ: Lawrence Erlbaum, pp.3–24.

Edgeworth, J and Carr, A (2000) 'Child Abuse', in A Carr (ed), *What Works with Children and Adolescents*. Abingdon: Routledge, pp.17–48.

Edwards, RT, Cailleachair, A, Bywater, T, Hughes, DA and Hutchings, J (2007) Parenting Programme for Parents of Children at Risk of Developing Conduct Disorder: *Cost effectiveness analysis. British Medical Journal*, Vol. 334, No. 7995, pp.682–85.

Egan, G (2002) *The Skilled Helper: A problem-management and opportunity-development approach to helping.* 7th edition. Pacific Grove, CA: Brooks/Cole.

Ekman, P (1998) Introduction to the Third Edition, in C Darwin, *The Expression of the Emotions in Man and Animals.* 3rd edition. London: HarperCollins, pp.xxi–xxxvi.

Ekman, P (2003) *Emotions Revealed: Understanding faces and feelings.* London: Weidenfeld & Nicholson.

Eliott, JA (2004) (ed), *Interdisciplinary Perspectives on Hope.* Hauppauge, NY: Nova Science.

Falloon, IRH, Laporta, M, Fadden, G and Graham-Hole, V (1993) *Managing Stress in Families: Cognitive and behavioural strategies for enhancing coping skills.* Abingdon: Routledge.

Farmer, RL (2009) *Neuroscience and Social Work: The missing link.* London: Sage.

Fisher, M, Newton, C and Sainsbury, E (1984) *Mental Health Social Work Observed.* London: Allen and Unwin.

Fisher, T, Gibbs, I, Sinclair, I and Wilson, K (2000) Sharing the Care: The qualities sought of social workers by foster carers. *Child and Family Social Work*, Vol. 5, pp.225–33.

Fonagy, P and Roth, A (2005) *What Works for Whom?: A critical review of psychotherapy research.* 2nd edition. London: Guilford Press.

Forrester, D, Kershaw, S, Moss, H and Hughes, L (2007) Communication Skills in Child Protection: How do social workers talk to parents? *Child and Family Social Work*, Vol. 13, pp.41–51.

French, S, Gillman, M and Swain, J (1997) *Working with Visually Disabled people: Bridging theory and practice.* Birmingham: Venture Press.

Fridlund, AJ and Russell, JA (2006) 'The Functions of Facial Expressions: What's in a face?', in V Manusov and ML Patterson (eds), *The Sage Handbook of Nonverbal Communication*. London: Sage, pp.299–319.

Frost, PJ, Dutton, JE, Worline, MC and Wilson, A (2000) 'Narratives of Compassion in Organizations', in S Fineman, (ed) *Emotion in Organizations*. 2nd edition. London: Sage, pp.25–45.

Gallese, V (2004) Intentional Attunement. The Mirror Neuron system and its role in interpersonal relations www.interdisciplines.org

Gallese, V (2005) '"Being Like Me": Self-other identity, mirror neurons and empathy', in S. Hurley and N. Chater (eds), *Perspectives on Imitation, Volume 1: From neuroscience to social science – mechanisms of imitation and imitation in animals*. Cambridge, MA: MIT Press. pp.101–18.

Gambetta, D (2005) 'Deceptive Mimicry in Humans', in S. Hurley and N. Chater (eds), *Perspectives on Imitation, Volume 2: From neuroscience to social science – imitation, human development and culture*. Cambridge, MA: MIT Press, pp.221–42.

Gardner, F, Burton, J and Klimes, I (2006), Randomised Controlled Trial of a Parenting Intervention in the Voluntary Sector for Reducing Child Conduct Problems: Outcomes and mechanisms of change. *Journal of Child Psychology and Psychiatry*, Vol. 47, No. 11, pp.1123–32.

Guardian, (2008) www.guardian.co.uk/society

Gerhard, S (2004) *Why Love Matters: How affection shapes a baby's brain*. Abingdon: Brunner-Routledge.

Gilbert, P (1992) *Depression: The Evolution of Powerlessness*. Hove: Lawrence Erlbaum.

Goffman, E (1963) *Behavior in Public Places*. New York: Free Press.

Golightley, M (2008) *Social Work and Mental Health*. 3rd edition. Exeter: Learning Matters.

Hall, J (2006) 'Women's and Men's Nonverbal Communication: Similarities, differences, stereotypes and origins', in V Manusov and ML Patterson (eds), *The Sage Handbook of Nonverbal Communication*. London: Sage, pp.201–218.

Hargie, O and Dickson, D (2004) *Skilled Interpersonal Communication: Research, theory and practice*. 4th edition. Abingdon: Routledge.

Harris, J (1997) *Deafness and the Hearing*. Birmingham: Venture Press.

Heard, D and Lake, B (1997) *The Dynamics of Attachment in Caregiving*. Abingdon: Routledge.

Henley, NM (1995) 'Body Politics Revisited: What do we know today?', in PJ Kalbfleisch and MJ Cody (eds), *Gender, Power and Communication in Human Relationships*. Hove: Lawrence Erlbaum, pp.27–61.

Henry, WP and Strupp, HH (1994) 'The Therapeutic Alliance as Interpersonal Process', in AO Horvath and LS Greenberg, (eds), *The Working Alliance: Theory, research and practice*. New York: John Wiley & Sons, pp.51–84.

Herth K (2004) 'State of the Science of Hope in Nursing Practice', in JA Eliott (ed), *Interdisciplinary Perspectives on Hope*. Hauppauge, NY: Nova Science, pp.169–211.

Hochschild, AR (1983, 2003) *The Managed Heart: Commercialization of human feeling*. 20th anniversary edition. Berkeley, CA: University of California Press.

Hooper, CA and Koprowska, J (2000) 'Reparative Experience or Repeated Trauma? Child sexual abuse and adult mental health services', in U McCluskey and CA Hooper (eds), *Psychodynamic Perspectives on Abuse: The cost of fear*. London: Jessica Kingsley, pp.275–90.

Hooper, CA, Koprowska, J and Milsom, R (1999) *Research on Adult Survivors of Childhood Sexual Abuse: Report on experiences of services*. York: North Yorkshire Health Authority.

Horvath, AO and Greenberg, LS (1994) Introduction, in AO Horvath and LS Greenberg (eds), *The Working Alliance: Theory, research and practice*. New York: John Wiley & Sons, pp.1–12.

Hurley, S and Chater, N (2005) 'Introduction: The importance of imitation', in S. Hurley and N. Chater (eds) *Perspectives on Imitation, Volume 1: From neuroscience to social science – mechanisms of imitation and imitation in animals*. Cambridge, MA: MIT Press. pp.1–52.

Hutchings, J, Bywater, T, Daley, D, Gardner, F, Whitaker, C, Jones, K, Eames, C and Edwards, RT (2007) Parenting Intervention in Sure Start Services for Children at Risk of Developing Conduct Disorder: Pragmatic randomised controlled trial. *British Medical Journal Online First*, Vol. 334, No.7995, pp.678–682.

Iacoboni, M (2009) 'The Problem of Other Minds is not a Problem: Mirror Neurons and intersubjectivity', in JA Pineda (ed), *Mirror Neuron Systems: The role of mirroring processes in social cognition*. Totowa, N.J.: Humana Press, pp.121–33.

Jones, DPH (2003) *Communicating with Vulnerable Children: A guide for practitioners*. London: Royal College of Psychiatrists.

Kadushin A and Kadushin, G (1997) *The Social Work Interview: A guide for human service professionals*. 4th edition. New York: Columbia University Press.

Kelly, A (2000) *Working with Adults with a Learning Disability*. Bicester: Speechmark.

Kitwood, T (1997) *Dementia Reconsidered*. Buckingham: Open University Press.

Knapp, M and Hall, J (2006) *Nonverbal Communication in Human Interaction.* 6th edition. Belmont, CA: Thomson Wadsworth.

Koprowska, J (2010) 'Are Student Social Workers' Communication Skills Improved by University-based Learning?', in H Burgess and J Carpenter (eds), *The Outcomes of Social Work Education: Developing evaluation methods.* Southampton, Higher Education Academy Subject Centre for Social Policy and Social Work. pp.73–87.

Koprowska, J (2000) 'Interviewing', in M. Davies, *The Blackwell Encyclopaedia of Social Work.* Oxford: Blackwell, pp.176–7.

Lakin, JL (2006) 'Automatic Cognitive Processes and Nonverbal Communication', in V Manusov and ML Patterson (eds), *The Sage Handbook of Nonverbal Communication.* London, Sage, pp.59–77.

Laming, H (2003) *The Victoria Climbié Inquiry.* London: The Stationery Office. Crown Copyright.

Lefevre, M (2010) *Communicating with Children and Young People: Making a Difference.* Bristol: The Policy Press.

Lefevre, M, (2008) 'Communicating and Engaging with Children and Young People in Care through Play and Creative Arts', in B Luckock and M Lefevre (eds), *Direct Work: Social work with children and young people in care.* London: British Association of Adoption and Fostering, pp.130–50.

Lishman, J (2009) *Communication in Social Work.* Basingstoke: Macmillan.

Love, C (2000) 'Family Group Conferencing: Cultural origins, sharing, and appropriation – a Maori reflection', in G Burford and J Hudson (eds), *Family Group Conferencing: New directions in community-centered child and family practice.* New York: Walter de Gruyter, pp.15–30.

Luborsky, L (1994) 'Therapeutic Alliances as Predictors of Psychotherapy Outcomes: Factors explaining the predictive success', in AO Horvath and LS Greenberg (eds), *The Working Alliance: Theory, research and practice.* New York: John Wiley & Sons, pp.38–50.

Luckock, B, with Stevens, P and Young, J (2008) 'Living Through the Experience: The social worker as the trusted ally and champion of young people in care', in B Luckock and M Lefevre (eds), *Direct Work: Social work with children and young people in care.* London: British Association of Adoption and Fostering, pp.1–20

Marchant, R (2008) 'Working with Disabled Children who Live Away from Home Some or All of the Time', in B Luckock and M Lefevre (eds), *Direct Work: Social work with children and young people in care.* London: British Association of Adoption and Fostering, pp.151–168.

Marsh, P and Crow, G (1998), *Family Group Conferences in Child Welfare.* Oxford: Blackwell.

Maslach, C, Jackson, S and Leiter, M (1996) *Maslach Burnout Inventory Manual.* Palo Alto, CA: Consulting Psychologists Press.

Mason, T and Chandley, M (1999) *Managing Violence and Aggression: A manual for nurses and health care workers.* Edinburgh: Churchill Livingstone.

Matsumoto, D (2006) 'Culture and Nonverbal Behavior', in V Manusov and ML Patterson (eds), *The Sage Handbook of Nonverbal Communication.* London: Sage, pp.219–35.

Mayer, JE and Timms N (1970) *The Client Speaks: Working class impressions of casework.* London: Routledge and Kegan Paul.

McCluskey, U (2003) 'Theme-focused Family Therapy: Working with the dynamics of emotional abuse and neglect within an attachment and systems perspective', in M Bell and K Wilson (eds), *The Practitioner's Guide to Working with Families.* Basingstoke: Palgrave Macmillan, pp.103–26.

McCluskey, U (2005) *To Be Met as a Person: The dynamics of attachment in professional encounters.* London: Karnac.

McMahon, L and Ward, A (2001) (eds) *Helping Families in Family Centres: Working at therapeutic practice.* London: Jessica Kingsley.

McNamara, S (2000) *Stress in Young People: What's new and what can we do?* London: Continuum.

Meltzer, H, Gatward, R, Corbin, T, Goodman, R and Ford, T (2003) *The Mental Health of Young People Looked After by Local Authorities in England.* London: The Stationery Office.

Meltzoff, AN (2005) 'Imitation and Other minds: The "like me" hypothesis', in S Hurley and N Chater (eds), *Perspectives on Imitation, Volume 2: From neuroscience to social science – imitation, human development and culture.* Cambridge, MA: MIT Press, pp.55–77.

Meyerson, DE (2000) 'If Emotions were Honoured: A cultural analysis', in S Fineman (ed), *Emotion in Organizations.* 2nd edition. London: Sage, pp.167–83.

Myers, S and Milner, J (2007) *Working with Violence: Policies and practices in risk assessment and management.* Basingstoke : Palgrave Macmillan.

Milner J and O'Byrne, P (2002) *Assessment and Social Work.* 2nd edition. Basingstoke: Palgrave.

Oberman, L and Ramachandran, VS (2009) 'Reflections on the Mirror Neuron System: Their evolutionary functions beyond motor representation', in JA Pineda (ed), *Mirror Neuron Systems: The role of mirroring processes in social cognition.* Totowa, NJ: Humana Press, pp.39–59.

Oliver, M (1990) *The Politics of Disablement.* Basingstoke: Macmillan.

Onyett, S, Pillinger, T, and Muijen, M (1997) Job Satisfaction and Burnout among Members of Community Mental Health Teams. *Journal of Mental Health,* Vol. 6, Part 1, pp.55–66.

Pally, R (2000) *The Mind–Brain Relationship.* London: Karnac.

Parker, JR (2010) *Effective Practice Learning in Social Work.* 2nd edition. Exeter: Learning Matters.

Parker, JR and Bradley, G (2007) *Social Work Practice: Assessment, planning, intervention and review.* 2nd edition. Exeter: Learning Matters.

Payne, M (1997) *Modern Social Work Theory.* 2nd edition. Basingstoke: Macmillan.

Petrie, S (2003) 'Working with Families where there are Child Protection Concerns', in M Bell and K Wilson (eds), *The Practitioner's Guide to Working with Families.* Basingstoke: Palgrave Macmillan, pp.168–87.

Pinker, S (1999) *Words and Rules: The ingredients of language.* London: Weidenfeld & Nicholson.

Pound, C and Hewitt, A (2004) 'Communication Barriers: Building access and identity', in J Swain, S French and C Thomas (eds), *Disabling Barriers – Enabling Environments.* 2nd edition. London: Sage.

Preston-Shoot, M (2007) *Effective Groupwork.* 2nd edition. Basingstoke, Palgrave Macmillan.

Qureshi, H, Patmore, C, Nicholas, E and Bamford, C (1998) *Overview: Outcomes of Social Care for Older People and Carers.* York: Social Policy Research Unit.

Race, DG (2002) Attempts at a social approach, in DG Race (ed), *Learning Disability: A social approach.* Abingdon: Routledge, pp.8–19.

Ramachandran, VS and Blakeslee, S (2998) *Phantoms in the Brain: Human nature and the architecture of the mind.* London: Harper Perennial.

Richards, S, Ruch, G and Trevithick, P (2005) Communication Skills Training for Social Work Practice: The ethical dilemma for social work education. *Social Work Education,* Vol. 24, Part 4, pp.409–22.

Rizzolatti, G and Sinigaglia, C (2006) *Mirrors in the Brain: How our minds share actions and emotions.* Oxford, Oxford University Press.

Roopnarine, JL, Johnson, JE and Hooper, FH (1994) *Children's Play in Diverse Cultures.* Albany, NY: State University of New York.

Ross, R (2000) 'Searching for the Roots of Conferencing', in G Burford and J Hudson (eds), *Family Group Conferencing: New directions in community-centered child and family practice.* New York: Walter de Gruyter, pp.5–14.

Ryan, M, Merighi, JR, Healy, B and Renouf, N (2004) Belief, Optimism and Caring: Findings from a cross-national study of expertise in mental health social work. *Qualitative Social Work,* Vol. 3, Part 4, pp.411–29.

Ryan, T and Walker, R (2007) *Life Story Work: A practical guide to helping children understand their past.* London: British Association of Adoption and Fostering.

Science to Service Taskforce (2007) *Practice Guidelines for Group Psychotherapy: A cross-theoretical guide to developing and leading psychotherapy groups.* New York: American Group Psychotherapy Association.

Schore, A (2003) *Affect Regulation and the Repair of the Self.* New York: WW Norton.

Shakespeare, T (2006) *Disability Rights and Wrongs.* Abingdon: Routledge.

Shannon, CE and Weaver, W (1964) *The Mathematical Theory of Communication.* Urbana, IL: University of Illinois Press.

Shaw, I (1999) 'Evidence for Practice', in I Shaw and J Lishman (eds), *Evaluation and Social Work Practice.* London: Sage, pp.14–40.

Shaw, I and Lishman, J (1999) *Evaluation and Social Work Practice.* London: Sage.

Simmonds, J (2008) 'Direct Work with Children: Delusion or reality?', in B Luckock and M Lefevre (eds), *Direct Work: Social work with children and young people in care.* London, British Association of Adoption and Fostering, pp.xiii–xxvi.

Simon, A and Agazarian, YM (2005) *SAVI® Grid.*

Simon, A and Agazarian, YM (2003) *SAVI® Definitions.* Philadelphia, PA: self published by Simon.

Simon, A and Agazarian, YM: www.SAVICommunications.com

Smith, PK, Cowie, H and Blades, M (2004) *Understanding Children's Development.* 4th edition. Oxford: Blackwell.

Snyder, CR (2002) Hope Theory: Rainbows in the mind. *Psychological Inquiry,* Vol 13, No. 4, pp.249–75.

Spiztberg, BH (1994) 'The Dark Side of (In)competence', in WR Cupach and BH Spitzberg (eds), *The Dark Side of Interpersonal Communication.* Hillside, New Jersey: Lawrence Erlbaum, pp.25–49.

START (2004) *Annual Report 2003–2004.* Plymouth: START.

Stein, M (1997) *What Works in Leaving Care?* Ilford: Barnardo's.

Sue, DW and Sue, D (2002) *Counseling the Culturally Diverse: Theory and practice.* 4th edition. New York: John Wiley & Sons.

Svanberg, PO (2005) Promoting attachment security in primary prevention using video feed-back: The Sunderland Infant Programme. Unpublished.

Swain, J French, S and Thomas, C (eds) *Disabling Barriers – Enabling Environments.* 2nd edition. London: Sage.

Thompson, N (2003) *Communication and Language: A handbook of theory and practice.* Basingstoke: Palgrave Macmillan.

Trevithick, P (2005) *Social Work Skills: A practice handbook.* 2nd edition. Buckingham: Open University Press.

Trevithick, P, Richards, S, Ruch, G and Moss, B (2004) *Teaching and Learning Communication Skills in Social Work Education – Knowledge Review 6.* London: SCIE/SWAPltsn/The Policy Press.

von Bertalanffy, L (1971) *General System Theory.* London: Penguin.

Vygotsky, L (1986) *Thought and Language.* London: MIT.

Walker, S (2003) *Social Work and Child and Adolescent Mental Health.* Lyme Regis: Russell House.

Watts, J and Priebe, S (2002) A Phenomenological Account of Users' Experiences of Assertive Community Treatment. *Bioethics,* Vol. 16, No.5, pp.439–54.

Watzlawick, P, Beavin JH and Jackson, DD (1967) *Pragmatics of Human Communication: A study of interactional patterns, pathologies and paradoxes.* New York: WW Norton.

Watzlawick, P, Weakland, JH and Fish, R (1974) *Change: Principles of problem formulation and problem resolution.* New York: WW Norton.

Weaver, HN and White, BJ (1997) 'The Native American Family Circle: Roots of resiliency', in PM Brown and JS Shallett (eds), *Cross-Cultural Practice with Couples and Families.* Bingharmton, NY: Haworth Press, pp.67–80.

Webb, NB (2003) *Social Work with Children.* 2nd edition. New York: Guilford Press

Webster-Stratton, C (1998) Preventing Conduct Problems in Head-Start Children: Strengthening parenting competencies. *Journal of Consulting and Clinical Psychology,* Vol 66, pp.715–30.

Webster-Stratton, C and Hammond, M (1997) Treating Children with Early-onset Conduct Problems: A comparison of child and parent training interventions. *Journal of Consulting and Clinical Psychology,* Vol 65, Part I pp.93–109.

West, A (1995) *You're on Your Own: Young people's research on leaving care.* London: Save the Children.

Whitaker, DS (2000) *Using Groups to Help People.* 2nd edition. Abingdon: Brunner-Routledge.

Wilder, S and Sorensen, C (2001) *Essentials of Aggression Management in Health Care.* New Jersey: Prentice Hall.

Williams, CR and Abeles, N (2004) Issues and Implications of Deaf Culture in Therapy, *Professional Psychology: Research and Practice,* Vol. 35, Part 6, pp.643–8.

Wilson, K, Kendrick, P and Ryan, V (1992) *Play Therapy: A non-directive approach for children and adolescents.* London: Bailliere Tindall.

Wincup, E, Buckland, G and Baylis, R (2003) *Youth Homelessness and Substance Use: Report to the drugs and alcohol research unit.* Home Office Research Study No. 258. London: Home Office.

Winnicott, DW (1958) 'Hate in the Countertransference', in DW Winnicott, *Through Paediatrics to Psychoanalysis.* London: Hogarth Press, pp.194–203.

Young, A Ackerman, J and Kyle, J (1998) *Looking On: Deaf people and the organisation of services.* Bristol: The Policy Press.

Zimbardo, P (2008) *The Lucifer Effect: Understanding how good people turn evil.* New York: Random House.

Index

Added to a page number 'g' denotes glossary.

Transforming Social Work Practice – titles in the series

Applied Psychology for Social Work (second edition)	ISBN 978 1 84445 356 6
Assessment in Social Work Practice	ISBN 978 1 84445 293 4
Collaborative Social Work Practice	ISBN 978 1 84445 014 5
Communication and Interpersonal Skills in Social Work (third edition)	ISBN 978 1 84445 610 9
Courtroom Skills for Social Workers	ISBN 978 1 84445 123 4
Critical Learning for Social Work Students	ISBN 978 1 84445 201 9
Effective Practice Learning in Social Work (second edition)	ISBN 978 1 84445 253 8
Equality and Diversity in Social Work Practice	ISBN 978 1 84445 593 5
Groupwork Practice in Social Work	ISBN 978 1 84445 086 2
Interprofessional Social Work: Effective Collaborative Approaches (second edition)	ISBN 978 1 84445 379 5
Introducing International Social Work	ISBN 978 1 84445 132 6
Loss and Social Work	ISBN 978 1 84445 088 6
Management and Organisations in Social Work (second edition)	ISBN 978 1 84445 216 3
Need, Risk and Protection in Social Work Practice	ISBN 978 1 84445 252 1
New Directions in Social Work Practice	ISBN 978 1 84445 079 4
Practical Computer Skills for Social Work	ISBN 978 1 84445 031 2
Proactive Child Protection and Social Work	ISBN 978 1 84445 131 9
Reflective Practice in Social Work (second edition)	ISBN 978 1 84445 364 1
Research Skills for Social Work	ISBN 978 1 84445 179 1
Safeguarding Adults in Social Work	ISBN 978 1 84445 148 7
Sensory Awareness and Social Work	ISBN 978 1 84445 293 4
Service User and Carer Participation in Social Work	ISBN 978 1 84445 074 9
Sexuality and Social Work	ISBN 978 1 84445 085 5
Social Policy and Social Work	ISBN 978 1 84445 301 6
Social Work and Human Development (third edition)	ISBN 978 1 84445 380 1
Social Work and Mental Health (third edition)	ISBN 978 1 84445 154 8
Social Work and Mental Health in Scotland	ISBN 978 1 84445 130 2

To order, please contact our distributor: BEBC Distribution, Albion Close, Parkstone, Poole, BH12 3LL. Telephone: 0845 230 9000, email: **learningmatters@bebc.co.uk**. You can also find more information on each of these titles and our other learning resources at www.learningmatters.co.uk